Frédérique Grim

**Integrating Grammar and Vocabulary in Second Language Cultural Content**

Frédérique Grim

# Integrating Grammar and Vocabulary in Second Language Cultural Content

Results of an Experiment at Intermediate French Levels

VDM Verlag Dr. Müller

**Impressum/Imprint (nur für Deutschland/ only for Germany)**
Bibliografische Information der Deutschen Nationalbibliothek: Die Deutsche Nationalbibliothek verzeichnet diese Publikation in der Deutschen Nationalbibliografie; detaillierte bibliografische Daten sind im Internet über http://dnb.d-nb.de abrufbar.
Alle in diesem Buch genannten Marken und Produktnamen unterliegen warenzeichen-, marken- oder patentrechtlichem Schutz bzw. sind Warenzeichen oder eingetragene Warenzeichen der jeweiligen Inhaber. Die Wiedergabe von Marken, Produktnamen, Gebrauchsnamen, Handelsnamen, Warenbezeichnungen u.s.w. in diesem Werk berechtigt auch ohne besondere Kennzeichnung nicht zu der Annahme, dass solche Namen im Sinne der Warenzeichen- und Markenschutzgesetzgebung als frei zu betrachten wären und daher von jedermann benutzt werden dürften.

Coverbild: www.purestockx.com

Verlag: VDM Verlag Dr. Müller Aktiengesellschaft & Co. KG
Dudweiler Landstr. 125 a, 66123 Saarbrücken, Deutschland
Telefon +49 681 9100-698, Telefax +49 681 9100-988, Email: info@vdm-verlag.de
Zugl.: Urbana-Champaign, University of Illinois, Diss., 2005

Herstellung in Deutschland:
Schaltungsdienst Lange o.H.G., Zehrensdorfer Str. 11, D-12277 Berlin
Books on Demand GmbH, Gutenbergring 53, D-22848 Norderstedt
Reha GmbH, Dudweiler Landstr. 99, D- 66123 Saarbrücken
ISBN: 978-3-639-05155-1

**Imprint (only for USA, GB)**
Bibliographic information published by the Deutsche Nationalbibliothek: The Deutsche Nationalbibliothek lists this publication in the Deutsche Nationalbibliografie; detailed bibliographic data are available in the Internet at http://dnb.d-nb.de.
Any brand names and product names mentioned in this book are subject to trademark, brand or patent protection and are trademarks or registered trademarks of their respective holders. The use of brand names, product names, common names, trade names, product descriptions etc. even without
a particular marking in this works is in no way to be construed to mean that such names may be regarded as unrestricted in respect of trademark and brand protection legislation and could thus be used by anyone.

Cover image: www.purestockx.com

Publisher:
VDM Verlag Dr. Müller Aktiengesellschaft & Co. KG
Dudweiler Landstr. 125 a, 66123 Saarbrücken, Germany
Phone +49 681 9100-698, Fax +49 681 9100-988, Email: info@vdm-verlag.de

Copyright © 2008 VDM Verlag Dr. Müller Aktiengesellschaft & Co. KG and licensors
All rights reserved. Saarbrücken 2008

Produced in USA and UK by:
Lightning Source Inc., 1246 Heil Quaker Blvd., La Vergne, TN 37086, USA
Lightning Source UK Ltd., Chapter House, Pitfield, Kiln Farm, Milton Keynes, MK11 3LW, GB
BookSurge, 7290 B. Investment Drive, North Charleston, SC 29418, USA
ISBN: 978-3-639-05155-1

To my Love, Joe

ACKNOWLEDGMENTS

There are numerous people I would like to thank for helping me produce this research project. Thank you to my committee members and colleagues Drs. Kim McDonough, Alice Omaggio Hadley, Peter Golato and Fred Davidson, who advised me and guided me throughout this adventure. I also want to thank my family and friends who supported me at all stage of my research.

Above all, I have to thank my husband Joe, who has always been there for me, during the trying times of my work and during the fun times. No word will ever express my gratitude and love for you. Your support and love are what has carried me through everything and has made my life so joyful.

Finally, I want to thank God who has blessed my life with His gracious and forgiving love and patience. I do not know who I would be without Him and without the ones He has brought into my life.

## TABLE OF CONTENTS

                                                                                                              Page

LIST OF TABLES ............................................................................................... vi

LIST OF FIGURES ............................................................................................. ix

CHAPTER ONE: Introduction .......................................................................... 1

    1.1 Introduction ........................................................................................ 1

    1.2 Communicative Language Teaching ................................................. 2

    1.3 Content-based instruction or content-enriched instruction ............ 4

CHAPTER TWO: Review of Literature on Focus-on-Form ........................... 15

    2.1 Introduction ...................................................................................... 15

    2.2 Defining Focus-on-form .................................................................... 15

    2.3 Theoretical background: Interaction, Output and Noticing hypotheses ... 21

    2.4 Experimental studies ........................................................................ 28

    2.5 Pedagogical implications .................................................................. 35

    2.6 Research questions ........................................................................... 38

    2.7 Definitions ......................................................................................... 40

CHAPTER THREE: Research Design and Methodology ............................... 42

    3.1 Participants ....................................................................................... 42

    3.2 Target structures .............................................................................. 44

    3.3 Materials ........................................................................................... 45

    3.4 Design ................................................................................................ 48

    3.5 Procedure .......................................................................................... 50

    3.6 Analysis .............................................................................................. 51

    3.7 Pilot study ......................................................................................... 53

CHAPTER FOUR: Qualitative Analysis of Teachers' Teaching Practice and

    Language Choice ..................................................................................... 54

    4.1 Introduction ...................................................................................... 54

    4.2 Teaching practices ............................................................................ 54

    4.3 L1 and L2: what role do they have in the classroom? .................... 77

    4.4 Summary .................................................................................................... 88

CHAPTER FIVE: Quantitative Results of the Integration of Focus-on-Form Instruction within Content-Enriched Instruction or Culture-based Lessons ................. 89

    5.1 Introduction ............................................................................................. 89

    5.2 Second-semester learners ........................................................................ 89

    5.3 Third-semester learners ......................................................................... 104

    5.4 Summary of findings .............................................................................. 119

CHAPTER SIX: Discussion and Conclusion ............................................................ 121

    6.1 Introduction ........................................................................................... 121

    6.2 The effectiveness of CEI at lower-level of foreign language teaching ....... 121

    6.3 Implications ........................................................................................... 136

    6.4 Limitations of the present study ............................................................. 143

    6.5 Conclusions ............................................................................................ 146

REFERENCES ....................................................................................................... 147

APPENDICES ....................................................................................................... 163

## LIST OF TABLES

| | Page |
|---|---|
| 3.1 Characteristics of the instructional approaches | 49 |
| 4.1 Episodes of Focus on Form: Totals of Vocabulary and Grammar for individual teachers - Focus on meaning groups | 75 |
| 4.2 Episodes of Focus on Form: Totals of Vocabulary and Grammar for individual teachers – Planned focus-on-form groups | 75 |
| 4.3 Episodes of Focus on Form: Totals of Vocabulary and Grammar for individual teachers – Incidental focus-on-form groups | 76 |
| 5.1 Descriptive data for each $2^{nd}$-semester group on each test on Vocabulary | 90 |
| 5.2 Descriptive data for each $2^{nd}$-semester group on each test on Focused-grammar | 91 |
| 5.3 Descriptive data for each $2^{nd}$-semester group on each test on Production-grammar | 92 |
| 5.4 Mixed Model Linear Analysis among tests for Vocabulary of $2^{nd}$-semester participants | 94 |
| 5.5 Mixed Model Linear Analysis among tests for Focused-grammar of $2^{nd}$-semester participants | 94 |
| 5.6 Mixed Model Linear Analysis among tests for Production-grammar of $2^{nd}$-semester participants | 95 |
| 5.7 Multivariate General Linear Model Analysis for Vocabulary pre-test of $2^{nd}$-semester participants | 96 |
| 5.8 Multivariate General Linear Model Analysis for Vocabulary post-test 1 of $2^{nd}$-semester participants | 97 |
| 5.9 Multivariate General Linear Model Analysis for Vocabulary post-test 2 of $2^{nd}$-semester participants | 97 |
| 5.10 Multivariate General Linear Model Analysis for Focused-grammar pre-test of $2^{nd}$-semester participants | 97 |
| 5.11 Multivariate General Linear Model Analysis for Focused-grammar post-test 1 | |

of $2^{nd}$-semester participants .................................................................. 98

5.12 Multivariate General Linear Model Analysis for Focused-grammar post-test 2 of $2^{nd}$-semester participants .................................................................. 98

5.13 Multivariate General Linear Model Analysis for Production-grammar pre-test of $2^{nd}$-semester participants .................................................................. 99

5.14 Multivariate General Linear Model Analysis for Production-grammar post-test 1 of $2^{nd}$-semester participants .................................................................. 99

5.15 Multivariate General Linear Model Analysis for Production-grammar post-test 2 of $2^{nd}$-semester participants .................................................................. 99

5.16 Descriptive data for each $2^{nd}$-semester group on each test on Culture ............... 100

5.17 Mixed Model Linear Analysis among tests for Culture of $2^{nd}$-semester participants .................................................................. 101

5.18 Multivariate General Linear Model Analysis for Culture pre-test of $2^{nd}$-semester participants .................................................................. 102

5.19 Multivariate General Linear Model Analysis for Culture post-test 1 of $2^{nd}$-semester participants .................................................................. 102

5.20 Multivariate General Linear Model Analysis for Culture post-test 2 of $2^{nd}$-semester participants .................................................................. 103

5.21 Descriptive data for each $3^{rd}$-semester group on each test on Vocabulary ......... 104

5.22 Descriptive data for each $3^{rd}$-semester group on each test on Focused-grammar .................................................................. 105

5.23 Descriptive data for each $3^{rd}$-semester group on each test on Production-grammar .................................................................. 106

5.24 Mixed Model Linear Analysis among tests for Vocabulary of $3^{rd}$-semester participants .................................................................. 108

5.25 Mixed Model Linear Analysis among tests for Focused-grammar of $3^{rd}$-semester participants .................................................................. 108

5.26 Mixed Model Linear Analysis among tests for Focused-grammar of $3^{rd}$-semester participants WITHOUT prepositions ............................................. 109

5.27 Mixed Model Linear Analysis among tests for Production-grammar of
3$^{rd}$-semester participants .................................................................................110

5.28 Multivariate General Linear Model Analysis for Vocabulary pre-test of
3$^{rd}$-semester participants .................................................................................111

5.29 Multivariate General Linear Model Analysis for Vocabulary post-test 1 of
3$^{rd}$-semester participants .................................................................................111

5.30 Multivariate General Linear Model Analysis for Vocabulary post-test 2 of
3$^{rd}$-semester participants .................................................................................112

5.31 Multivariate General Linear Model Analysis for Focused-grammar pre-test of
3$^{rd}$-semester participants ................................................................................ 112

5.32 Multivariate General Linear Model Analysis for Focused-grammar post-test 1 of
3$^{rd}$-semester participants .................................................................................113

5.33 Multivariate General Linear Model Analysis for Focused-grammar post-test 2 of
3$^{rd}$-semester participants .................................................................................113

5.34 Multivariate General Linear Model Analysis for Production-grammar pre-test of
3$^{rd}$-semester participants .................................................................................114

5.35 Multivariate General Linear Model Analysis for Production-grammar post-test 1
of 3$^{rd}$-semester participants ............................................................................. 114

5.36 Multivariate General Linear Model Analysis for Production-grammar post-test 2
of 3$^{rd}$-semester participants ............................................................................. 114

5.37 Descriptive data for each 3$^{rd}$-semester group on each test on Culture ................115

5.38 Mixed Model Linear Analysis among tests for Culture of 3$^{rd}$-semester
participants ........................................................................................................ 116

5.39 Multivariate General Linear Model Analysis for Culture pre-test of 3$^{rd}$-semester
participants ........................................................................................................ 117

5.40 Multivariate General Linear Model Analysis for Culture post-test 1 of
3$^{rd}$-semester participants .................................................................................117

5.41 Multivariate General Linear Model Analysis for Culture post-test 2 of
3$^{rd}$-semester participants .................................................................................118

## LIST OF FIGURES

    Page

3.1 Overview of procedure for FR102 and FR103 courses .................................................. 51

5.1 Bar chart of $2^{nd}$-semester Vocabulary mean scores ................................................... 90

5.2 Bar chart of $2^{nd}$-semester Focused-grammar mean scores ....................................... 92

5.3 Bar chart of $2^{nd}$-semester Production-grammar mean scores ................................. 93

5.4 Bar chart of $2^{nd}$-semester Culture mean scores ......................................................... 101

5.5 Bar chart of $3^{rd}$-semester Vocabulary mean scores .................................................. 105

5.6 Bar chart of $3^{rd}$-semester Focused-grammar mean scores ....................................... 106

5.7 Bar chart of $3^{rd}$-semester Production-grammar mean scores ................................. 107

5.8 Bar chart of $3^{rd}$-semester Culture mean scores ......................................................... 116

5.9 Summary of the results .................................................................................................. 120

# CHAPTER ONE

## Introduction

### 1.1 Introduction

With a goal of improving the understanding of second language acquisition and second language instruction, researchers and teachers have investigated the benefits of communicative language learning (Brown, 1994, 2000; Cook, 1996, 2001; Lee & VanPatten, 1995; Omaggio, 1983; Omaggio Hadley, 2001; Savignon, 1972, 1983, 1991, 1997), which attempts to create practical and applicable techniques to bring the outside world into the classroom. Within the framework of communicative language teaching, a combined focus on language structures and meaningful messages has been at the center of many research studies and discussions over the past few years (Doughty & Varela, 1998; Doughty & Williams, 1998a; Long, 1991; Long & Robinson, 1998) as this combination has been shown to promote more accuracy in learners' output. Communicative language teaching, as a methodological approach, encourages the use of realistic messages in order to present linguistic features (Brown, 1994, 2000; Cook, 1996, 2001; Omaggio, 1983; Omaggio Hadley, 2001; Savignon, 1972, 1983, 1991, 1997); yet, the reality of language courses often seems to differ from the original goal of fostering the development of communication strategies (Cook, 1996, 2001). One example of this divergence of practice from goal statement is the presentation of cultural items during the early years of second language (L2) learning. As Ballman (1997) and Shook (1998) have noticed, many beginning language textbooks present culture in the L1, therefore missing the opportunity to use culture to teach the L2. This reflects a tendency to separate and isolate the two aspects of the message: culture and language – and thus grammatical and lexical forms. However, research has shown that combining a focus on language forms with a meaningful message produces more positive results in learners' output than if instruction is focused on forms alone (Doughty & Williams, 1998a; Long, 1991; Long & Robinson, 1998, Swain, 1985, 1991, 1996, 2001). Teaching methodologies and curricula have been designed to integrate meaning and forms. For instance, one major methodology -- content-based instruction (CBI) -- has emphasized the integration of content and linguistic components at advanced levels of L2 instruction. However, it is not clear if the same findings from previous research on upper-level content-based instruction (Brinton, Snow & Wesche, 1989; Davison & Williams, 2001; Mohan, 1986; Mohan & Beckett, 2003; Rodgers, 2006; Short, 1999; Snow & Brinton, 1997) would be obtained in early levels of L2 instruction. Content can be interpreted in many ways, but the most common contents used in L2 teaching are Literature, History, Geography, Business, Civilization, Culture, etc. Because of the nature of the current experiment (beginning and intermediate levels of French courses), culture has been chosen to be the content of this study, due to the flexibility of its focus: topics are numerous and can branched to a array of cultural possibilities. Consequently, this book will focus on 1) the use of cultural content to introduce language structures (i.e., grammatical and lexical items) at the early levels of French L2 classes, and 2) the types of instruction that will promote the acquisition of those same language structures. Furthermore, as a secondary analysis, the data collected will also provide the opportunity to observe teachers' behavior regarding their first and second language use, as well as their application of instructions.

Before presenting in more detail the core research supporting this study, a short overview will be given of the impact communicative language teaching has had on pedagogy. This will be followed by a more thorough description of content-based instruction.

## 1.2 Communicative Language Teaching

Research on second language acquisition has influenced the direction that language teaching has taken during the past three decades (Brown, 1994, 2000; Cook, 1996, 2001; Krashen, 1981, 1982; Lee & VanPatten, 1995; Omaggio, 1983; Omaggio Hadley, 2001; Savignon, 1972, 1983, 1991, 1997; VanPatten, 1985). One major contribution of theoretical research has shown that instruction should be oriented towards a more meaningful content in order to facilitate L2 learning (Long, 1991; VanPatten, 1985). In the past, teaching methods would often lack focus on developing communicative skills, limiting the speakers' abilities to express themselves in the foreign language. For instance, one very widespread method, which focused on rule memorization and translation, is the Grammar Translation Method. This methodology has been used for centuries (see for example the discussion in Musumeci, 1997) and its impact is still felt in some teaching techniques, such as drill activities and translation exercises (Brown, 2000, Omaggio Hadley, 2001). Based on behaviorist theories, the Audiolingual Method (also referred to as ALM; Lado, 1964) sought to automatize the comprehension and production of language through drill activities and memorization of native-like prompts that could be produced by the teacher or listened to on tapes. Once automatization occurred, the assumption was that learners would be able to apply what they had learned outside of the classroom. However, ALM did not satisfy teachers and L2 practitioners, since it lacked a focus on developing communicative ability (Savignon, 1997). Because of perceived failure in attaining real-world proficiency using older approaches and a need to use language for communication, language teaching began to switch towards different objectives, which were argued to be more communicative.

However one major question arose from the discussion concerning the type of language competence that learners acquire during their training. Researchers, such as Hymes (1972) and Savignon (1972) argued that communicative competence should not be based on idealized notions of the way a language should be spoken (i.e., prescriptively) but rather on how it was in fact spoken (i.e., descriptively). Savignon (1997) claimed that learners have to use their knowledge to create a proper message and learn to share it through adequate strategies of communication. Because language teaching and communicative competence still needed to be concretely connected to each other in order to foster effective teaching, Canale and Swain (1980; and then Canale, 1983) evaluated the research literature and proposed a theoretical framework to better define communicative competence. In their earlier framework (Canale & Swain, 1980), three components were identified as representing communicative competence: 1) grammatical competence (mastering the linguistic code of the L2 and its lexical items and morphological, syntactic, semantic and phonological rules); 2) sociolinguistic and discourse competence (the faculty of producing and interpreting specific communicative functions); and 3) strategic competence (strategies learners apply to resolve a situation where communication could be interrupted due to performance factors or to shortfalls in other components of competence). A later evaluation added discourse competence. The impact of this framework on L2 teaching practices has been considerable (Brown, 2000, Omaggio Hadley, 2001; Savignon,

1997), especially as it appears to give valuable guidance for fostering a communicative environment inside and outside of the L2 classroom.

Today, communicative language teaching is applied in most language programs, with the goal of combining meaningful content and linguistic structures. One major approach that has widely attempted to emphasize the integration of meaning and form within the Canale and Swain theoretical framework of communicative competence is the *content-based instruction* approach. My research interest in this book concerns the combination of a message, such as cultural content, and of language structures, such as grammar and vocabulary, with the types of instruction that would make L2 learning efficient. Content-based instruction has characteristics that seem to be relevant for the inquiries of such a study. Therefore, a concise description of this approach is now presented.

## 1.3 Content-based instruction or content-enriched instruction

### 1.3.1 Benefits of content-based instruction (CBI)

Approximately 30 years ago, *content-based instruction* (CBI) emerged in immersion and bilingual programs, where needs to combine content and language instruction were felt in order to properly educate children (Cook, 2001; Musumeci, 1993; Rodgers, 2006; Savignon, 1972, 1983, 1997; Snow & Brinton, 1997; Stoller, 2004; Swain, 1985, 1991, 1996, 2001). Immersion programs in Canada and bilingual programs in the United States have employed this technique primarily from kindergarten through high school (K-12) levels but also in college curricula, targeting foreign students, immigrants, and others who have had the desire to learn an L2 intensively (Cammarata, 2007; Kowal & Swain, 1997; Pessoa, Hendry, Donato, Tucker & Lee, 2007; Rhodes, Christian & Barfield, 1997; Snow & Brinton, 1997; Stoller, 2004; Swain, 1985, 1991, 1996, 2001; Swain & Johnson, 1997). With content-based instruction, the second language is taught and a specific curriculum (i.e., content) is integrated. In most language programs using content-based instruction, such as immersion programs in Canada and bilingual programs in the United States, the content is based on subject matters that native speakers have to also learn (such as mathematics, sciences, history, etc.), but in their native language. In those specific programs, a process enabling the L2 learners to gradually be integrated into the courses is established; these learners eventually are expected to reach a level of comprehension and production comparable to that of native speakers. It is important to point out that these types of programs strive to bring the learners' second language proficiency as close as possible to that of the native speakers with the understanding that those learners might not reach that goal; however, the fact that the L2 learners are in environments strongly supporting their L2, and that they are often in the critical age period (Colombo, 1982; Lenneberg, 1967), encourages L2 practitioners and instructors to hope for comparable levels of language between the native speakers and L2 speakers. Besides provising a content for language learning, CBI is also a support for cognitive processing and for existing school curriculum (Pessoa et al., 2007).

Other L2 programs, and more specifically general-purpose courses at the college level, often do not specify course content in most beginning and intermediate courses. Most language textbooks have thematic chapters in which the aim is to acquire the four skills (speaking, writing, reading and listening) through the teaching of the language in a communicative way while using different themes to insure lexical diversity and practicality. Yet, there is generally no overall focus on a given domain of content, as it is understood in content-based instruction curricula. The diversity of the thematic chapters in a general purpose course allows learners to receive an overview of everyday lexis. However, if communicative ability in the L2 is the goal, then I would contend that a content-based course may also be beneficial if integrated into the L2 lower-level sequences.

The ACTFL Proficiency Guidelines (1999) associate each level of proficiency to different abilities learners have attained. The novice proficiency level is characterized by a very minimal level of ability to function in the language, using a small amount of memorized material, with many problems in output accuracy. As abilities grow, learners become increasingly more spontaneous and less dependent upon memorized language. However, it is not until learners achieve the more advanced proficiency levels that a predominantly focus-on-form approach changes to a focus on content (e.g., Literature, Business, Culture L2 courses); such higher proficiency courses are a good representation of content-based instruction, that is courses in which a content area is chosen as the focus for the syllabus, and where the L2 is the vehicle of instruction. This method of L2 teaching is found in many different environments (e.g., very commonly at the level of K-12 with bilingual programs, in magnet schools, English for Academic Purposes, and occasionally in colleges with ESL courses, English for Specific Purposes or sheltered programs), but its goal stays very uniform: teaching a second language through the teaching of a specific, and often non-linguistic, subject-matter.

Davison and Williams (2001) believe that one justification for integrating content and language in the classroom is that it follows the "current 'communicative' trends in language teaching that emphasize the meaningful use of language in appropriate contexts in the language classroom" (p. 53). Defining language and content, they add that while looking at the field of ESL, language has often been seen as the means to "communicative competence" (Bachman, 1990; Canale & Swain, 1980; Hymes, 1972; Savignon, 1991) and content as the message or the meaning of communication. When looking at previous research, Davison and Williams state that research studies " indicate that content presented through a second language improves second language proficiency and delivers content knowledge and skills just as efficiently as L1 instruction (Brinton et al., 1989; Wesche, 1993)" (p. 53).

Wesche (1993) presents the impact and implications that discipline-based courses, a kind of content-based instruction, have on learning. Reviewing previous research, she concludes that, despite the complexity of implementing such programs, the positive overall results make the effort worthwhile when learners are motivated to concurrently learn content and language.

The previous comments are also supported by quantitative and qualitative studies that have also encouraged the use of content-based instruction. I will turn now to a review of results from some of these studies.

1.3.2 Results from research on content-based instruction

Many studies and reviews (Met, 1991; Pica, 2002; Swain, 1996, 2001; Swain & Lapkin, 2000) have looked at L2 learning in CBI, such as mathematics, social sciences, history, etc., and the impact it has on learning. Most of those concern courses at the K-12 level. Results have shown that CBI can be effective, but particularly if learners are made aware of their language use.

Met (1991) reviewed CBI in the elementary school curricula when, at the time of her article, it had started to be an accepted teaching trend in immersion and bilingual programs. Based on her observations of past studies, she attributes a positive role for CBI among children in immersion programs who, through CBI, were able to learn not only the content, but L2 as well.

Swain (1996) examined several studies that she and others conducted. She noticed that in immersion classrooms, content is often presented; however, while intending to target the foreign language through content, teachers have a tendency to separate the content from the form and present either one or the other. Swain proposed two types of tasks that allow integration of content and language teaching: the dictogloss (the learners reflect on their output, through collaboration) and the jigsaw task (the learners have to negotiate in order to figure out the message through reordering chunks of phrases or images).

Swain and Lapkin (2000) examined the use of two task formats (the dictogloss and the jigsaw puzzle) when form and content are integrated. They hypothesized that the dictogloss task would bring the learners to focus more on form than the jigsaw puzzle task, either using the L1 or the L2. They investigated whether creating opportunities for output through the tasks would trigger L2 learning. Two classes (D and J; $n=75$) from a grade 8 French immersion program participated in their study. The data were collected over a 5-week period: the first week, a pre-test was administered; during the second week, the learners were exposed to tasks similar to those used in the experiment (jigsaw puzzle for class J and dictogloss for class D); during the third week, a grammatical lesson was given and pair-work was tape-recorded; during the fourth week, the post-test was developed based on the recordings; during the last week, the post-test was administered. Results suggested that the dictogloss task encouraged greater amount of negotiation in French within practice of vocabulary, language-use, organization, accuracy, and discourse structure. English was also used for metalinguistic usages. According to the authors, the L1 occurrences were put to good use. They suggested that the L1 was an efficient tool for comprehension, for focusing attention on language form, and for organization.

These results have supported the claim that a more directed task within a certain context would help learners notice and better acquire the targeted language forms.

Swain (2001) further reviewed two additional studies (LaPierre, 1994; Swain & Lapkin, 2000), with tasks inviting learners to focus on meaning and form. The purpose of the tasks in both studies was based on bringing meaning to the content of the course through metatalk between learners. Her research question focused on the benefit of metatalk in the L1 and of its possible effects on acquisition. From the results of LaPierre (1994) and Swain and Lapkin (2000), Swain (2001) wanted to demonstrate that integrating form has a place in collaborative tasks. Her research focus was on "considering teaching strategies which might focus immersion students' attention on the accuracy of their spoken and written L2, while still maintaining the 'philosophy' of immersion education – that is, that second language learning be embedded in a contextually rich, content-based curriculum" (p. 53). Because of the immersion environment, the content was entirely centered on the topic of the course. During the tasks, the learners who were working in groups were negotiating meaning and, as lexical, morphological and syntactic problems came up, they also focused on the forms of the language. The tasks were communicatively oriented but encouraged the learners to look at their language use when producing output. She concluded that teaching grammar separately from content might hinder the learners from developing a native-like proficiency, as the content brings learners to negotiate meaning and language; therefore "language instruction needs to be systematically integrated into content instruction" (p. 58).

Interest in immersion, bilingual or sheltered programs has been the focus of those specific programs (Freeman & Freeman, 1997; Grabe & Stoller, 1997; Kowal & Swain, 1997; Rhodes, Christian & Barfield, 1997; Snow & Brinton, 1997; Stoller & Grabe, 1997; Swain, 1985, 1991, 1996, 2001; Swain & Johnson, 1997); in the United States, at the college level, despite the fact that content-based instruction has not widely been implemented, a few studies (Burger & Chrétien, 2001; Crandall, 1987; Grandin, 1993; Pica, 2002; Rodgers, 2006; Wesche, 1993) have shown the impact of CBI in courses, such as Literature, Culture, Civilization, Geography and Business. In an overview of past research, Grabe and Stoller (1997) noted that content-based approaches motivate learners in postsecondary situations, and that a few well established second language programs have been quite successful in combining content and language (e.g., at Eastern Michigan University or at the University of Minnesota). These authors strongly supported content-based practice, as CBI simultaneously exposes learners to language and content and increases their motivation (Grabe & Stoller, 1997). Eastern Michigan University has implemented such programs for a few decades now (Palmer, 1993) with L2 courses such as Business, Export and Trade Studies, International Trade, and Economics. At the University of Minnesota, courses in Geography, History, Political Science, and Sociology are taught in foreign languages (French, German, Italian, Russian, and Spanish) (Metcalf, 1993). However, it is necessary to point out that all these content-based courses are carried out at a more advanced level of L2.

Burger and Chrétien (2001) have explored the role of content and language in Canadian college Psychology courses conducted in French, in a CBI setting, and their effects on oral production when content is topical for the course. The data, collected over two semesters, were recorded in order to examine content, speed of delivery, pronunciation, grammatical accuracy, and precision of vocabulary within an elicited imitation task (i.e., reconstitution of a sentence) and a discussion task on a psychology-related topic. Burger and Chrétien's results indicated that when a French course was linked to a course that was part of the curriculum (such as Psychology), the learners appeared to make measurable progress in their oral production in terms of both fluency and accuracy. These findings support the idea of using content-based instruction while teaching a language.

In a recent study, Pica (2002) examined the impact of two high-intermediate ESL content-based courses on L2 learning. The contents of the courses were Literature & American Culture and Film & American Culture. Pica attempted to see if discussion of the content between teachers and learners triggered modified interaction and provided input, feedback, and production of modified output all of which would draw attention to developmentally difficult relationships of L2 form and meaning. The data were based on observations, coded according to teacher and student utterances and following specific features. The results showed that learner attention was mainly drawn to the course content, which was their primary motivation for taking the course. However, the discussions did not seem to bring enough opportunities to the teachers for input and feedback from the modified interaction, and learners did not appear to make use of the modified output as expected. Pica suggested two approaches that could vary the outcomes of such a technique. First, teachers could be guided in their teaching practice to learn a type of response that would produce more input, feedback, and production of student output. Second, teachers could use the discussions in order to present the content and introduce activities that would offer more opportunities for the anticipated input, feedback, and student production of modified output. Pica supported the efficiency of content-based instruction, as long as activities brought learners to notice the linguistic forms in addition to the content.

In a rare study of CBI at intermediate level of college L2 instruction, Rodgers (2006) examined if content would solely develop in learners' production, or if linguistic (form-function abilities) skills would also develop after a semester of instruction. Forty-three learners from $3^{rd}$-semester Italian Geography courses participated. After 10 weeks of instruction, learners showed significant improvements in their content and linguistic knowledge.

With a qualitative perspective, Pessoa et al. (2007) studied two Spanish teachers of $6^{th}$ grade content-based classes in order to analyze "teachers' discursive practices on content-based instruction, the goals of instruction, and the students' linguistic development". They saw that the tendency of the teachers was to focus more on the language than the content, possibly caused by a lack of knowledge in the content. When comparing the two classes, the researchers noticed that the students (the first class) who were mainly exposed to content, with form as a background support, outperformed the students who mostly focused on form (with content as a vehicle for form, rather than form complimenting the content as more often done in the first class) in all assessed criteria (function, text, impact, vocabulary, comprehension and language control).

One essential drawback of content-based instruction resides in the fact that many studies concerning immersion and bilingual programs have shown that learners do not entirely acquire the forms intended. The content of such courses takes over the entire objective of the class, leaving language buried under meaning. Swain (1985) and Short (1999) addressed this problem and examined some possible solutions to better integrate content and language in the same context. Looking at content-based classrooms in immersion programs in Canada, Short (1999) and Swain (1985, 1988, 1993) discovered that simply learning in context, without precise focus on the language form, would not help learners to attain the expected proficiency level. For example, through a large-scale observation, Short (1999) noticed that many teachers in ESL programs did not have any training in teaching non-English speaking students. The instruction from such teachers was based on content only and lacked language instruction. The consequence Short observed was that learners seemed to lack accuracy in language form. Therefore, she offered parameters for integrating language and content in the type of ESL programs within which she worked. For instance, she suggested making a connection between the necessary material to teach and the students' prior knowledge and personal experiences. Additionally, Short suggested that offering multiple ways of checking learners' newly acquired content knowledge might have positive implications. Those parameters have allowed teachers to better implement an effective syllabus.

As the previous studies have demonstrated, CBI has been shown to be effective at all levels of language learning, especially in immersion-type programs. However, this method is not meeting all needs of all language courses.

1.3.3 Another option for lower levels of college L2 courses: "content-enriched instruction" (CEI) (Ballman, 1997)

Generally speaking, the CBI method has seldom been used in beginning-language programs at the college level. Shook (1996) attempted to do this, though he only looked at how textbooks met the objective of integrating language and form with content. Literature is a common way to make use of CBI, as reading and writing often give learners simultaneous content and linguistic foci. In the majority of the cases though, it is offered at more advanced stages, as teachers often feel that student cognitive and proficiency levels are not advanced enough until $5^{th}$ semester courses when the content can be handle with sufficient sophistication and maturity (Ballman, 1997, Shook, 1996). However, scholars (to name a few: Byrnes & Kord, 2002; Frantzen, 2002; Shook, 1996) proposes that some literary texts can also be presented, to some degree, at the beginning stages of language teaching. Redmann (2005) suggests using an interactive reading journal to instill in students a sense of literary analysis from the beginning levels of instruction, which better prepares learners for more successful comprehension. Exploring the *what* (i.e., comprehending the components of a literary text: grammar, vocabulary and culture) and *how* (i.e., presenting a literary text through selecting appropriate material and preparing accompanying tasks) of foreign language literature will help literary texts have a positive effect on learning (Shook, 1996). Pre- and post-reading activities with personal applications and with an opportunity to look at the target language culture are necessary to bring higher comprehension. After looking at Spanish textbooks, Shook strongly encourages language teachers to integrate literary texts in their curriculum, in order to enrich language learning. However, as he also mentions, there is insufficient research to categorically encourage teachers and L2 practitioners to continue in the trend of including literature (content) in beginning foreign language courses.

Past studies have supported the notion that CBI appears to be an appropriate technique for integrating cultural issues within the study of specific language structures. The communicative approach, which often claims that meaning and form should be combined in order to make learning successful, is still in use. CBI presents a specific and meaningful content (e.g., culture) while still working with the forms (i.e., grammar and vocabulary) of the second language. However, all of those studies have assumed a complete integration of language and form in a specific course curriculum (i.e., Mathematics, Literature, Psychology), which is not representative of what might happen at lower levels of foreign language instruction in which learning the linguistic features of the L2, rather than the content taught with the L2, is the stated goal of the course. Because choosing the proper content to cover an entire course syllabus might be problematic, a slightly different perspective might need to be considered. Ballman (1997) proposes an alternative to presenting content early on: *content-enriched instruction*, which integrates the instruction of grammar and vocabulary within content. In particular, she refers to culture, as it is most commonly found at beginning-level L2 courses and is a flexible and integrative component for a curriculum not fully focusing on content; however, other types of content could be interchangeable. Since culture is being enhanced instead of representing the whole curriculum (as is the case with CBI), Ballman calls teaching culture at the early-level content-*enriched* instruction (CEI). It makes up only a fraction of the total set of course objectives, rather than being the sole objective. Since content is one element of instruction, she suggests a four-stage model lesson plan that facilitates the incorporation of culture, grammar and vocabulary. The first stage is called *setting the stage*, where the learners receive some type of warm-up using their existing knowledge. The second stage, *providing input*, presents the cultural, grammatical and lexical information, through an oral lesson supported by different kinds of visual media (pictures, gestures, written texts). This part is the essential component of the lesson for providing input. *Guided participation*, the third stage, encourages learners to work with partners in order to apply the new knowledge given to them. The tasks focus on the new features learners learned and provide additional input. The fourth stage is the *extension activity*. Here, learners are encouraged to use all of the new knowledge in a combined activity. The outcome allows for more open-ended and creative answers. The model Ballman proposes is an example of enhancing content at the lower level in L2 curricula. However, this is not a set lesson and modifications are possible. One major critique of the CEI approach, and one that motivated this study, is that no experimental studies have examined the efficacy of this type of instruction in the lower-level L2 classrooms. However, since CEI can be interpreted to be a variation of CBI, the research done investigating CBI might be partially applicable to CEI. The main differences between both types of approach are that: 1) the content in CEI is not part of a curriculum, but is a topic chosen by the teacher that can be interchanged throughout a semester, where form is integrated; and 2) it occurs at the lower level of L2 teaching, unlike CBI which is typically introduced at higher levels of proficiency (Ballman, 1997).

Because of the traditional meaning of CBI, the perspective on CBI needs to be slightly reoriented for this present study, as the concentration will be on early L2 courses at the college level. Since the study does not concern immersion, bilingual, ESL, or sheltered programs, CEI (Ballman, 1997) is a more appropriate term concerning this present study. Within college L2 classrooms at beginning and intermediate levels, a particular content aside from the thematic chapters can be incorporated in order to make the communicative setting more significant and rich in meaning, even though not being the whole focus of the class. The teaching of culture is an obvious means for having some occasional CEI in the communicative language teaching classroom in beginning-level college courses (Ballman, 1997).

The previous research on CBI still applies to CEI since in both cases, the principle behind teaching content in the classroom is similar. Even though CEI calls attention to the cultural, grammatical and lexical information related to a specific topic, the same concern remains as for CBI regarding production accuracy, with no apparent experimental research proving otherwise. The L2 pedagogical approach that may help resolve part of the issue on the lack of accuracy and that may direct learners' attention to language form using a CEI approach is focus-on-form (Long, 1991; Long & Robinson, 1998).

Therefore, in the next chapter, the literature and research about *focus-on-form* will be presented in order to acquire a better understanding of how focus-on-form could be an essential tool in CEI. After the review of literature (Chapter two), the chapters will comprise the methodology of the study (Chapter three), a qualitative perspective (in the format of a journal) on teachers' applications of instruction and first and second language choice in the context of the study (Chapter four), the results of the quantitative analysis comparing types of instructions in a content-enriched lesson (Chapter five), and a discussion of the results followed by a conclusion (Chapter six).

## CHAPTER TWO
## Review of Literautre on Focus-on-Form

**2.1 Introduction**

Research on content-based instruction and, likewise, content-enriched instruction has shown possible problems in the lack of accuracy in learners' production, as content becomes the center of the instruction, leaving aside linguistic issues such as grammar (Swain, 1985, 1991, 1996, 2001). Emerging from the notion of communicative competence and aiming to address the issue of accuracy, focus-on-form is a perspective that seeks a balance between meaning and form in L2 instruction. The questions examined in this book are motivated by this notion, and are supported by theories that show that second language acquisition occurs through attending to and producing linguistic forms in a communicative context. The present study investigates the effects of combining content and linguistic forms at early levels of L2 instruction. The first question concerns the effect of this combination of form and content on the acquisition of grammatical and lexical features. The second objective is to investigate the type of form instruction that would actually encourage grammatical and lexical acquisition.

To review the theories behind focus-on-form, the section on previous literature is divided into four sections. First, a general presentation of focus-on-form will be given. Then, since the Interaction Hypothesis (Gass, Mackey & Pica, 1998; Long, 1985, 1996, 1997; Pica, 1994), the Output Hypothesis (Harley, 1988; Harley, Allen, Cummins & Swain, 1990; Harley & Swain, 1978; Swain 1993, 1995; Swain & Lapkin, 1995) and the Noticing Hypothesis (Schmidt, 1990, 1995, 2001) have theoretically motivated the concept of focus-on-form, a brief description of these three hypotheses will follow. The third section will be comprised of a discussion of empirical studies on focus-on-form as an instructional strategy. Finally, the pedagogical implications of the research done on focus-on-form will be discussed.

**2.2 Defining Focus-on-form**

    2.2.1 The foundation of focus-on-form

After conducting extensive empirical research on how to implement grammar instruction in order to improve L2 accuracy, researchers have supported three major perspectives (Krashen, 1981, 1982; Long, 1991; Terrell, 1977, 1982). Long (1991) gives an overview of the approaches that argued for focus-on-form. One of the early movements has claimed that grammar should be presented as clearly and as basically as possible; therefore, any obstructions, such as communicative functions, should not interfere when linguistic forms are presented. Subsequently, this approach is categorized as *focus-on-formS* with a capitalized "s" (Long, 1991), as the grammar rules receive focus outside of a meaningful communicative context to ensure their understanding. The *grammar translation method* is an example of such an approach utilizing the concept of focusing principally on linguistic forms often through literary works. Because of a lack in the development of communicative skills among students being taught with this approach, other researchers (Krashen, 1981, 1982, 1985, 1989; Long, 1985, 1996; Swain, 1993, 1995) have maintained that the ability to communicate a message should be the primary goal in learning a language. Consequently, the *focus-on-meaning* approach became prevalent. In this view, learners' communicative needs are what enable them to communicate in the real world; therefore it is essential to attempt to equip them with those communicative strategies, and not to trouble them with the grammatical features of the language. In this approach, accuracy is not as much of a concern at the beginning levels of instruction. The input that is given will eventually be acquired and produced to allow communication. Approaches embodying this philosophy, such as the Natural Approach (Terrell, 1977, 1982) or the Total Physical Response method (Asher, 1972), have been popular and still can be found today in some instructional settings. Even though the approach appears to increase expressive skills, such as speaking, a lack of production accuracy has been found in some studies (Lim, 2001; Swain, 1993, 1995).

However, Long (1991, 1997) propose an approach for integrating language form in meaning-based instruction, which he called *focus-on-form*. He defines focus-on-form as an instructional approach that "overtly draws students' attention to linguistic elements as they arise incidentally in lessons whose overriding focus is on meaning or communication" (Long, 1991, pp. 45-46). He claims that the focus should not only be on the linguistic forms or the meaning, but that a balance between both should be found in order to focus on form. That is, there should be an alternation between forms and meaning. Forms cannot be avoided, but including them in a more functional setting would make them more communicative, and therefore more authentic. Long believed that the practice of integrating forms into meaning would lead to more positive results in terms of learner proficiency level. As opportunities come up during a lesson, the forms are presented in such a way as to draw the attention of the learner to them.

A few years later, Long and Robinson (1998) slightly reoriente the definition of focus-on-form. Instead of advocating an attention to forms due to problems occurring incidentally, the newer definition, which has become the more widely accepted one, left room for degrees of interpretation:

> *Focus on form* refers to how focal attentional resources are allocated. Although there are degrees of attention, and although attention to forms and attention to meaning are not always mutually exclusive, during an otherwise meaning-focused classroom lesson, focus on form often consists of an occasional shift of attention to linguistic code features – by the teacher and/or one or more students – triggered by perceived problems with comprehension or production (Doughty & Williams, 1998, p. 23).

This latter definition allowed L2 practitioners and researchers to use the term in a broader manner; instead of waiting for the problem to arise, the definition called for "an occasional shift" to, which could be interpreted either by an incidental attention to form, as the first definition mentioned, or as a planned look at form. Ellis, Basturkmen and Loewen (2001, 2002) define focus-on-form similarly to Long and Robinson (1998). As in focus-on-form, "the treatment of linguistic form in the context of performing a communicative task" occurs. For Ellis et al. (2001, 2002), the form does not only consist of grammar but of phonology, vocabulary and discourse as well.

The term "focus-on-form" has taken on an important role in the teaching of foreign languages. Variations of the original definition have been proposed in order to meet different styles of teaching. The most widely cited variations of the original definition are presented next.

### 2.2.2 Other types of focus-on-form

In their book *Focus on form in Classroom Second Language Acquisition,* Doughty and Williams (1998c) refer to one occasion of focus-on-form in a manner similar to Long's original definition, through what they call *proactive focus-on-form*; this occasion is opposed to a definition of a different type of focus-on-form, which Doughty and Williams term *reactive focus-on-form*. Reactive focus-on-form represents the technique some teachers use for pointing out form in an implicit teaching approach, when learners (and not the teacher) raise questions concerning elements of grammatical or lexical form; however, if learners do not mention problems they have, opportunities for bringing the form to attention are not provided. Put differently, proactive focus-on-form emphasizes the difficulties of the language, even before (and whether or not) the learners experience problems. Doughty and Williams (1998a) believe that focus-on-form is a necessary step for language acquisition, as it pushes "learners beyond communicatively effective language toward target-like second language ability" (p. 2).

During the past few years, as Spada (1997) and Doughty and Williams (1998b) have noted, focus-on-form has often been confused with form-focused instruction. According to them, form-focused instruction is more planned than focus-on-form. Spada (1997) defines form-focused instruction as "any pedagogical effort which is used to draw the learners' attention to language form either implicitly or explicitly" (p. 73). Doughty and Williams (1998b) refer to form-focused instruction as "instruction that is, in fact, formS-focused but sometimes can refer to instruction involving what we are calling *focus-on-form*. Thus, the phrase *form-focused* instruction is variously used to denote the teaching of linguistic formS in isolation, as well as to describe teaching that integrates attention to forms, meaning, and use" (p. 4).

Ellis (2001) also agrees that the terminology of form-focused instruction and focus-on-form have been mixed; nevertheless, he claims that both notions are used synonymously and have actually merged into one. He defines form-focused instruction as "any planned or incidental instructional activity that is intended to induce language learners to pay attention to linguistic form." (p. 1-2) He more precisely categorizes form-focused instruction as being one of three types. The first is called *focus-on-forms*, which refers to the sole focus on linguistic forms without implementing any meaningful context. The second and third types, under the category of focus-on-form, have been of greater interest for researchers (Doughty & Varela, 1998; Long & Robinson, 1998; Williams & Evans, 1998). *Planned focus-on-form* (or *proactive focus-on-form*, Ellis, et al., 2001) draws learners to the forms through enriching the input, for instance through input flooding or input enhancement, while bringing meaning to the language. The teacher selects in advance the form that will be in focus and the manner and the tasks to introduce it. The last type, *incidental focus-on-form,* arises when a problem of communication or of form occurs in unfocused tasks, defined as "communicative tasks designed to elicit general samples of the language rather than specific forms" (Ellis et al., 2002). Two kinds of incidental focus-on-form are defined: *pre-emptive focus-on-form* and *reactive focus-on-form*. With pre-emptive focus-on-form, the teacher takes time out from a communicative task by bringing attention to a form that the teacher anticipates will be problematic. The problem of communication is resolved through negotiation between the teacher and the students, or among students. With reactive focus-on-form, the teacher provides feedback to the students only after an error is perceived (Ellis, 2001; Ellis et al, 2001, 2002). These categories, even though partially similar to Doughty and Williams' (1998c) categories, allow a more complete coverage under one umbrella of the same concepts with more related and precise terms. In the rest of this study, *focus-on-form* will be operationalized following Ellis' (2001) terminology. However, some research articles categorized as studies of form-focused instruction will also be presented below, since Ellis (2001) describes form-focused instruction as pre-emptive focus-on-form. Figure 2.1 (page 26) provides a summary of the different definitions of focus-on-form.

    Nassaji (1999) argues that even though teachers are often encouraged to use focus-on-form activities, difficulties arise when the teachers are not instructed on how to create such activities. According to him, using tasks that focus on both meaning and form could be a solution to the lack of accuracy in learners' interlanguage. In order to help teachers prepare their tasks, Nassaji (1999) offers two types of methods, based on Long's definition of focus-on-form (1991). The first method is what he names the 'design' method: the teacher plans in advance which forms in the activities that the learners would have to use in order to convey the message. These types of activities are meaning-focused but with a strong focus-on-form when the learners are asked to use certain linguistic items. The second method is the 'process' method, which encourages the idea that teachers should present the form as the situation arises from the learners' needs during the activities. These two methods coincide with Ellis's (2001) definition of planned focus-on-form and incidental focus-on-form.

Focus-on-form is a pedagogical approach, since it suggests bringing to attention the form that teachers want to introduce or that learners encounter. However, there are different ways for this bringing to attention to happen. Most often, teachers generate focus-on-form, as they promote the language by presenting it and by assessing it (Basturkmen, Loewen & Ellis, 2002). Another way for focus-on-form to happen is through student initiatives. Basturkmen et al. (2002), Williams (1999), and Leeser (2004) have examined the attention to form within student negotiation events. Basturkmen et al. (2002) observe that most uptake within negotiation occurs within student-initiated episodes. Williams (1999) and Leeser (2004) demonstrate that among learners with different proficiency levels, student-generated focus-on-form, especially that which is lexically related to focus-on-form, can occur. However, Williams (1999) notes that even though student-generated focus-on-form seems to occur at all levels of proficiency, the focus becomes more frequent and grammatical at increasingly higher proficiency levels. At beginning levels, students seem to rely more on the instructor and appear to struggle more with the lexis than with the grammar.

As it has been previously stated, focus-on-form presents linguistic forms in a meaningful environment. However, a theoretical background is necessary in order to discuss in concrete terms and motivate the implications of focus-on-form in second language learning. To this end, I will next present three major theories that surface from focus-on-form. I will present the Interaction Hypothesis (Gass, 1992; Long, 1994; Pica, 1994), as negotiating with others might bring a focus-on-form and as focusing on form could facilitate occurrences of interaction. A concise presentation of the Output Hypothesis (Harley, 1989; Harley, Allen, Cummins, & Swain, 1990; Harley & Swain, 1978; Swain, 1993, 1995; Swain & Lapkin, 1995) follows, which supports the fact that production is beneficial for learning. Finally, a section on the Noticing Hypothesis (Schmidt, 1990, 1995, 2001; Schmidt & Frota, 1986) is provided because of its implication for noticing language form during instruction.

## 2.3 Theoretical background

### 2.3.1 The Interaction Hypothesis

Long (1985, 1996, 1997) has found that besides the input learners are receiving, interaction (or negotiation, in the sense of Hatch's definition, 1978) is an important component for acquiring the L2. The *Interaction Hypothesis* developed by Long (1985, 1996) claims that comprehensible input is facilitated by the modified interaction that occurs between speakers, which stimulates input comprehension and acquisition. Interaction thus facilitates the development of the L2. Pica (1994) provided further evidence in favor of the interaction hypothesis through a review of the literature on negotiation and its effect on L2 acquisition. She suggested that theories oriented towards learners and language, such as comprehensible input and output, attention to L2 form through enhanced L2 input, and feedback, seem to encourage the use of negotiation. Through examples of discourse between native speakers and non-native speakers, Pica demonstrated that negotiation provides occasions for learners to attend to form and meaning. As Gass (1997) also stated, "the input to the learner coupled with the learners' manipulation of the input through interaction forms a basis of language development" (pp. 86-87). She added that "conversational interaction in a second language forms the basis for the development of syntax" (p. 104). Gass saw a strong benefit in the role of interaction: it is not just to practice what has been acquired; it is really a way to negotiate what was learned. Gass, Mackey and Pica (1998) pointed out that it is really when learners receive incomprehensible input that they are more likely to recognize a difference between their interlanguage and the second language, and, as a result, attempt to negotiate with their interlocutors.

From attempts to apply this theoretical idea in the classroom, researchers (Doughty & Williams, 1998a; Gass et al., 1998; Pica, 1994) have suggested some practical techniques to elicit forms while staying in a communicative milieu. The following techniques are mentioned: group work, task-based instruction with the integration of input enhancement and implicit negative feedback. Such techniques allow the teacher to communicate their message without interrupting the flow of communicative instruction. One example of concrete application to language teaching is offered by Omaggio (1983; Omaggio Hadley, 2001) in a set of hypotheses, one of which strongly emphasizes the use of interaction and accurate structures. Omaggio (1983, Omaggio Hadley, 2001) stated that opportunities to use the language among students and in the classroom in general need to be abundantly created in situations similar to those encountered in the target language, with attention to the eventual development of "precise and coherent language use" (p 90-91). The Interaction Hypothesis motivates opportunities for interaction between speakers in order for them to analyze their peers' input, notice form, and produce negotiated output.

Swain (1998) claimed that production, among learners or between teachers and learners, might induce the conscious recognition of linguistic problems. For this reason, Swain (1993, 1995, 1998) has called more structured output, using comprehensible and targeted tasks. Pica (1994) also pointed out that comprehensible output is a condition for second language acquisition to occur.

### 2.3.2 The Output Hypothesis

The Output Hypothesis posits that students need to recognize forms in order to notice the gap between their interlanguage output and the output of native speakers. In looking at immersion programs in Canada, Swain (1993, 1995) and Swain and Lapkin (1995) realized that although their comprehension skills (listening and reading) are comparable to those of their French-speaking peers, children learning French are still lacking accuracy in their writing and speaking. This observation leads to the formulation of the hypothesis that teachers must encourage learners to produce in order to apply what they have learned. What the *Output Hypothesis* (Swain, 1985) maintains is that opportunities for using the language are necessary in order to increase the learners' focus on accuracy: in a comprehension task, a general understanding (top-down processing) of the message might be sufficient, but in a productive task, syntactic accuracy is necessary to bring clearer meaning to the message, i.e., to the semantics. According to Swain (1995), output provides three functions: the noticing/triggering function, the hypothesis-testing function and the metalinguistic function. Each of these functions assumes that the learners will attend to their own production and improve their intake. Several studies (Harley, 1989; Harley et al., 1990; Harley & Swain, 1978) have supported the need for integrating output in the classroom. Swain (1998) has outlined the role of output in focus-on-form: with production and interaction, learners may attend to form and acquire it, while still comprehending the meaning.

Because the Interaction Hypothesis and Output Hypothesis highlight the need for learners to attend to the language they use, either by negotiating or by producing, the Noticing Hypothesis becomes central to theoretically motivating focus-on-form. The next section presents how the Noticing Hypothesis argues for the necessary attention for learning to occur.

### 2.3.3 The Noticing Hypothesis

Schmidt (1990, 1995, 2001) stated that in order for acquisition to take place, a meaningful message is necessary, and furthermore, for that message to be of any use, a certain amount of attention is indispensable to allow the learners to acquire the second language[1]. One study that inspired Schmidt (1990, 2001) to argue for the importance of noticing input form order to acquire language is a diary study about his experiences learning Portuguese in Brazil (Schmidt & Frota, 1986). Studying his own diary, he realized that he really progressed and acquired new forms when he noticed those forms and wrote them down in his diary. Noticing the gap between the interlanguage and the target language is a major step for acquisition, as efforts are more likely to be made if there is conscious knowledge of the information to learn. Schmidt (2001) strongly emphasized the fact that "noticing is therefore the first step in language building, not the end of the process" (p. 31). It is important for learners to notice language forms in order to understand them, but afterwards, producing those forms in a meaningful message might help them become part of the interlanguage. Schmidt (1990, 2001) also maintained that input given to a learner will not be acquired if it is not noticed. Learners must be consciously noticing forms of language for acquisition to happen. When input is integrated into the learners' interlanguage, it has become *intake*; according to Schmidt, intake is that part of the input that the learners have noticed.

---

[1] However, there are authors (Bialystok, 1994; Schwartz, 1993; Zobl, 1995) who argue that awareness is not a necessary component of language acquisition, especially if the view of a two-component learning system (such as Krashen's learning and acquisition notions) is implied.

Schmidt (1990) described consciousness according to three major categories, which correspond to three different conceptions of consciousness: consciousness as awareness, consciousness as intention and consciousness as knowledge. *Consciousness as awareness* is also divided into three degrees of awareness. First of all, awareness is looked at as *perception*, meaning that a mental system is created in order to store internal representations of existing information. Perception does not imply consciousness. Awareness can also have a degree of *noticing*. Noticing is when learners are able to verbally point out what they have just learned. However, as Schmidt has expressed, there are some types of knowledge that we are fully able to decipher, without being able to verbally articulate them. In this last case, this is still noticing, as the person is fully aware of a difference. He gave an example to illustrate the distinction of being able and being unable to verbalize noticed knowledge: it is possible to notice the accent of some speakers, but we might not be able to explain the specific characteristics of the accent. The third degree of awareness is *understanding*. Once the noticing processing has occurred, the learners start analyzing and understanding. By understanding, what is meant is that learners are able to compare their current interlanguage with their previous interlanguage, and build onto the present one. These three degrees of awareness have been fundamental to the foundation of the noticing hypothesis, as being aware of the language forms will apparently guide the learner to understanding, and therefore will contribute to intake.

Schmidt (1990) equated consciousness with *intention*; when someone does something consciously, they actively intended to do it. However, there can be passive awareness, such as when we are not conscious of what we do. In order to exemplify this type of consciousness, let us imagine that someone has just moved to a new home. One day, that person decides to drive to the store. On his way back, he realizes that he drove back to his old home. This showed that he was not really conscious of where he was going but his mind led him back to his old home, instead of going to the new one. While dealing with an L2, it can happen that a person integrates a word from their L1 into the L2 or from their L2 into their L1 without being conscious of this happening. This is called code-switching, and can happen for many different reasons. The last category defining consciousness refers to consciousness as *knowledge*. It is often believed that if one knows something, he or she is consciously aware to know the thing in question. However, this conception should be discarded as one can have unconscious knowledge of something.

In his most recent paper on attention, Schmidt (2001) mentioned that learning can occur through subliminal processes; however, noticing does not produce the whole learning process but is instead the first step in language acquisition. Schmidt asked the following question: "Can there be learning based on unattended input as well as attended input?" (p. 23). It seems that in order to learn, one must attend to the input, but the fact of attending does not have to be intentional. However, from the perspective of the teacher, intentional presentation of specific forms might be a practical way to lead learners to attend to those forms. It appears that learning is more likely to happen if the forms are made more salient through explicit instruction, which leads the learners to focus on specific forms and meanings in the input.

Tomlin and Villa (1994) described attention with a slightly different perspective. In their model, attention is comprised of three components. The first is *alertness*, meaning that the learner is ready to receive information. This is often associated with the motivation and the readiness learners might have in order to learn. The second component is *orientation*: the attention of the learners is directed towards certain information and excludes other information. The third component is *detection*: the information is registered. This last aspect of attention is the closest to what Schmidt meant by "noticing" and "understanding". However, Tomlin and Villa (1994) purposefully made a distinction with Schmidt's definitions, as they believe that alertness and orientation are not necessary for detection. Put differently, Tomlin and Villa held that learning without awareness is possible. This is a strong claim that some (Rosa & O'Neill, 1999; Schmidt, 2001; Simard & Wong, 2001) have not agreed with, as these authors have seen awareness as a crucial component in the learning process.

Leow (1998) examined Tomlin and Villa's (1994) article and accordingly conducted an experiment that would use their model of attention processing. His goal was to integrate the model into a task-based approach in order to operationalize the model in second language acquisition. Eighty-three first-year Spanish students participated in the experiment. The targeted form was the irregular third person and plural preterit forms of stem-changing *–ir* verbs in Spanish (p. 137). The tasks were crossword puzzles that were manipulated in order to test the three variables of the model (i.e., alertness, orientation and detection). Each crossword puzzle was different in order to stimulate different aspects of attention. The first group's crossword puzzle triggered alertness but neither orientation nor detection; specifically, the puzzle was not modified and the subjects did not need to know the irregular forms of the verbs, thus this condition only stimulated alertness. The second group's puzzle task triggered alertness and orientation, but not detection, as part of the instructions was bolded and two choices (one correct, one incorrect) were given. Subjects' attention was directed to the incorrect forms through clues. The third group's task triggered alertness, orientation and detection. Partially bolded instructions, with additional clues to guide the subjects to the correct stem-changing vowels in the irregular verbs, were presented to orient learners' attention. The fourth group's task triggered alertness and detection, but not orientation. Similar in design to the third crossword puzzle, the fourth one did not have any boldface instructions. The two groups who received the trigger for detection performed significantly better than the groups who were not led to detect the forms. Leow's results supported Tomlin and Villa's (1994) analysis of attention in second language acquisition, as detection seemed to be crucial for learning, while awareness, alertness and orientation did not appear to have been necessary. Later, however, Leow (2000) provided evidence for the necessity of awareness to learn targeted forms.

  Simard and Wong (2001) looked at the research that Tomlin and Villa (1994) and Leow (1998) carried out and examined the reasons why the argument they make on the non-necessity of alertness and orientation might not be fair. In particular, Simard and Wong (2001) examined Tomlin and Villa's claim that "neither awareness nor alertness nor orientation is required for detection to occur" (p. 198). Simard and Wong found that the Tomlin and Villa model is not properly based on the studies (Carr & Curran, 1994; Curran & Keele, 1993), which they used as the basis for their ideas. Simard and Wong further contended that Tomlin and Villa's interpretation of previous research was not accurate. The two authors also pointed out that while Leow (1998) attempted to give support to Tomlin and Villa (1994)'s claim, he was not able to do so as his research design was not appropriate to answer the questions he had asked. One major problem that Simard and Wong argued was that the component of alertness was always present in each of the groups, therefore making the assessment of the presence of alertness impossible. They also criticized Leow's definitions, stating that they were not clearly operationalized. Thus, to summarize, Simard and Wong argued that Leow's study did not give strong support to Tomlin and Villa's (1994) study.

In their study, Rosa and O'Neill (1999) examined the presence or absence of attention during explicit and implicit instruction and the role it had on intake. Their rationale was that research in cognitive psychology (Curran & Keele, 1993; Nissen & Bullemer, 1987) and in second language acquisition (Robinson, 1995; Schmidt, 1990, 1995) seemed to show more evidence of a need for some type of attention in the learning process. Rosa and O'Neill (1999) mentioned Tomlin and Villa's (1994) study, with their attention model, which claimed that attention was an important factor for learning but was not necessary. Contending that there was in fact a need for attention in SLA, Rosa and O'Neill (1999) carried out a study in order to observe what learners actually do. In their study, 67 native English speakers in fourth-semester Spanish courses participated. The data were gathered through a multiple-choice recognition test and a questionnaire. The linguistic focus was on Spanish contrary-to-fact sentences in the past. The participants were assigned to five different groups that received different treatments. All groups were taught the targeted form, while only two of those groups received explicit formal instruction. What Rosa and O'Neill found was that compared to implicit instruction, explicit explanation of linguistic form appeared to have a positive effect on intake processing. They also noticed that the participants who explained the rules aloud seemed to retain the targeted forms better and to process them more accurately. Finally, when exposed to formal instruction and to the search of rules, participants performed better than the groups who did not have those treatments. The researchers concluded that instructed participants performed significantly better than those who were in an implicit condition and that noticing had a significant impact, giving strong support to Schmidt's noticing hypothesis.

The issue of how learners notice specific forms of language and the methods used for drawing learner attention is an additional focus of research. Sharwood-Smith (1993, 1995) claimed that one efficient way to bring the input to attention is to enhance it. In his earlier work (1981), Sharwood-Smith called this procedure *consciousness-raising*, as some type of saliency causes the forms to be noticed. Later on (1993, 1995), Sharwood-Smith changed the name of that procedure to *input enhancement*, as he realized that only input could be modified by the teacher or researcher, while intake is really a learner-controlled construct independent from the teacher or researcher. Input enhancement consists of bringing input to the attention of a learner by emphasizing it in one of the following manners: by altering the auditory characteristics (amplitude, pitch) of the targeted words or forms, by accentuating the font of a written text (bolding, italicizing, underlying, coloring) (Doughty, 1991), or by using gestures. Other varieties of input enhancement include a metalinguistic explanation (Fotos, 1993), a higher frequency of the targeted form (White, 1998; Williams & Evans, 1998), explicit or implicit error correction (Spada & Lightown, 1993), or simplification of written and oral texts (Leow, 1993, 1995). Enhancing the linguistic forms leads the learners to notice the new information, and presumably to notice the gap that exists between their interlanguage and the second language.

From these last remarks drawn from the research literature, it becomes clear that attention could be a factor that allows for successful focus-on-form. If learners are not implicitly or explicitly made aware of language form, the Noticing Hypothesis claims that their acquisition of form and meaning might not occur. It seems also apparent that the type of input given during focus-on-form instruction is a factor in the success of any administered instructional treatments. To concretely illustrate examples of research studies investigating focus-on-form instruction, I will turn now to the experimental studies that have investigated the efficacy of focus-on-form.

**2.4 Experimental studies**

To verify the impact of focus-on-form on the acquisition of a second language, many studies have used techniques to introduce the forms of the language with specific treatments (Muranoi, 2000; Samuda, 2001; Schulz, 1996; Swain & Lapkin, 2000). In recent years, studies on focus-on-form have been mainly oriented towards the integration of focus-on-form in communicative tasks.

Lightbown and Spada (1990) examined whether form-focused instruction was beneficial for classroom learners of a second language. In their study, there were approximately 100 participants who were native speakers of French between the ages of 10 and 12 and who were students in communicative-based ESL classrooms in Quebec. The listening, reading and speaking skills of these children were analyzed. Their results showed that the class whose teacher had provided the most form-focused instruction performed the best on the different skills. The class that received almost no focus-on-form had the lowest accuracy score. However, for the latter class, comprehension level was as good as or better than other classes. Lightbown and Spada's conclusion was that focus-on-form instruction might help the development and improvement of some linguistic aspects, but that a communicative context was needed to bring meaning to any form. They further stated that the development of accuracy, fluency and communicative skills was mainly stimulated through instruction based on meaning and accompanied with focus-on-form activities. Finally, they raised the question that the efficiency of form-focused instruction might depend on the linguistic feature presented. In a later study, Spada and Lightbown (1993) reached the same conclusion with a different form in focus. Form-focused instruction appeared to be beneficial when it was embedded in a communicative language teaching framework. Their studies provided strong evidence concerning the efficacy of form-focused teaching; however, clear information on the instructional techniques was missing. One suggestion to improve the acquisition of forms is to integrate more specific and relevant content with the targeted forms.

Using recasts as a procedure for focusing on form, Doughty and Varela (1998) checked the effect on accuracy of providing recasts to learners. The participants were 34 intermediate level middle-school ESL students from two science classes. The experiments consisted of teaching pedagogical science labs during which the treatment group received additional focus-on-form, while the control group only had the science instruction. In order to investigate the influence of the focus-on-form treatment, the students' written and oral output of weekly science assignments was gathered and analyzed. The results supported a focus-on-form approach as learners who received recasts improved the most in their accuracy compared to the control group who did not receive any recasts. The authors concluded their study by stating that integrating a relatively implicit focus-on-form technique into a content-based classroom was both possible and beneficial. In this case, communicative teaching combined with a technique that brings attention to a form was apparently more effective than a simple focus on meaning or on forms.

Muranoi (2000) investigated the integration of and the effects of formal instruction in a communicative task among 91 EFL students through interaction enhancement, defined as implicit negative feedback given during an interactive problem-solving task. In particular, he examined the role of formal instruction on the acquisition of English articles in a communicative task, and looked at the effects of formal debriefing on the acquisition of this grammar feature. One of his research questions asked if interaction enhancement would influence the learners' restructuring of the focused forms. The groups that received the implicit negative feedback both in the explicit formal debriefing and the meaning-focused debriefing situations (two of his treatments) performed significantly better than the control group, which was involved in purely meaning-oriented interaction. Therefore, Muranoi concluded that a focus on a specific form, when kept in a communicative teaching framework, was beneficial compared to a total absence of focus-on-form. According to those results, meaning needs to be present in teaching, but without integrating any formal focus-on-form, focusing on meaning alone seems to decrease learners' accuracy. This study brings support to the fact that a language form can be acquired when integrated within a specific context. However, it seems to also encourage the idea of not using an instructional approach that focuses on meaning alone, as theis results in learners missing an opportunity to acquire a form, while still learning a meaning. Muranoi noted that the explicitness of the form instruction might have an important role in learners' interlanguage development; however, the experiment did not consider the use of implicit form instruction, which could have produced similar results. That is, the researcher's main goal was reached since he targeted meaning and form in one specific condition and showed that meaning with form seems to give the best overall results. In this present context, this study is important in that it shows that content-based teaching might have a stronger impact when a focus on form is added.

Using collaborative tasks that brought attention to both form and meaning, Samuda (2001) studied the relationship between form and meaning and the type of enhancement necessary to cause learning. In particular, Samuda looked at the role of the teacher in the outcomes of the implicit introduction of focus-on-form. The participants were 9 ESL students who were in small groups and, in an information exchange activity, were asked to negotiate the identity of a person. They were to verbally report their findings and then make a poster that would explain their results. The teacher encouraged some language focus throughout the task, either implicitly (using targeted forms while attending to the meaning generated by the learners' utterances) or explicitly (bringing attention to language forms themselves). Samuda found that when the teacher implicitly introduced new forms within a conversation among learners, they seemed to accept it as part of the ongoing interaction since the general meaning gave support to the new form, without disrupting the exchange. She called this action of the teacher "leading from behind", as the teacher slowly led the conversation to come to the form he/she wanted to point out, pursuing the flow of the conversation established by the learners. Looking more explicitly at instances of teacher's input, it appeared that it was beneficial when meaning was still used and was first introduced through implicit form input. The author explained that "the implicit language focus gave free rein to meaning, but only when meaning had been extensively rehearsed was the teacher ready to bind meaning to form more explicitly" (p. 133). The form might need to be explicitly introduced in some cases, but an implicit background has to be solidly established in order to make the teaching salient. Samuda's conclusions strengthen the approach of focusing on form, when meaning is at the center of instruction.

Williams (2001) examined the effect of spontaneous (i.e., incidental) focus-on-form on learners' retention and use of targeted forms through their interaction with the teacher and other learners. She studied language-related episodes of interaction among learners of English and between the learners and the teacher over 8 weeks of an intensive English program class. Those language-related episodes were based on either students' or teacher's questions or comment about the students' language. She observed that learners mainly focused on the meaning that was part of the negotiation; however, the higher the learners' proficiency, the more frequent and beneficial the focus-on-form became. According to Williams (2001), the level of proficiency appeared to be a factor in the amount of meaning and form learnability, regardless of the initiators of the language-related episodes. Furthermore, she noticed that when language-related episodes came from the teacher's feedback or students' questions, the focus-on-form still had a similar positive effect. When it came from peers, the attention to form increased even further. This was found at all levels. Williams concluded by encouraging the use of attention to form within communicative events, when learners interacted with other learners or their teacher. The negotiation seemed to have a positive effect on form noticing in this case. Spontaneous, or incidental, focus-on-form appears to be successful in a communicative environment.

Prompted and based by the many research studies on the effectiveness of instruction from the past decade or two, Norris and Ortega (2000) wrote a synthesis and thorough meta-analysis. Specifically, they addressed the questions of (1) how effective L2 instruction was overall and relative to simple exposure or meaning-driven communication, and (2) what effects had different instruction types and categories. They also looked at the factor of time in the retention of instruction. Of the studies they reviewed, 49 were deemed to have sufficient data for inclusion in the meta-analysis. They classified those studies according to their characteristics of explicit vs. implicit instruction and of focus-on-form, focus-on-forms and focus on meaning. They further looked at subtypes of instructional treatment to better understand what really impacted acquisition (e.g., input flood, enhancement, recasts, consciousness raising, input processing, garden path, traditional explicit, traditional implicit, input practice, etc.). For the results of their synthesis and meta-analysis, they reached the following conclusions. Regarding their first research question, the differences of effects between the pre-treatment and the post-treatment actually showed that instruction was effective. Compared to situations where no instruction was present in the experiment, the results of the instructed groups were significantly higher than the groups who did not receive instruction. The second research question looked at the instruction types of focus-on-forms (solely on the forms) and focus-on-form (within a meaningful context). What was found was that the instruction types were not significantly different. The implicitness and explicitness of the instruction were also observed and it was shown that explicit teaching appeared to be more effective than implicit teaching. One secondary issue Norris and Ortega explored concerns learners' retention of instruction. They observed that even though the learners did lose a great amount of knowledge between the treatment and the second post-test, they still showed some retention of the items presented, therefore showing that intake occurred.

Empirical results give support to focus-on-form, as it is able to integrate meaning and form in the same element. However, understanding how teachers and students perceive this technique is important, as they are the ones who apply it in the classroom. From an ethnographic perspective, Schulz (1996) investigated the attitudes of teachers and learners toward the teaching of grammar through focus-on-form. Using a multiple-choice questionnaire, she found that most students (out of 824 students from different language backgrounds) seemed to favor the idea of having a focus on language form in the classroom. Teachers had more divided beliefs on focus on grammar: some believed it is essential for language learning, while others believed communicative skills should be the focus. Schulz's study is important in that it offers a perspective on what teachers and students appreciate in L2 teaching and learning. Those opinions might help us refocus and reconsider some aspects of instruction. However, as Schulz (1996) mentioned, while opinions are not sufficient to establish facts about efficiency, they still need to be taken into consideration as they lead researchers towards the reality of successful acquisition of language form in the everyday classroom, and not just on specific days and environments determined by the experimenters. That is why studies have been carried out and still need to be carried out in order to fully understand the role of focus-on-form in L2 acquisition and its application in teachers' hands.

One major criticism to keep in mind of the focus-on-form approach is that if meaning and form are attended to simultaneously, one might occur at the expense of the other. More specifically, VanPatten (1985, 1990) has argued that if the learners are attentive while processing meaning, they will not be able to attend to form. Because of learners' limited capacity for processing, VanPatten does not believe that when they process input for meaning, beginning and intermediate learners can pay conscious attention to form. In his 1990 study, he tested the claim that if the attention of beginning and intermediate learners was directed to form, the comprehension of meaning (or content) would be negatively affected. Two hundred two students of Spanish from $1^{st}$ semester, $4^{th}$ semester and $3^{rd}$-year conversation courses were divided into four groups. Each group had to listen to two passages and was assigned a specific task: Task I required learners to listen for content only; Task II asked learners to listen for content and look for key words; in Task III, learners were told to listen for content and look for articles; finally Task IV consisted of listening for content and looking for a verb morpheme. VanPatten found that when early-level L2 learners were exposed to grammatical form and meaning at the same time, they did not record information as well as learners who were only exposed to meaning or to meaning and lexis. The intermediate learners, however, did not seem to encounter the same difficulties, especially between Tasks III and IV, where Task III did not significantly lower their level of comprehension. This study supported the proposal that bringing attention to form and meaning simultaneously might not be a beneficial task, as input processing might be overloaded with an excess of information.

VanPatten's input processing model (1993, 1996, 2003a) proposes that meaning will be processed before form, making form less probable to be acquired if the learners' input processing is already overloaded with meaning. The level of proficiency does have an effect, as the less proficient learners will struggle more with form acquisition when meaning is present. In support of VanPatten's claim, Leeser (2004) also suggested that the learners' level of proficiency might allow more or less focus-on-form. From language-related episodes, he examined the effect of pairing learners with either similar or different levels of proficiency. Forty-two participants of a fourth-semester L2 Spanish content-based course (Geography) were paired using the following dyads: dyads with two higher proficiency learners, dyads with one higher proficiency and one lower proficiency learner, and dyads with two lower proficiency learners (the proficiency level being based on the teachers' judgments). Due to a larger number of language-related episodes focusing on form at the higher proficiency level and on meaning at the lower proficiency level, Leeser suggested that the level of proficiency might have been the reason for the difference in focus: the more proficient the learners were, the more likely they were to realize the form, while learners with lower levels of proficiency had a tendency to focus only on meaning. His findings support VanPatten's input processing theory that stated that learners would initially process the meaning. The form would be processed only if the meaning had become less cognitively demanding. Despite these findings, however, there is still great need to investigate lower proficiency learners when they are exposed to instruction focusing on form in a content-enhanced environment.

## 2.5 Pedagogical implications

Deciding on the type of focus-on-form instruction is not always evident, even if theories partially guide the bases of the decisions. The Interaction, Output and Noticing Hypotheses have had a significant impact on the motivation for the use of focus-on-form instruction; however, finding practical ways to apply it in the classroom has been another source of discussion. Doughty and Williams (1998c) have listed six decisions L2 practitioners should be aware of when making a decision to focus-on-form: 1) whether or not to focus-on-form, 2) reactive versus proactive focus-on-form, 3) choice of linguistic form, 4) explicitness of focus-on-form, 5) sequential versus integrated focus-on-form and 6) role of focus-on-form in the curriculum (p. 199). Only the decisions that pertain to the topic of the present study will be explained in more detail. The first one is reactive versus proactive focus-on-form. As was mentioned earlier, Ellis (2001) makes a distinction between planned and incidental focus-on-form. Doughty and Williams (1998c) make a similar distinction with reactive focus-on-form, occurring as learners' needs arise; by contrast, proactive focus-on-form is planned in advance so that learners are drawn to form. The authors have concluded that both approaches appear to be equally efficient and the choice of one over the other might depend on the classroom circumstances and needs. The third decision described by Doughty and Williams (1998c) is to choose the linguistic form. For example, some (Ellis, 1993) believe that the problematic forms should guide the decisions. Others (Tomaselli & Schwartz, 1990) suggest that, based on Universal Grammar, an order in the presentation of form is more appropriate for acquisition. Still others (Hawkins, 1989; Tarallo & Myhill, 1983) believe that acquisition is based on processing constraints, both inside and outside of the classroom. The fifth decision Doughty and Williams (1998c) mention is about sequential versus integrated focus-on-form. Because of focusing on form, there is a danger of extracting the form totally from the meaning, which would become what Long (1991) calls focus-on-formS, the traditional way to focus on grammar rules. One solution to avoid the separation is to keep the tasks in a communicative environment. The last decision on the role of focus-on-form in the curriculum is discussed. The long-term effect of focusing on form is questioned; however, as Doughty and Williams have noted, not much research has looked at that particular point. Yet, questions are raised on the effectiveness of focus-on-form related to its length or intensity, or on the tasks and techniques that facilitate the integration of focus-on-form in the curriculum. Lengthy instructional emphasis is not always necessary for acquisition to occur (Trahey, 1996), but if integrated throughout the curriculum, it might be more beneficial than short-term instruction (Harley, 1989; Spada & Lightbown, 1993). Focus-on-form finds its place in the language classroom to bring attention to form, while still having a communicative goal. Among the six decisions Doughty and Williams list, a few seem to be relevant for this study, as they shed more light on the justification for this study and its materials design.

Doughty and Williams (1998c) also offered a large number of techniques they consider useful and practical when designing a focus-on-form task. They advise that tasks should be designed around the following components of focus-on-form: (1) the learning context, with the availability of input and classroom constraints; (2) the learners, considering their age, their proficiency, their educational background, and their educational goals; (3) the form, with its inherent characteristics (nature of rule, frequency of input, and relation to L1 form) and its status in the interlanguage; and finally (4) the learning process to be included: noticing meaning, noticing gaps and holes, cognitive comparison, restructuring, hypothesis testing and automatization (pp.259-260). These components should promote successful second language acquisition. A number of techniques have been suggested in order to present a specific point of language. In order to stay organized and consistent, the following presentation of possible focus-on-form techniques has been broken down following the categories of Ellis (2001) of planned and incidental focus-on-form. First of all, some researchers have suggested techniques that can be planned by the teachers to bring up the potential language difficulties. Doughty and Williams (1998c) refer to different major techniques that have been used throughout research studies to present focus-on-form. From the least obstructive to the flow of communication to the most obstructive, they mention input flood, task-essential language, input enhancement, negotiation, recast, output enhancement, dictogloss, consciousness-raising tasks, input processing and garden-path.

Long and Robinson (1998) also present a few techniques in which focus-on-form can easily be integrated into classroom language activities without divorcing form from meaning. *Input enhancement*, a notion introduced by Sharwood-Smith (1991, 1993) and adhering to Schmidt's Noticing Hypothesis, is one main pedagogical tool for bringing the intended form to the learner's attention. Ways to enhance a form include reinforcing the aspect of a form, by altering the pitch or intonation of the spoken targeted words or forms, by accentuating the font of a written text (bolding, italicizing, underlining, coloring) (Doughty, 1991), or by using gestures. Another technique is *input flood*, where the frequency of the targeted lexical items is increased in a written or oral text. The higher the frequency, the more salient the items will become to the learners and the greater the likelihood will be for noticing the forms. Doughty and Williams (1998c) and others (White, 1998; Williams & Evans, 1998) support the input flood technique, as they believe that the more opportunities there are in the input to notice the form, the more likely learners will notice it. It is crucial for the learning process to present learners with as many instances as possible related to the targeted form. However, White (1998) mentions that an input flood might not be sufficient, and that additional tasks are necessary for form to be noticed. Another procedure Long and Robinson (1998) mention uses explicit negative feedback: a teacher who hears an error draws the attention of the learners to the right form. To this, there is a more implicit counterpart: implicit negative feedback, which calls for the teacher to recast (to repeat the structure with the correct form), hoping that the learner will notice and repeat the right form. Studies have shown positive effects on L2 development from being exposed to implicit negative feedback (Oliver, 1995; Ortega and Long, 1997). Other varieties of input enhancement can include a metalinguistic explanation (Fotos, 1993), explicit or implicit error correction (Spada & Lightown, 1993), and simplification of written and oral texts (Leow, 1993, 1995). Enhancing the linguistic forms will lead the learners to specifically notice the new information, and therefore notice the gap that exists between their interlanguage and the second language. By using a multitude of enhancing techniques, the likelihood of noticing is increased.

In the case of incidental focus-on-form, techniques, such as corrective feedback, negotiation of meaning and form (through tasks such as role plays, jigsaw puzzles, discussions, debates; Ellis et al. 2001), and recasts also have a role. Furthermore, one last technique that is meaningful for bringing learners to the form is *interaction enhancement* (Muranoi, 2000), which attempts to integrate focus-on-form in an interactive situation, where the negotiation of meaning is being emphasized through interaction. The mismatch between the learners' interlanguage and the target language are indicated by the teacher, with the intention of having learners realize and modify their erroneous speech.

Focus-on-form, through theoretical support and experimental research carried out over the past several decades, seems to be an appropriate and efficient approach in teaching a second language in a proficient way. However, finding proper content through which to teach form might be problematic at times, especially if the level of proficiency is considered. The content needs to be comprehensible so that meaning and form can be taught, without interfering with either one. To select the target structure for focus-on-form, Harley (1993) and Williams and Evans (1998) have noted guidelines. They suggest that the items chosen for an experiment should: 1) "differ in nonobvious ways from the learners' first language"; 2) not be "salient because they are irregular or infrequent in the input"; 3) not be "important for successful communication"; 4) be "likely to be misinterpreted or misanalyzed by learners" (Williams & Evans, 1998, p. 140). These guidelines serve as a useful reference for the selection of forms by researchers.

## 2.6 Research questions

Focus-on-form research has shown that drawing learners' attention to form within a meaningful context facilitates L2 learning (Doughty & Williams, 1998; Williams & Evans, 1998; Ellis, 2001; Long, 1991; Long & Robinson, 1998; Muranoi, 2000; Nassaji, 1999; Samuda, 2001; Swain, 1998). However, despite some evidence, possible negative effects could occur if learners' attention is directed concurrently to form and meaning (VanPatten, 1985, 1990). Yet, continuing to search for a better and successful approach is a persistent need. Content-based instruction, an approach that bases its teaching on the integration of form and meaning, can lead to problems of accuracy in learners' production (Pessoa et al., 2007; Swain, 1985, 1993, 1996, 2001; Swain & Lapkin, 2001). One possible way to resolve this issue is to introduce *focus-on-form* in a meaningful content. As several scholars have shown (Doughty & Williams, 1998c; Sharwood-Smith, 1995; White, 1998), one way to bring learners attention to the targeted form is by using noticing techniques, such as input enhancement. A large body of research has examined both content-based instruction and focus-on-form; however, the combination of both in one research project has not been frequently seen, especially at the lower levels of foreign language instruction. Since this study concerns lower-level foreign language instruction, the notion of CBI will be replaced by content-enriched instruction (Ballman, 1997) in order to better represent the objectives of the research (i.e., levels of instruction, fraction of a course, etc.). The literature has shown that even though much has been investigated and supported by concrete results relevant to the effects of focusing on form, there are still many pieces of the puzzle to be resolved, specifically when looking at the setting proposed in this study. Additionally, I would like to point out that at the early L2 levels in American colleges, the combination of content-enriched teaching and focus-on-form is not commonplace in instructional practices. Even though there have been calls for this kind of research at the lower levels of instruction (Ballman, 1997; Williams, 2001), very little research of this kind has actually been done. The present study seeks to shed light on what can be done in this particular L2 classroom context. The present study will address the following research questions:

1. Does the integration of focus-on-form in content-enriched lessons facilitate the acquisition of grammar and vocabulary in intermediate French L2 classes?
2. If integrating focus-on-form in content-enriched lessons does facilitate acquisition, which type of focus-on-form instruction is more effective at promoting the acquisition and production of grammar and vocabulary in intermediate French L2 classes?
3. What effect, if any, does focus-on-form instruction have on learners' acquisition of cultural content?

This study tests the prediction that integrating focus-on-form into content-enriched lessons through input enhanced material presented by the teacher and through proper explanations from the teacher is most effective at facilitating the acquisition of the target language forms. Along with explicit teaching of language form, the presence of input enhancement will increase the likelihood of form acquisition; however, incidental focus-on-form instruction, responding only to problems and questions raised by the students, will still allow learning. Finally, the prediction will be tested that the absence of input enhancement and of all sorts of focus-on-form instruction (planned and incidental) will further diminish the probability of form acquisition. It is expected that, under the condition of focus on meaning, only content will be noticed and acquired. The reason for these hypotheses is partially based on the noticing hypothesis, which states that a form is acquired when noticed (Schmidt, 1990, 2001). With the presence of some type of input enhancement and planned focus-on-form from the teacher, it is hypothesized that the learners will have a better opportunity to notice the forms. When the enhanced forms are removed, and the focus-on-form becomes incidental, the noticing is predicted to decrease. If the incidental focus-on-form is also taken away from the instruction, it is hypothesized that the learners will have little chance to notice the forms at all, as the meaning will become the sole focus of instruction. I also hypothesize that the content (i.e., culture) that is presented in the lesson will be learned; therefore the focus-on-form instructions will have positive effects, as they will allow the learning of language forms (syntactic and lexical forms) and content.

## 2.7 Definitions

Throughout this research, several terms are employed. In order to clarify understanding and remove any confusion, operational definitions are listed next.

- **Content-based instruction:** the instruction of content in language courses, often found in immersion and bilingual programs. Theoretically, the curriculum taught in the L2 replaces a curriculum normally taught in the L1, with an emphasis on language forms.
- **Content-enriched instruction (CEI):** the instruction of culture or other possible content at early-level L2 college courses, where grammar and vocabulary are integrated

(Ballman, 1997). Theme-based foreign language classes could be categorized under CEI as the content is secondary, as opposed to the primary focus in CBI.

- **Focus-on-form:** form can focus on grammar, phonology, vocabulary or discourse (Ellis et al., 2001, 2002). Ellis (2001) has divided the definition of focus-on-form under *planned focus-on-form* and *incidental focus-on-form*
    - **Planned focus-on-form:** learners are drawn by teachers' pre-planning of the forms to those same forms through enriching the input with input flood or input enhancement, while being focused primarily on meaning to the language.
    - **Incidental focus-on-form:** This type of focus-on-form arises when a problem of communication or of form occurs; it combines *pre-emptive focus-on-form* and *reactive focus-on-form*. With pre-emptive focus-on form, the teacher interrupts the students during a communicative task by bringing attention to a form that is anticipated to be problematic. With reactive focus-on-form, the teacher provides feedback to the students only after an error is made.
- **Form-focused instruction:** synonym of focus-on-form (Ellis, 2001)
- **Focus-on-meaning:** entire focus on the meaning of the message, without looking at the language forms, as accuracy is not as much a concern. Accuracy is thought to eventually be acquired with time and practice of the meaning.
- **Focus-on-formS:** sole focus on linguistic forms without reference to any meaningful context

To present the core of this study, the next chapter will describe the methodology used in order to integrate content-enriched instruction and focus-on-form, and appropriately analyze the data collected.

# CHAPTER THREE

## Research Design and Methodology

### 3.1 Participants

#### 3.1.1 French as a foreign language student participants

At the beginning of the study, 258 undergraduate students agreed to participate. They were all enrolled in second-semester and third-semester French courses at a large university in the United States. One hundred and fifty-two (N=152) of them were kept for the study. One elimination procedure was done based on pretest scores: students with scores above 90% in the different components of the tests were removed from the data collection. The percentage might be considered high but it can be justified by the fact that the pretests appeared to be too easy for the participants, as the grammatical tasks, in particular, did not really test the ability of producing the forms[2]. Another requirement for the participants was that they had to attend all days of the experiments (i.e., for the pre-test, the cultural day, and both post-tests) to remain in the data collection. This last requirement excluded a large number of students who had initially volunteered to participate.

The participants were mostly between the ages of 17 and 38 (mean = 20.12), and spoke English either as their first language or at a very high-proficiency level. Following Magnan's (1986) operationalization of participant proficiency level, the second-semester learners' proficiency (N = 60) represented learners who were hypothesized to be between the range of Novice-Mid and Intermediate-Mid (ACTFL Proficiency Guidelines, 1999), while third-semester learners (N = 92) between the range of Intermediate-Low and Intermediate-High. Magnan's study was on oral proficiency, but she raised an issue likely true for all language skills: within one level of study, different levels of proficiency can be found, and students of the same proficiency level are also found at different levels of study. This suggests that even in tightly controlled studies, an accurate estimate of participant proficiency levels will necessarily reveal overlapping proficiency ranges. The participants were recruited in the spring, summer and fall of 2004.

---

[2] The adjectives for the second-semester group and the prepositions for the third-semester group were already given out which might have reduced task demands (see Appendices I and R for a clear example).

The vast majority of the participants all took the first and / or second semesters of French in the same institution using the same manual and material. However, a few of the students might have tested into the class because of having taken French in high school. Such cases are less common, as most students who have had French in high school and do not score high enough to enter the second or third semester of French go to the accelerated beginning class (FR105: a combination of first and second semester taught in one semester).

The choice for the levels of instruction investigated in this study (second-semester French and third-semester French) was based on the rationale that the second and third semesters of French are a transitional time for the learners in terms of the amount of L2 input they receive. Their textbook (*Rendez-vous*, Muyskens & Omaggio Hadley, 2002) transitions to full instructions in the L2 at the end of the first semester. Teachers might also be in situations where the L1 can be practically excluded, as learners are estimated to have reached at least an intermediate-low level, making a content lesson in the L2 more possible. Furthermore, while a few researchers have encouraged more studies on focus-on-form at the early levels (VanPatten, 1990, Williams, 2001), the precise nature of that phenomenon at low level is not yet well understood.

### 3.1.2 Teacher participants

There were 15 teacher participants. Two of them had double teaching assignments, resulting in a total of 17 classes in this study. The teachers were graduate teaching assistants (14) and a lecturer (1) in the French department of the same large university. They were pursuing or had pursued graduate study in fields such as French Studies, French Linguistics, Second Language Acquisition and Teaching, Advertising, and English Literature. They were native or near-native speakers of French. Because of the diversity of interest and training backgrounds, the range of teaching experiences also varied greatly. All of them had attended foreign language training courses offered and required by the French department. In order to properly match teachers to the treatments based on their teaching style, the researcher observed each one and decided on that basis to which treatment condition each should be assigned. The goal was to match as closely as possible the teaching styles with the treatments in order to bring as much ecological validity as possible to the study.

## 3.2 Target Structures

### 3.2.1 Grammar

Harley (1993) and Williams and Evans's (1998) guidelines have been in part followed in order to select the target forms to be taught (see page 43 in this book). One French grammar feature that appears to satisfy these criteria for second-semester learners is the comparative and superlative forms of adjectives, as 1) it differs slightly from the English language (the L1), 2) it is not a high frequency structure, 3) the meaning would still be conveyed if the comparative or superlative form was not properly used, and 4) it could generate some confusion because of English's own structure of the comparative or superlative (e.g. in English for short adjectives, the suffixes –er and –est are added directly at the end and for long adjectives (more than two syllables), the preposition (e.g., more, less, the most, the least) has to be used, while in French, the length of the adjectives does not change the rule). According to the syllabus established in this specific language program, the comparative and superlative adjectives are taught during third-semester French (chapter 13).

For third-semester learners, certain relative pronouns that are relatively infrequently used, especially at the intermediate level, were introduced. Earlier, the participants learned relative pronouns such as "qui", "que", "dont", but the more complex relative forms used as objects of prepositions, such as "lequel" (and its agreements in gender and number), are not presented at this stage of learning. The choice for these specific structures followed the four criteria Doughty and Evans (1998) mention. The relative pronouns used as objects of prepositions ("lequel" and its agreements in gender and number) 1) differ somewhat from English but in a subtle way, 2) are infrequent in spoken input, though they are occasional found in literary works, 3) do not contribute significantly to the general meaning of the sentence in which they appear, and 4) could be misinterpreted by the learners as the structures require a careful understanding of the context. Even though some potential previous knowledge of these features of French might be present, it is unlikely that it is well developed and fully accurate, as the grammar items should not yet have been formally presented to students at this level. However, as was mentioned in the "participants" section, students with high scores on the pretest were eliminated from the pool to exclude any participant with potential knowledge of the forms.

### 3.2.2 Vocabulary

The vocabulary introduced in each treatment was related to the country being discussed in the cultural lesson. Cultural topics, related to francophone countries, are only occasionally presented during class, as they are not the primary objective of the textbook *Rendez-Vous* (Muyskens & Omaggio Hadley, 2002). Instructors had to use, at least once, the targeted lexical items during the cultural presentations, exposing the participants to those words at least once. A few of the words are present in the textbook, though they appear either as secondary vocabulary (not in the list of vocabulary to memorize) or in later chapters. All the words are draw from the standard French lexicon, which is the most common form of French taught in American universities. For the second-semester French participants, the words "roi" (*king*), "flamand" (*Flemish*), "pouvoirs" (*powers*), "moules-frites" (*mussels-fries*), "gaufres" (*waffles*), "fêtes" (*holidays*) and "bandes dessinées" (*comic books*) were targeted. For the third-semester French participants, the lexical focus was on: "campagne" (*countryside*), "champs" (*fields*), "amère" (*bitter*), "fer" (*iron*), "oeuvres" (*works, masterpieces),* "camion" (*truck*), "course" (*race*).

## 3.3 Materials

### 3.3.1 Teaching materials

Because information about the Francophone world is an important part of any curriculum in French, the content-focus of the teaching materials was related to cultural themes about Francophone countries. Discussing francophone countries allow the instructors to present a wide range of cultural differences and interesting facts. Such lessons are often motivating for learners, as they represent current events and situations, and can be experienced through travel.

A different country was presented at the second-semester and third-semester levels. France as a country was excluded from the choice, as the students are more familiar with France than with any other Francophone country. For the second-semester French courses, Belgium was the country of choice, as it is one of the European Francophone countries that is often overlooked during cultural presentations and in textbooks. A review of three popular French textbooks (*Thèmes*, Harper et al., 2000; *Paroles*, Magnan et al., 1998; *Rendez-vous*, Muyskens & Omaggio Hadley, 2002) revealed that there was no particular or extensive mention of Belgium in the textbooks' cultural presentation boxes[3]. In the third-semester French courses, the country of Senegal was chosen for its leading role in Francophone Africa. It is a country presented in *Rendez-Vous*; however the presentation is done in a general manner, with a short description on Dakar (the capital of Senegal) and three short testimonies of Senegalese inhabitants.

The content for both levels concerned cultural facts about Belgium and Senegal, such as: geography of the country, population, currency, type of government, politics, weather, cuisine, celebrities in music and/or literature, comic book characters, holidays, and traditions. Recordings of two Belgian singers (Jacques Brel, Renaud) and a Senegalese singer (Youssou N'Dour), and poems of a Senegalese poet (Léopold Sédar Senghor) were included. The accuracy of the Senegalese information was verified by a Senegalese graduate student in the French Department and for the Belgium presentation, information accuracy was verified by a Belgian exchange student in the English Department[4]. To bring more reality to the information conveyed and to enhance conceptualization, I also included visual supports, such as comic books, currency, maps, as well as photos of monuments, landscapes and people extracted from the Internet[5]. This extra visual material was intended to better illustrate the lessons and make them more relevant and interesting to learners. Early (1991) mentions that visual resources help learners comprehend content better as they are dealing with language. Therefore, since

---

[3] Belgium was only mentioned in *Rendez-vous*, but only to present the origin of a French-speaking celebrity and to refer to the difference in numbering (e.g. "septante" instead of "soixante-dix" in standard French).

[4] I am grateful to Awa Sarr and to an anonymous reader from Belgium for verifying the content and accuracy of the information for me.

[5] I received permission of the photographers to use their pictures, but they are not included in this book for copyright purposes.

adequate audiovisual materials could be found from different sources, they were included in the lessons.

### Lesson plans

The lesson plans were created by the researcher, based on Ballman (1997)'s suggestions of lesson planning for content-enriched instruction. They consisted of four sections. The first section was a short warm-up with questions suggested to the teachers to ask their students, in order to bring attention to the topic (i.e. *setting the* stage, Ballman, 1997). This was followed by a teacher-fronted presentation of the content (i.e. *providing input*, Ballman, 1997), with the help of transparencies containing the cultural, grammatical and lexical items and with pictures and recordings about the culture of Belgium or Senegal (e.g., maps, monuments, food, music). The third part of the culture lesson had a listening task based on Belgian songs and an oral reading task based on poetry for Senegal (i.e. *guided participation*, Ballman, 1997) (Appendices G and Q). Finally, during the last section students in groups of 2 or 3 were asked to write a picture-based production activity (i.e. *extension activity*, Ballman, 1997) (Appendices H and R). The entire lesson took the full class period (approximately 50 minutes). The lesson plans for each treatment conditions can be found in the appendices for Belgium (Appendices C-E) and for Senegal (Appendices L-N).

### 3.3.2 Testing materials

Three tests were created, all following the same format and designed according to test specification principles (Davidson & Lynch, 2002). The specifications of those tests can be found in the appendices (H and Q). All tests presented discrete-point items and one open-ended writing item. The pre-test had began with 7 items testing the content through knowledge questions, 7 items testing the vocabulary through translation and 7 items testing the grammatical items through sentence fillers (i.e., focused-grammar). The second part of the pre-test asked the participants to produce a short paragraph according to a given topic (on the last break) in order to test the application of their acquired grammatical knowledge (i.e., production-grammar). After the administration of the pre-test, it was observed that distracters might have been a good addition in order to avoid an overgeneralization of the example given in the instructions; it was then decided to add three distracters to the focused-grammar portion of the post-tests for each level. Therefore, the two post-tests contained, in a first part, 7 items testing the content through knowledge questions, 7 items testing the vocabulary through translation and 10 items testing focused-grammatical items through sentence fillers. Furthermore, the focused-grammar section had to be slightly modified between the pre-test and both post-tests, as it was observed that in the pre-test, participants seem to easily fill in the blanks, not with their previous knowledge, but using logical reasoning: the targeted items appeared to be too obvious and too discrete-point oriented. In the post-tests, the grammar section became slightly more open-ended, and more challenging to the participants in that it asked them to translate longer sets of items (i.e. comparative or superlative *with* the adjectives for the second-semester learners; preposition *and* relative pronouns for the third-semester learners). The production-grammar part followed similar directions, except that each test had a different composition topic for each post-test (pre-test: what students did during their last break (winter or summer); post-test I: what students did during another break (summer or winter); post-test II: on the most enjoyable vacation students have had) in order to avoid repetition and boredom. The tests can be found in the appendices (Appendices I-K and Appendices R-T).

**3.4 Design**

This study employed a pre-test-post-test design to measure the effect of different instructional activities on the learners' content knowledge, vocabulary and grammar. The independent variable of this study is the type of instructional activity, which has three levels: planned focus-on-form, incidental focus-on-form and focus on meaning. There are three dependent variables: learners' scores on cultural knowledge, grammatical knowledge and lexical knowledge, with all scores resulting from the pre-test and post-tests. Two student levels are included, as the participants were from second-semester and third-semester French courses.

The instructional approaches were planned focus-on-form, incidental focus-on-form, and focus on meaning. The planned and incidental focus-on-form approaches are based on categories described in Ellis (2001). The distinction between planned focus-on-form and incidental focus-on-form is that when the focus-on-form is incidental, the instructor answers questions that are raised during the lesson, but that he or she had not specifically intended on covering. Planned focus-on-form occurs when instructors plan to go over a linguistic point that they find essential to cover or problematic to acquire. An important point to mention is that in all three treatments, an input flood was provided as the learners had visual support (transparencies) as well as the teacher's verbal presentation. Because it was present for all groups, the factor of input flood was not studied as a potential effect. The instructional approaches are summarized in Table 1, and are described in more detail below.

Table 3.1 Characteristics of the instructional approaches

|  | Planned focus-on-form | Incidental focus-on-form | Focus-on-meaning |
|---|---|---|---|
| **Content** | Yes | Yes | Yes |
| **Form-focus** | Yes | Yes | No |
| **Enhanced forms** | Yes | No | No |

The planned focus-on-form group was given materials that had been enhanced by bolding and coloring the different forms that had been targeted for acquisition. The lexical items were bolded and colored in green or blue, depending on the level. The grammatical items were colored in red and bolded. The rest of the text was in black. The teachers for this group knew in advance what forms were the targets of instruction, as the researcher had briefly explained what was to be presented. The lesson plans for both levels (second and third semesters) can be found in the appendices (Appendices C-E and Appendices L-N).

The second group was the incidental focus-on-form group. The material for this group contained the same information on culture, lexis and grammar, but no enhancement was present on the transparencies (the content of the transparencies is found in the teachers' lesson plans: Appendices C-E and Appendices L-N). The instructors for this group were told to present the content material and answer students' questions. The focus-on-form was a reactive (i.e., incidental) focus-on-form, meaning that the teachers alone provided the feedback learners requested or that was motivated by what teachers believed to be important.

The third group was the focus-on-meaning group. The instructors were only told to present what information was included on the transparencies, without any additional comments on the forms included in the transparencies.

The observations looking at teaching styles, previously done by the researcher, were then useful in determining to whom to attribute the different treatments. The teacher for the focus-on-meaning group had to have a natural tendency not to deviate from the lesson plan and not to provide supplementary feedback. The incidental focus-on-form treatment was matched to instructors who did not focus on the forms, except when their students asked questions or made an error. The planned focus-on-form was especially given to teachers who clearly pointed out the grammar and the vocabulary of the chapter studied in class.

## 3.5 Procedure

In the spring and fall semester of 2004, the cultural lesson took place after about two months of instruction, a period of time I deemed sufficient to allow teachers and students to become familiar with the class, their teacher, and each other. The cultural lesson was presented during the regularly-scheduled cultural days on the syllabus. Three weeks prior to the cultural lesson, a consent form and a language background questionnaire (Appendices A and B) were filled out by the participants. Eleven days before the presentation, the pre-test was given to each participant. The background questionnaire/consent forms took approximately 15 minutes of class time, while the pre-test took about 20 minutes for the participants to complete. The researcher provided all the lessons plans and materials to the instructors about ten days in advance to make sure they had a chance to become familiar with the content. Then, on the cultural day, the instructors carried out their lessons as planned. The lesson and the activities lasted the class period (approximately 50 minutes). All classes were videotaped to verify the proper administration of the approaches and to collect as much data as possible for more reliable and richer analysis. One day after the cultural lesson, the first post-test was given. Two weeks later, the second post-test was given in order to check the long-term effects of the teaching conditions. The administration of each posttest took approximately 20 minutes. Interviews with some of teachers were conducted afterwards, so that the researcher could deepen her understanding of their teaching practices.

The experiment that occurred during the summer session of 2004 followed similar procedures, except that the time periods between the tests and the experiment day were shortened. Because the students had only 4 weeks of classes in FR102, the pre-test and the cultural lessons were conducted on the second week. The first post-test was administered during the third week and the second post-test during the last week. The number of instruction hours was followed as closely as possible in order to respect the timing of the experiments of the spring and fall semesters.

The experimental procedure is summarized in Figure 3.1.

Figure 3.1 Overview of procedure for FR102 and FR103 courses

| Day 1 | Pretest |
| --- | --- |
| Day 10 | Culture lesson |
| Day 11 | Posttest 1 |
| Day 24 | Posttest 2 |
| Following weeks | Interviews with teachers |

## 3.6 Analysis

### 3.6.1 Student data

The first three sections of the tests were scored according to pre-set scales. In order for the tests to be as valid as possible, prior to the experiment the researcher sought the help of a group of testing specialists. Their advice was that instead of awarding either 1 point or 0 point for a right or wrong answer (respectively), a partial credit scale might be more appropriate and representative of the participants' knowledge. Therefore, I adopted such a method for scoring the pre- and post-tests. As mentioned earlier, in the pre-test, there were 7 questions on the cultural knowledge presented through the teaching material, to be answered in English. Each one of those questions was worth one or two points depending on the amount of information to be provided. The lexical items were tested by asking participants to translate 7 words from English to French. Each item was worth one point. The focused-grammar section consisted of 7 fill-in-the-blank items, based on an English translation situated below each blank. Each item was worth up to 4 points (4 points being the highest score). The last section consisted of a free writing task based on a given topic with instructions to use a minimum of 4 grammatical target structures; these instructions were given in order to observe participants' ability to integrate those structures at the production level. Up to 16 points were possible in this section (4 points for each form). The total scores for the pre-test were thus 9 points for culture, 7 points for vocabulary, 28 points for focused-grammar items and 16 points for the production-grammar task. Both post-tests were nearly identical to the pre-test, except that three distracters were added in the focused-grammar section; the distracters did not receive any point value.

In order to increase the validity of the data, a subset of the test data were scored by another researcher (agreement rate = 99.8%).

To test the first research question, a Mixed Model Linear Analysis was used as it allowed the analysis of the within-group effect over the period of the three tests. The second research question was analyzed through a series of Multivariate General Linear Model post hocs tests, to compare the effects of instruction types between groups. Alpha was set at .05 for all statistical tests. The choice for those analyses was based on the fact that the effects among groups and between groups were necessary, and this is a very common practice in classroom-setting studies. Furthermore, a test of interaction effects was not essential, as evidence from the qualitative observations (chapter 4) showed that teachers were not controlled in such a way to make the tests of interaction effects appropriate for this study.

### 3.6.2 Teacher data

The teacher data were collected by videotaping the lessons, conducting questionnaires (Appendices U and V), and personal interviews between the researcher and the teachers. Because some teachers could not answer the questionnaires or participate in an interview due to a busy schedule, I was not able to collect answers from all teachers. The video recordings provided adequate support to check the application of the instructional approaches.

Additionally, it helped the researcher to better understand teachers' choices in applying the instructions. The teachers' responses on the questionnaires and during the interviews served to elucidate their online decision-making during the culture lesson. The qualitative analysis of all the teacher data, found in chapter 4, provides insights on their awareness of their teaching, on their applications of the provided instructions and on their language choice.

## 3.7 Pilot study

Before conducting the data collection, I was interested in knowing if the teaching material would be efficient and what teachers thought of the content and procedure. Therefore, a semester prior to the experiments, the cultural lesson, inserted in the syllabi of second- and third-semester French, served as a pilot study of the material used for the future experiment. A few days before the cultural lessons, the researcher gave the lesson plans on Belgium to the second-semester teaching assistants and the lesson plans on Senegal to the third-semester teaching assistants. Due to a strict syllabus (followed by several sections), the researcher asked two teaching assistanta at the second-semester level and two at the third-semester level to teach the lessons with different instructional approaches. As explained earlier, learning the cultural content was the intended goal for all groups; changes occurred at the level of focus-on-form, and the types of instruction of the linguistic forms in order to compare their effects. After the cultural lesson, the researcher individually contacted each teaching assistant in order to elicit constructive feedback. Overall, the impression given by the teaching assistants showed satisfaction with the content of the material. They found the cultural information interesting and relevant to the course. However, for some of them, the quantity of information was such that they were unable to organize their time efficiently, due to the additional activities following the teacher-fronted presentation. As a result of these comments, the researcher shortened the length of information and attempted to make the activities more comprehensible. The teaching assistants also received a satisfied reaction from their students.

CHAPTER FOUR

Qualitative analysis of teachers' teaching practice

and language choice

**4.1 Introduction**

During the gathering of the data for the quantitative analysis of this research project and to ensure the validity of the treatment types (focus on meaning, planned focus-on-form, incidental focus-on-form), video recordings of all the cultural lessons were made. In order to analyze teaching practices and application of instruction, this chapter addresses two main questions: 1) Did the teachers apply the material according to the instructions provided by the treatment they were assigned? 2) Because of their need to communicate information, were they confronted by a language choice (L1 or L2) in order to facilitate instruction? To answer those questions, this chapter is divided into two sections. The first section investigates the application of the instructions by teachers and their teaching practices. The second section covers the language choice involved in the instructors' discourse.

**4.2 Teaching practices**

The instructors responsible for teaching and presenting a language have their own personal conceptions and teaching philosophy, based on their previous experience and/or on the training they receive. Because of the different backgrounds instructors have, their resulting teaching philosophies and practice can differ greatly (Borg, 2003; Breen, 2002; Breen, Hird, Milton, Oliver & Thwaite, 2001; Nunan, 1992; Pessoa et al., 2007; Richards, 1994; Schulz, 1996, 2001; Wray, 1993, Zucker, 2005). Richards (1994) describes belief systems that teachers develop and bring to the classroom, based on "information, attitudes, values, theories and assumptions about teaching and learning" and based on "experience, school practice, personality, educational theory, reading and other sources" (p. 4). These shape the way teachers apply the teaching of language or any other topic. There is a text (i.e., instruction written or taught) at the base of the teaching, but the way it is presented depends in part on the teacher's perceptions and decisions (Shulman, 1987). In the present study, it was observed that despite similar instructions for the intended cultural lessons, the presentation of the information varied from teacher to teacher. In order to analyze their practice, it is important to observe how they taught. Research in second language teaching has not been very fruitful in the area of teachers' cognition and beliefs. Most of the studies have specifically focused on the teaching of grammar (Andrews, 1994, 1999; Borg, 1998a, 1998b, 1999a, 1999b, 2003, Johnston & Goettsch, 2000; Williamson & Hardman, 1995). Since the present research attempts to integrate grammar and vocabulary within culture, it is important to examine how teachers reacted when faced with the teaching of form, especially for the teachers involved in the focus-on-form groups.

According to Breen et al. (2001), teachers acquire a set of teaching principles from personal theories, based on pedagogical and theoretical knowledge. Those principles influence the interaction between the learners, the teacher and the course content. Despite the variety of principles, the researchers also noticed many similarities among those teachers, such as the importance of individual differences among learners.

One can speculate that a good teacher is a teacher who, in part, understands the foreign language clearly and deeply, and is therefore a teacher who is aware of the details of the language. In the research literature, the matter of grammatical and linguistic knowledge on the part of the teachers has been studied (Borg, 1998a, 1998b, 1999b, 2003; Chandler, Robinson & Noyes, 1988; Johnson & Goettsch, 2000; Pessoa et al., 2007; Zucker, 2005). Many studies on the issue of teacher cognition are overviewed in Borg (2003), who notes that in several studies, teachers show a lack of grammatical knowledge of the language they teach. He refers to that lack of knowledge as "detrimental to the effectiveness of the formal instruction teachers provide" (p.100). However, as Borg also mentions, the types of methods used in the teaching are more important. If the teaching method is communicative, the ability to give explicit grammatical explanation might not be a necessary skill to possess. If the teaching is focusing more on form, the issues raised by Borg (2003) might be problematic. In the case of my study, the general teaching philosophy of the lower-division courses is based on communicative language teaching, with the support of a fairly explicit grammar explanation in each chapter of the textbook. The instructors of this study were not tested on their grammatical knowledge of French, since the purpose was to simply view their natural teaching methods. The manner they applied the instructions provided to them is important to describe, as doing so furthers our understanding of teachers' practices in communicative language classrooms.

4.2.1 Data collection and expectations

The total time of recordings in this study amounted to 17 hours, with 8 hours recorded at the second-semester level and 9 hours at the third-semester level of French. As previously mentioned, the topic of the cultural content and the grammatical and lexical foci depended on the level of instruction and on the groups. At the second-semester level, Belgium was the country introduced, while for the third semester, it was Senegal. Each level was divided into three treatment groups: focus on meaning, incidental focus-on-form and planned focus-on-form. Each teacher was given instructions on how to carry out their lesson; however, in order not to disturb the natural predilections of the teachers, those instructions were kept limited and general (see Appendices C-E and Appendices M-O). Instructions varied depending on the treatment the teachers were assigned to, as seen in the appendices.

I carefully watched each video to ensure proper administration of the instruction. However, I noticed that some teachers did not carry out the lesson the way I had planned; for example, some teachers who were asked to only present the information, without any special focus, would focus on some lexical items; while another who should have brought a stronger focus to the grammatical items did not mention them to her students. This was not due to a lack of involvement and interest in the study; instead, I believe that the interpretation of the instructions might have diverged from how I had expected them to be interpreted. I was conscious that if I gave too many details in the instruction, I could interfere with the natural teaching style of the teachers. I wanted to avoid any such interference in order to observe as realistically as possible the teachers' application of CEI. Therefore, depending on the treatment, I told the teachers to either present what was on the transparencies, to answer students' questions or bring to their attention what they might believe to be important, or to present the transparencies while specifically introducing the enhanced target grammatical and lexical items.

It is important to recall that most instructors were assigned to the treatment based on observations I had previously done. Given the three treatments included in the study, I expected two or three different types of teaching practice from the teachers. With the focus-on-meaning treatment, I had planned that teachers would only present the cultural content, without explaining specific language forms. The incidental focus-on-form treatment directed teachers to respond to students' errors or questions through feedback or to bring up areas they found problematic. Finally, the role of planned focus-on-form treatment was to provide explanations on the marked (input enhanced) structures, which were grammatical and lexical. The written instructions to teachers (see Appendices C-E and Appendices M-O) showed that most of the instructions were the same, except in the case of the planned focus-on-form instruction, which contained an additional paragraph (bolded in the instructions): "Comme tu peux le remarquer, il y a des choses qui sont soulignées de différentes couleurs. Essaye d'insister dessus en pensant que certains points sont sur des informations culturelles, sur du vocabulaire ou sur de la grammaire. Essaye de tous les présenter aussi bien que tu peux, mais ne passe pas trop de temps"[6]. In addition to this paragraph, during our first meeting, I explicitly told those teachers that they had to point out the colored and bolded information. It was imperative that teachers follow my instructions, as this ensured that the students would receive the intended treatment and thereby allow me to test my research questions. Furthermore, research on teachers' practices is necessary in the field of language instruction. Studies (Borg, 1998a, 1998b, 1999b, 2003; Breen, 2002; Breen et al., 2001; Johnson & Goettsch, 2000) have emphasized that more of such research is needed in order to better understand the teachers and their role in the application of teaching methods. My close examination of teacher practice should further our knowledge of the role of teachers in the application of teaching methods.

---

[6] Translation: *as you can notice, there are some things that are highlighted with different colors. Try to focus on them, thinking that some points are cultural information, vocabulary or grammar. Try to present them all as well as possible, but don't spend too much time either.*

In the next subsection, a description of what happened among the types of instructional treatment (i.e., focus on meaning, incidental focus-on-form, planned focus-on-form) is displayed; this is a summation of the actions and decisions that each teacher made. The videotapes were analyzed according to the following method. All the language episodes specifically involving lexical and grammatical foci were transcribed and analyzed in relation to the treatment assigned to the teachers. The language episodes were coded according to presence of incidental focus-on-form, brought up by the situation, or of planned focus-on-form. The metalinguistic explanations of teachers were also marked down, to view uses of explicit teaching. Examples illustrating the findings are given in each type of treatment category.

4.2.2 Focus-on-meaning group

In the second-semester sections, Monique, Céline and Alexandra (all names throughout this chapter are pseudonyms) are the teachers with the focus-on-meaning treatment. Although Monique presented the information from the transparencies as carefully as possible, she nonetheless created opportunities for the students to ask questions. For example, one student asked for the meaning of "flamand" (*Flemish*). Another wondered about the monarchy of Belgium. In both cases, Monique took time to respond. One common way she verified students' knowledge of their lexical comprehension was by asking them the meaning of words or expressions (examples 1-3). This practice involved the students in the lesson and allowed a more interactive presentation.

> Example 1:
> Monique:  L'horloge de Bruges, vous savez ce que ça veut dire 'horloge'?
>              *[The Bruges bell tower, do you know what it means 'bell tower']*
> *Students negotiate some meaning but not understandable*
> Monique:  Oui, *bell tower*.
>              *[Yes, bell tower]*
>
> Example 2:
> Monique:  Voilà les moules-frites
>              *[Here are the mussels-fries]*
> Student:    *What's* moules?
>              *[What's mussels?]*

>     Monique: Moules? *Mussels*
>     Student: *Fries and mussels!*
>
> Example 3:
>     Monique: Que veut dire 'ne me quitte pas'?
>              *[What does 'don't leave me' mean?]*
>     Student: *Don't leave me.*
>     Monique: Oui, *don't leave me.*
>              *[Yes, don't leave me]*

This type of decision is natural for the teacher: even though no encouragement was made on my part to bring forms to attention, Monique brought attention to some vocabulary she assumed students might have difficulty with.

Monique was not purposefully aware of the focused grammatical structure of my research, as I did not refer to it when I met with her. And this is exemplified when she went over one of the items, without focusing on the grammar, but rather on its lexical meaning (example 4).

> Example 4:
>     Monique: La Belgique est aussi grande que le Maryland, donc c'est relativement petit.
>              *[Belgium is as big as Maryland, so it is relatively small.]*

As was expected, Monique followed the instructions given to her, but when exposed to a need for lexical clarification, she did not hesitate to make use of a type of reactive focus-on-form. She naturally transforms material that is solely focusing on meaning into one that incidentally focuses on form.

As for Céline, her students did not initiate any questions at all. The lack of student participation can be attributed to the fact that the students were part of the summer session, and therefore had to be in French class for four hours four days a week. This means that their level of oral French might not have been be as advanced as most $2^{nd}$-semester classes, since the acceleration of a summer course does not allow for as much oral participation. Yet, the linguistic knowledge and written production should be relatively equal to regular semester, as learners followed the same curriculum, and had the same number of course hours. Moreover, the students might have not been as familiar with their instructors. Monique had been teaching her class for almost 2 months during a regular semester, while Céline had only been teaching her class for 2 weeks during an intensive summer session. Similarly to Monique, Céline asked a few clarification questions on the vocabulary and the cultural items, but her principal strategies were either to use English, or to paraphrase (examples 5-6).

> Example 5:
> Céline: On a une photo d'une gaufre belge que l'on ne voit pas très bien. Mais vous savez-ce que c'est qu'une gaufre? Vous connaissez les gaufres? Nan? *['nan' is a familiar way to say 'non']*The Belgian waffles. Ce sont des gaufres.
> *[We have a picture of a Belgian waffle that we can't see very well. But do we know what a waffle is? Do you know waffles? No? The Belgian waffles. These are waffles.]*

> Example 6:
> Céline: Ici vous avez des moules-frites. Donc des moules-frites. Les moules, c'est un fruit de mer. D'accord? Oui.
> *[Here, you have some mussels-fries. So some mussels-fries. Mussels are a type of seafood. Okay? Yes.]*

Because Céline's students did not indicate any difficulties, she only focused on what she believed they did not understand. Similarly to Monique, she also brought a few lexical forms to attention, but no indication from the students was given that they noticed them, since she never checked for comprehension, and they never asked for clarification.

Alexandra acted very much like Monique in bringing students' attention to forms, either by paraphrasing, by writing difficult words on the board, or by asking for a translation (example 7). However, most of the language episodes that showed negotiation of meaning were not among the items targeted in the planned focus-on-form material.

> Example 7:
> Alexandra: Il y a des canaux à Bruges, avec donc de l'eau, ici, *water*, et donc vous voyez ici, les maisons, ici ce n'est pas la rue, c'est de l'eau. *It is water, okay?* Il y a des canaux à Bruges.
> *[There are canals in Bruges, with water, here, water, and then you can see here, the houses, here, it is not a street, it is water. It is water, okay? There are canals in Bruges.]*

Alexandra's students were very active and asked questions, mainly regarding the culture (about Belgian beer, endives). She was also trying to make sure her students understood the content of the message and to often bring lexical forms to their attention.

For the 3rd-semester classes, Aurélie and Marie were the instructors. Aurélie's teaching style was very consistent in the two classes she taught. As did the second-semester instructors, Aurélie brought a few (non-targeted) lexical items that she believed might be problematic to her students' attention (examples 8-10).

> Example 8:
> Aurélie: Un autre mot pour ça (pirogue), c'est un bateau
> *[Another word for that is boat.]*
> Example 9:
> Aurélie: Vous comprenez le mot 'mouton'?
> *[Do you understand the word 'sheep'?]*
> Student: Sheep
> Aurélie: Oui, béééé
> *[Yes, baaaa]*
>
> Example 10:
> Aurélie: Vous comprenez 'amer'? (*silence*) *bitter*, ça veut dire que le thé est amer.
> *[Do you understand 'bitter'? Bitter, it means that the tea is bitter.]*

Among the words Aurélie pointed out to her students, three of the words were part of the seven target words of the study: Aurélie considered those words to be a possible comprehension obstruction, supporting my initial assessment of the words as items not known by the students. One student in Aurélie's first class also asked a question on a verb form (example 11). This appears to be the only focus on a grammatical form during her class, but closer inspection reveals that it is in fact a focus on word meaning, as the true question turns on what "élu" means:

> Example 11:
> Student: 'élu' est-ce que c'est le passé composé de '*elect*'?
> *['elect', is it the past tense of 'elect'?]*
> Aurélie: Oui, le sens en anglais, c'est '*elect*', mais le mot en français c'est 'élire'.
> *[Yes, the meaning in English is 'elect', but the word in French is to elect'.]*

Then Aurélie spells the word in French.

Another time, Aurélie used a similar technique to communicate the idea of the Senegalese national holiday (example 12).

> Example 12:
> Aurélie: Le 4 avril, c'est comme le 4 juillet aux USA.
> *[The 4$^{th}$ of April, it is like the 4$^{th}$ of July in the USA.]*

Marie might have been the only teacher who closely adhered to the information on the transparencies, without interrupting the flow by checking comprehension or paraphrasing. She only translated three words in order to help with comprehension (examples 13 and 14).

> Example 13:
> Marie: 'Course', c'est comme le Tour de France, race.
> *['Race', it is like the Tour de France, 'race'.]*

> Example 14:
> Marie: Des champs très différents, *fields*, des champs très différents qu'ici, en Illinois.
> *[Some very different fields, fields, some fields very different than here, in Illinois.]*

Nunan (1992) comments that teachers make interactive decisions principally for student understanding, student motivation and involvement and instructional management. This appears to be true in most of the teaching presented above: teachers were not told to answer students' questions or check their comprehension, but they still brought the problematic lexical items to their students' attention. Focus-on-form seems to be spontaneous and natural in most teaching; despite no particular indication on my part to help students this way, the teachers I videotaped felt a strong need to do it. However, these instructors did not make reference to grammar. The vocabulary was the only source for negotiations.

Other examples show that the teachers in the focus-on-meaning condition would expand on meaning through providing more information on some cultural or personal issues. For instance, Monique talked about Belgian waffles (example 15), while Aurélie spent time describing the pictures of Senegal she was showing (example 16):

> Example 15:
> Monique: Vous connaissez 'les gaufres belges'? Elles sont très délicieuses!
> *[Do you know 'Belgian waffles'? They are very delicious!]*

Example 16:
Aurélie :   Beaucoup de couleurs...les Sénégalais aiment nager...
            *[Many colors ... the Senegalese people like to swim...]*

Expanding on meaning is an expected technique of focus on meaning, as meaning is being clarified for the learners through more extensive explanations. Focusing on meaning entails that only meaning is discussed, not forms. This is where the distinction between lexical forms and vocabulary meaning needs to be made. Vocabulary, an essential feature of comprehending the cultural message, was always the cause of the focusing. Yet, the reason for focusing on vocabulary was not to understand each work individually, as a focus-on-form treatment might entail, but rather to understand the general message. It is a support for communication, for clarity of meaning.

### 4.2.3 Incidental focus-on-form groups

The second treatment, incidental focus-on-form, was carried out by Annabelle, Jeanne, and Danielle in the second-semester, and Eddy and Julie in the third-semester. I had encouraged them to stimulate students' questions, to respond to upcoming difficulties and to students' errors through feedback.

At the beginning of the lessons, they told their students to ask questions if they had any (examples 17-20), which was the statement that was encouraging students to interrupt if necessary.

Example 17:
Annabelle: Si vous avez des questions, vous pouvez m'interrompre.
            *[If you have any questions, you can interrupt me.]*

Example 18:
Eddy:      N'hésitez pas à poser des questions.
            [Don't hesitate to ask questions.]

Example 19:
Julie:     Je vais parler seulement en français donc si vous avez des questions, posez-les.

> [I will only speak French, so if you have any questions, ask them.]

**Example 20:**
Julie: Est-ce qu'il y a des questions? Vous comprenez?
[Are there any questions? Do you understand?]

In most classes, very few students took advantage of this opportunity. More often than not, it was the teachers who generated the incidental attention to forms (examples 21-25).

**Example 21:**
Eddy: Qu'est-ce que c'est qu'une pirogue? C'est une sorte de...
[What is a pirogue? It is a sort of....]
Student: Bateau.
[Boat.]
Eddy: Oui.
[Yes.]

**Example 22:**
Eddy: Vous comprenez 'champs'?
[Do you understand 'fields'?]
Student: Field
Eddy: Très bien!
[Very good!]

**Example 23:**
Julie: Qu'est-ce que c'est le phosphate?
[What is phosphate?]
Student: Phosphate.
Julie: Oui c'est vrai.
[Yes, it is true.]

**Example 24:**
Julie: Qu'est-ce que c'est le fer?
[What is iron?]
Student: Iron.

**Example 25:**
Julie: Qu'est-ce que c'est une pirogue?
[What is a pirogue?]
Student: Boat
Julie: Oui, *a bark, a boat*.
[Yes, a bark, a boat.]

Concerning the teaching of vocabulary, the application of the instructions followed my expectations. Answering students' questions and bringing up possible problems was the goal under the heading incidental focus-on-form.

The grammar was explained by only one teacher. Even though Anabelle did not know that this study was introducing the comparative and superlative, she brought this form several times to students' attention through comparing and paraphrasing the grammatical form (examples 26-29). She also attempted to stimulate the learners' interest during the lesson by asking questions, but very few of her students were answering, either because of lack of comprehension or lack of enthusiasm. However, it is obvious she was making sure learners understood the information by paraphrasing or by repeating sentences several times.

Example 26:
Annabelle: Elle est aussi grande que...elle est la même que... la même chose, similaire.
*[It is as big as... it is the same than... the same thing, similar.]*

Example 27:
Annabelle: Plus chaud ... plus élevé.
*[Warmer ... higher.]*

Example 28:
Annabelle: Il y a moins de fromages qu'en France, il y a plus de fromages en France.
*[There are fewer cheeses than in France, there are more cheeses in France.]*

Example 29:
Annabelle: Renaud est plus contemporain, Brel n'est pas aussi nouveau que Renaud.
*[Renaud is more contemporary, Brel is not as new as Renaud.]*

By this method of paraphrasing, Annabelle actually covered the grammatical targeted forms (comparative and superlative of adjectives) that, unbeknownst to her of, were of interest in the study. Unlike the other instructors, she did not bring specific vocabulary to attention, but rather grammatical forms. She did not explicitly present those forms; her method (repetition and paraphrasing) is more implicit. In the instructions I had given her, I had specifically pointed out to Annabelle to tell her students not to hesitate if they had any questions on the cultural facts, the grammar or vocabulary.

Jeanne was probably the most experienced teacher of the group (with 10 years of previous teaching) and had taught an extensive variety of beginning to advanced courses. Her class was small compared to the other experimental classes, which allowed her to get to know all of her students quite well. During the presentation of the cultural lesson, Jeanne took a few opportunities to add some cultural information or make personal comments on Belgium, as she had spent a year abroad in Belgium several years prior to the study. Despite a very enthusiastic involvement throughout the presentation, she did not produce any type of incidental focus-on-form, as all the focus was brought to bear on meaning. Likewise, the learners did not ask any questions, but instead only acknowledged Jeanne's explanations and personal remarks by laughter. This behavior might actually support a phenomenon that I have personally experienced: when presenting culture, the teaching of any other aspect of the language ceases. Having to deal with more complex structures and new vocabulary while introducing new content might force the teacher to make a choice on what becomes priority, to their understanding. Since Jeanne knew that she had to introduce cultural information about Belgium that became her focus. She was very enthusiastic about the content, as she stated "it was so great to have an opportunity to share about the country I love so much". However, due to her lack of incidental focus-on-form, Jeanne was switched from the original group to which she had been assigned to the group of focus-on-meaning treatment, in order to better match her actual behavior to the treatment objectives.

Subsequent to the presentation, Julie said that she did not really enjoy teaching the lesson, as it did not match her style: "it was difficult to teach in a way that was not natural to me". This comment is significant, because it tells me that she did not use a technique that she was used to. It is also felt by her tone of voice, which, during the presentation itself (and not during the activities), was not natural. I was hoping that the teachers would integrate their own teaching style into the lesson. Yet, even if Julie tried, she felt like she was forced into lecturing too much, and that the interactions between her and the students were not initiated by the lesson. For Julie, the interference of my instructions was felt too strongly. It is important to know that teachers cannot be forced to deliver certain kinds of instruction if enthusiasm and effectiveness are expected. However, all the other teachers told me they enjoyed the cultural lesson, as it was informative and they believed their students appreciated the different class format.

Overall, the expectations I had regarding what teachers did in order to incidentally focus-on-form were met, as teachers pointed out many lexical items they found difficult for their students. The reason given for the focus-on-meaning treatment, as why vocabulary was focused, is probably also true here, as most lexical items were pointed out by the teachers in order to convey the general message of the cultural content. However, because very few opportunities for incidental focus-on-form arose, the teachers did not often respond to questions or errors. This is probably explained by the nature of a teacher-fronted lesson, which did not provide many opportunities for teachers and students to interact.

### 4.2.4 Planned focus-on-form group

The planned focus-on-form group was the group that received the most instructions as the teachers were instructed to provide explanations on the marked (input enhanced) structures. Thierry taught two sections of the second-semester classes and Emilie, Blanche, Alice and Nicole taught the third-semester levels. The reason for having so many teachers in the third-semester courses teaching the planned focus-on-form treatment was to have a similar number of student participants compared to the other two third-semester treatment groups.

Thierry taught his two classes in a slightly different manner, especially regarding the focus-on-form. With his first section, when he went over a superlative structure, Thierry first stressed the structure with his voice (noted by capitalized words n transcripts), then repeated it by adding some metalinguistic talk (example 30).

> Example 30:
> Thierry: Bruxelles la ville la PLUS importante (...) La PLUS importante, ça veut dire, c'est ce que l'on appelle superlatif.
> *[Brussels the most important city (...) The most important, it means, it is what we call superlative.]*

Grammatically speaking, this was all he mentioned. The rest of the time, he paraphrased one of the early comparative expressions and checked the comprehension of another one (examples 31 and 32).

Example 31:
Thierry: 'Aussi grande', vous comprenez? Pas plus, pas moins.
['As tall', do you understand? Not more, not less.]

Example 32:
Thierry: Vous comprenez la phrase 'plus petite, plus rustique, ouais, c'est clair?
[Do you understand the sentence 'smaller, more rustic, yeah, it is clear?]

For the vocabulary, Thierry brought attention to a few items by asking students if they understood. In a few instances, a student directly asked for meaning (examples 33-36).

Example 33:
Thierry: C'est quoi une horloge?
[What is a bell tower?]

Example 34:
Thierry: Gaufre en anglais?
[Waffles in English?]
Student: Waffles

Example 35:
Thierry: Le roi n'a pas tous les pouvoirs, vous comprenez 'pouvoirs'? En réalité c'est le Premier Ministre, c'est comme en Angleterre.
[The king does not have all the powers, you understand 'powers'? In reality, it is the Prime Minister, it is like in England.]
Student: Pouvoirs?
[Powers?]
Thierry: Quoi?
[What?]
Student: Pouvoirs?
[Powers?]
Thierry: C'est quoi 'pouvoirs'? C'est lui qui dit qu'il a tout le pouvoir, vous comprenez? Power.
[What is 'powers'? It is he that says that he has the power, do you understand? Power.]

Example 36:
Thierry: Voilà une photo des moules et des frites. Qui aime ça? Elizabeth, vous aimez les moules?
*[Here is a photo of some mussels and some fries. Who likes those? Elizabeth, do you like mussels?]*
Student: Oui.
*[Yes.]*
Thierry: Vous autres? Lindsay? Et les frites?
*[You, others? Lindsay? And fries?]*
Student: Qu'est-ce que 'moules'?
*[What is 'mussels'?]*
Thierry: Moules? Vous ne pouvez pas voir? Puisque vous aimez, Elizabeth, expliquez c'est quoi les moules?
*[Mussels? You can't see? Since you like them. Elizabeth, explain what mussels are.]*
Student: *I am not sure what* moules *is.*
Other student: *Mussels*
Thierry: Ouais, qui aime les moules, maintenant ? Très populaire à Quebec aussi.
*[Yeah, who like mussels, now? Very popular in Quebec too.]*

This focus-on-form is very similar to that provided by most teachers previously mentioned; however, in this case, Thierry could see that the forms were important by their enhancement, so he mentioned some of them.

Thierry's second class was conducted very similarly, except for the fact that since in his previous class, some students had difficulties with words such as "powers", he brought the vocabulary up himself by asking for their meaning. With the grammatical focus, however, Thierry did very little explicit instruction. He did give a brief explanation once in both of his classes (example 37).

Example 37:
Thierry: Vous comprenez 'plus importante, la plus importante'? *It's superlative.* Il n'y a aucune ville plus importante. La Belgique est aussi grande que l'état de Maryland, donc c'est assez petit, okay?
*[Do you understand 'more important, the most important'? It's superlative. There is no other city more important. Belgium is as big as the state of Maryland, so it is rather small, okay?]*

At the third-semester level, often at the beginning of the lesson and then less frequently, Emilie pointed out the relative pronouns with preceding prepositions. Her manner was explicit in that she used metalinguistic explanations to bring the grammatical forms to attention and/or she repeated the grammatical target form, as if it might have helped students understand better. Her metalinguistic talk included words such as relative pronouns (which could be obscure for some students) or feminine, masculine, singular, or plural forms (very comprehensible to students) (examples 38-41).

Example 38:
Emilie: La capitale dans laquelle se trouve le centre est Dakar. Ici, par exemple, vous voyez le pronom relatif "dans laquelle" c'est parce que la capitale, c'est un nom féminin, *it's a place* so on utilise 'dans, dans laquelle'. Alors on va voir plus d'exemples.
*[The capital in which the center is found is Dakar. Here, for example, you see the relative pronoun 'in which', it is because the capital is a feminine noun, it's a place so we use 'in, in which'. So we will see more examples.]*

Example 39:
Emilie.: Il y a environ 10 millions d'habitants parmi lesquels on trouve une grande diversité ethnique. Ici, vous voyez par exemple 'parmi lesquels'. Pourquoi c'est 'lesquels'? C'est parce qu'on parle de habitants (?), n'est-ce pas? Les Sénégalais, c'est masculin pluriel alors on fait l'accord, 'parmi lesquels, among whom'.
*[There are about 10 million inhabitants among whom we can find a great ethnic diversity. Here, you see for example 'among whom'. Why is it 'whom? It is because we talk of inhabitants (?), isn't it? The Senegalese people, it is masculine plural, so we make the agreement, 'among whom, among whom'.]*

Example 40:
Emilie: Aujourd'hui, c'est une république dans laquelle il y a un président élu démocratiquement, alors ici, vous voyez aussi 'une république dans laquelle' parce que 'république' est un nom féminin et puis singulier alors, donc on utilise 'dans laquelle' or 'in which' or 'at which'.
*[Today, it is a republic in which there is democratically elected president, so here, you also see 'a republic in which' because 'republic' is a feminine noun, and singular at that, so we use 'in which' or 'in which' or 'at which'.]*

Example 41:
Emilie: La saison des pluies pendant laquelle, par exemple, ici 'laquelle' par exemple parce que c'est une saison, c'est féminin singulier...
*[The rainy season during which, for example, here 'which' for example because it is a season, it is feminine singular ...]*

With the vocabulary, she did not ask question to check students' comprehension; rather, she just directly translated the words she considered complex (examples 42-47).

Example 42:
Emilie: 'Fer', qu'est-ce que c'est en anglais?
[Iron, what is it in English?]

Example 43:
Emilie: 'Campagne', ça veut dire *like 'country'*.
['Country', it means like 'country'.]

Example 44:
Emilie: 'Champs', qu'est-ce que c'est en anglais? Like fields.
['Field', what is it in English? Like fields.]

Example 45:
Emilie: On mange du mouton. Vous comprenez 'mouton'? On mange du mouton en anglais like mutton en anglais.
*[We eat mutton. Do you understand 'mutton'? We eat mutton in English like mutton in English.]*

Example 46:
Emilie: Amer, c'est *like bitter*.
[Bitter, it is like bitter.]

Example 47:
Emilie: On va à la mosquée pour prier, *to pray*.
[We go to mosque to pray, to pray.]

Except for one instance when a student asked for the translation of a word he noticed and did not understand (example 48), Emilie initiated all foci on vocabulary.

Example 48:
Student: Qu'est-ce que ça veut dire 'amer'?
[What does 'bitter' mean?]
Emilie: Amer? *Bitter*.
[Bitter? Bitter.]

Nicole also gave some metalinguistic explanations to highlight the grammatical forms (examples 49-51).

Example 49:
Nicole: Cette structure, on va voir plusieurs fois, nous avons 'lequel, laquelle, lesquels' comme pronom interrogatif pour demander *'which one'*. Ici on l'utilise comme pronom relatif comme 'que, qui, dont' avec une préposition. Donc 'dans laquelle' qu'est-ce que ça veut dire?
*[This structure, we will see several times, we have 'which (masculine singular), which (feminine singular), which' (masculine plural) as an interrogative pronoun to ask 'which one'. Here, we use it as a relative pronoun as, that, who, of which, with a preposition. So 'in which" what does it mean?]*
Student: *In which*

Example 50:
Nicole: Parmi lesquelles? (...) parmi, ça vous dit quelque chose? Among une grande diversité, 10 millions d'habitants parmi lesquels, among which on trouve une grande diversité.
*[Among which? (...) among, does it mean something? Among a great diversity, 10 millions inhabitants, among which, among which we can find a great diversity.]*

Example 51:
Nicole: Pendant laquelle. Laquelle s'accorde avec quoi? Féminin singulier, une saison, il faut regarder le nom qui vient avant une saison.
*[During which. Which one agrees with what? Feminine singular, a season, you need to look at the noun that comes before a season.]*

However, she only pointed out three of the enhanced words on the transparencies.

In the case of Alice, her teaching style for focusing on form was unique when compared to the other teachers in the planned focus-on-form group. Instead of going over each enhanced grammatical and lexical form while teaching, she mentioned at the beginning of class that they needed to be careful with the red words, which meant that they were about grammar, and with the green words, which meant they were new vocabulary. She directed their attention to these features right at the beginning, but very rarely during the lesson. Since Alice drew the students' attention to the input enhancement technique, it can still be interpreted as presenting a planned focus-on-form. The students did not receive any type of explicit instructions on the red forms (grammar) and very few on the green ones (vocabulary) (examples 52 and 53).

Example 52:
Alice: C'est quoi le fer?

>   *[What is iron?]*
>   Student: *Silver?*
>   Alice: Non *[no]*, but it is a metal.
>   Other student: *Iron*
>
> Example 53:
>   Alice: Le thé est très fort et amer. Amer, qu'est-ce que ça veut dire 'amer'? Quand on fait des choses, ce que l'on mange, est amer. Le citron… quelque chose qui n'est pas sucré est amer. Qui a un example?
>   *[The tea is very strong and bitter. Bitter, what does 'bitter' mean? When we do things, what we eat, is bitter. Lemon… something that is not sweet is bitter. Who has an example?]*
>   Student: *Strong coffee or strong tea without sugar.*
>   Alice: Oui, *strong coffee or strong tea without sugar, and you don't put sugar in it, it can be bitter.*

She probably focused on the highlighted words that she believed to be more difficult to understand, even with the context.

The last teacher in the group of planned focus-on-form was Blanche. She was very dynamic and told me that she found the lesson very interesting. However, Blanche did not at all focus on the grammatical targeted forms. She went over the content, as if nothing but the vocabulary could obstruct the flow of the lesson. She did highlight some of the lexical items, but ignored the grammatical ones. Due to this methodological difference, a decision had to be made in order to accurately analyze the quantitative data. Because Blanche's class was first assigned to the planned focus-on-form group and because she did not use planned focus-on-form techniques with the grammatical items, it was decided that Blanche's students would be grouped with the incidental focus-on-form group, as Blanche brought up upcoming difficulties that were not marked, and did not especially focus on the marked forms (examples 54 and 55).

> Example 54:
>   Student: Fer, *what is it?*
>   *[Iron, what is it?]*
>   Blanche: *Iron.*
>
> Example 55:
>   Blanche: Est-ce que vous comprenez 'amer'? C'est *'bitter'*.
>   *[Do you understand 'bitter'? It is 'bitter'.]*

Blanche's practice was surprising, especially since I had based my choice of having her do a planned focus-on-form treatment on the observation I had previously made of her class. During that observation, she had been giving detailed explanations on grammar. However, Blanche was also a teacher who had a strong background in second language acquisition, and told me recently that she had been very interested in content-based instruction. This interest might have influenced her teaching, as she saw a content to communicate when the grammar was not required for comprehension. Another hypothesis is that she, like Jeanne, might have felt overwhelmed with the different components to cover, and therefore selected what may have been the most interesting and fundamental one to her: culture.

When looking at the teachers' practice of instruction, even though the presentations were in the form of lectures, most of them included personal questions or comments. I believe it is important that, even when they are given instructional materials and textbooks, teachers understand the possibility they have of bringing their personal styles into their teaching. It also seems that most teachers performed some kind of incidental focus-on-form, which they initiated when they saw an upcoming comprehension problem. All non-planned foci were on vocabulary or cultural facts, which are the foundation of a meaningful message.

### 4.2.5 Conclusion

In summary, this study has been challenging, but yet illuminating for the following quantitative section: some of the instructions were not applied as I had expected, and therefore some changes had to be made in the organization of the treatment groups. Tables 4.1 through 4.3 represent the number of the focus-on-form episodes that occurred in the different groups, giving more support to choosing certain teachers for certain treatment conditions and to switching two teachers to different treatment groups, in order to better match their behavior with a specific treatment conditions.

Table 4.1 : Episodes of Focus on Form: Totals of Vocabulary and Grammar for individual teachers - Focus on meaning groups

| Teacher | Total FonF Vocabulary | Total FonF Grammar | Total FonF All | Student questions |
|---|---|---|---|---|
| Monique (Sem 2) | 4 | 0 | 4 | 0 |
| Céline (Sem 2) | 1 | 0 | 1 | 0 |
| Alexandra (Sem 2) | 3 | 0 | 3 | 0 |
| **Total Semester 2** | **8** | **0** | **8** | **0** |
| Aurélie (Sem 3) #1 | 3 | 0 | 3 | 0 |
| Aurélie (Sem 3) #2 | 3 | 0 | 3 | 0 |
| Marie (Sem 3) | 3 | 0 | 3 | 0 |
| **Total Semester 3** | **9** | **0** | **9** | **0** |
| **GRAND TOTAL** | **17** | **0** | **17** | **0** |

Table 4.2: Episodes of Focus on Form: Totals of Vocabulary and Grammar for individual teachers – Planned Focus-on-Form groups

| Teacher | Total FonF Vocabulary | Total FonF Grammar | Total FonF All | Student questions |
|---|---|---|---|---|
| Thierry (Sem 2) #1 | 6 | 2 | 8 | 1 |
| Thierry (Sem 2) #2 | 8 | 1 | 9 | 0 |
| **Total Semester 2** | **14** | **3** | **17** | **1** |
| Emilie (Sem 3) | 7 | 8 | 15 | 1 |
| Nicole (Sem 3) | 5 | 4 | 9 | 0 |
| Alice (Sem 3) | 2 | 1 | 3 | 1 |
| Blanche (Sem 3) | 3 | 0 | 3 | 2 |
| **Total Semester 3** | **17** | **13** | **30** | **4** |
| **GRAND TOTAL** | **31** | **16** | **47** | **5** |

Table 4. 3: Episodes of Focus on Form: Totals of Vocabulary and Grammar for individual teachers – Incidental Focus-on-Form groups

| Teacher | Total FonF Vocabulary | Total FonF Grammar | Total FonF All | Student questions |
|---|---|---|---|---|
| Annabelle (Sem 2) | 9 | 0 | 9 | 1 |
| Danielle (Sem 2) | 10 | 0 | 10 | 3 |
| Jeanne (Sem 2) | 6 | 0 | 6 | 0 |
| **Total Semester 2** | **25** | **0** | **25** | **4** |
| Eddy (Sem 3) | 2 | 0 | 2 | 2 |
| Julie (Sem 3) | 3 | 0 | 3 | 2 |
| **Total Semester 3** | **5** | **0** | **5** | **4** |
| **GRAND TOTAL** | **30** | **0** | **30** | **8** |

Most teachers followed the instructions they were provided: the teachers from the focus-on-meaning treatment produced 17 episodes of lexical focus-on-form. The teachers for the planned focus-on-form group produced 31 episodes of lexical focus-on-form and 16 grammatical ones. They were the only group, as planned, who highlighted the targeted grammatical items. One exception is Blanche, who did not show any focus-on-form on grammar. However, since some of her students asked some questions, she was included in the incidental focus-on-form. The teachers of the incidental focus-on-form treatment produced 30 lexical focus-on-form episodes, which is almost twice as much as for the focus-on-meaning teachers. They also responded to students' questions, when comprehension problems were raised. However, in the case of Jeanne, no incidental focus-on-form occurred, which shows support for including her data in the focus-on-meaning group.

This study shows that, in a classroom setting, it is very difficult to control what happens during the experiment. The teachers have their personal styles and experience that they apply in their own teaching, and this is reflected in instructional behavior despite any directions they might receive. Most teachers highlighted problematic lexis to attention in identical ways (i.e., asking learners for the translation of a specific word, directly translating a word, eliciting for the meaning of a word); this might be due to personal and common beliefs they hold on vocabulary acquisition (Breen, 2002; Breen et al., 2001). My hopes are that this small study will shade some light on the understanding of teachers' decisions in their teaching. As Breen et al. (2001) mentioned, it is not possible to predict teachers' behavior from their own perceptions, but as more comparisons are made between classroom observations and teachers' explanations for their decisions, this will become more obvious and clear; hopefully this will results in teachers being better informed about teaching behavior (and their own behavior in particular) in their early training.

Observations by an outsider alone cannot determine teachers' metalinguistic knowledge of the target language. Only a few of them used metalinguistic talk that signaled their expertise in the focused grammatical items of the study. However, if their personal beliefs are that the L2 should be taught through an implicit teaching approach, their personal beliefs may take precedence over the directions they are given for methodology, as in Blanche's and Jeanne's case.

From this examination at teachers' application of instruction, another question arises about teachers' practice. It has been observed in research that when teachers are confronted with a comprehension problem or when they want to give extensive explanations, they might use the L1 to facilitate communication between their students and themselves (Atkinson, 1993; Duff & Polio, 1990; Franklin, 1990; Levine, 2003, forthcoming; Polio & Duff, 1994; Swain & Lapkin, 2000). The experimental lessons recorded for this study have provided rich data to also analyze the language choice teachers made, in order to present meaning and forms or to give feedback. An analysis of their language choice is presented in the next section.

### 4.3 L1 and L2: what role do they have in the classroom?

#### 4.3.1 Introduction

The focus of this present experiment is to observe the effects of different types of treatment on students' learning of both form and content in a cultural lesson. In the section above, it was shown that instructors applied and interpreted with their own style the instructions given out to them. Another factor that needs to be analyzed is the choice of using the L1 instead of the L2 during instruction. This becomes part of focusing on form, as the reasons for choosing the L1 are often caused by checking comprehension, giving feedback, or bringing forms to attention.

Some of the decisions foreign language teachers have to make include the choice of teaching methods and styles; the role of the L1 in their teaching is another. This issue has often been raised but is by no means resolved as many teachers, practitioners and researchers still discuss the role of the L1 in an L2 classroom (Castelloti, 2001; Cook, 2001; Levine, 2003, forthcoming; Macaro, 2001; Moore, 2002; Picker, 2005; Rell, 2005; Thompson, 2006; *Turnbull, 2001;* Turnbull & Arnett, 2002). Methodologies differ drastically in this regard. Some allege that using the L2 exclusively is the only way to achieve accurate learning (Atkinson, 1987; DES (Department of Education and Science), 1996, cited in Cook, 2001; Krashen, 1981, 1985, 1989; Krashen and Terrell, 1983; Macdonald, 1993); others claim that the L1 is fundamental for learning the L2 and should not be separated during instruction (See the *New Concurrent Method,* Jacobson & Fattis, 1990, cited in Cook, 2001; Giauque & Ely, 1990; *Community Language Learning*, Curran, 1976, cited in Cook, 2001; *Dodson's Bilingual Method* – Cook, 2001); finally, the balance between those two principles is that the L2 should be mostly used, but the L1 should not be banned as it is part of the learner's repertoire of strategies of understanding (Atkinson, 1993; Cook, 1999, 2001; Duff & Polio, 1990; Franklin, 1990; Levine, 2003, forthcoming; Polio & Duff, 1994; Rolin-Ianziti & Brownlie, 2002; Swain & Lapkin, 2000; Turnbull & Arnett, 2002). This last belief appears to be the most accepted among researchers and teachers. Observations show that some teachers decide to use only the L2, while others make the choice of using the L1 in order to "facilitate" comprehension or interaction (Cook, 2001; Duff & Polio, 1990; Macaro, 2001; Levine, 2003; Polio & Duff, 1994). Macaro (1997), as well as Levine (2003), refer to the L1-L2 use in the classroom as a continuum going from *"bain de langue"* (full use of L2) to teaching almost entirely in the L1 with the help of L2 recorded materials.

In the present study, 15 teachers were observed through video recording, which provided the researcher with hours of language production on the part of the teachers (the focus of the camera was on the teachers and very little of students' speech was recorded). Attempting to explain the linguistic choice of the teachers and find a possible pattern linked to focus-on-form episodes is the goal behind my inquiries into language use. Furthermore, the use of the L1 is an issue that many L2 teachers and teacher educators wonder about. Therefore, an analysis and categorization of the participating teachers' L1 speech is presented below. Along with this analysis, the few studies on language choice in the L2 classroom will be compared to my results to check for similarities or differences in the findings.

In the department of French of the university where this study took place, no specific policy was mandated to the teachers, it is well understood that the use of the L2 should be maximized as much as possible since the goal is to teach communication in the L2. However, the L1 is not forbidden when needed. This was represented in a previous study (Grim, 2004) in which instructors and professors from the same French department who filled out a questionnaire mentioned that the L2 was the most important language to use; the same questionnaire also indicated that teachers felt the L1 was necessary when difficulties of grammar, vocabulary, and comprehension arose. After watching the recordings provided in this present research, it is obvious that the objective of maximal L2 is well understood by the teachers, as they use very little English (the L1) in the classroom.

### 4.3.2 Data analysis

After collecting all the L1 episodes, a coding system had to be defined in order to classify them. The codes were inspired by previous studies, specifically those of Duff and Polio (1990), Polio and Duff (1994), Rolin-Ianziti and Brownlie (2002) and Levine (2003)[7]. However, due to the results of this present study, the category names differ from the studies in which they originally appeared. Instances are listed below with possible interpretations. The categories are operationalized as:

- Immediate translations: the teacher uses the L1 to give the translation of a word or expression, without asking students for the meaning or taking time to check students' comprehension. This mainly focuses on lexical forms.

---

[7] Only the categories relevant to this study are mentioned. However, the speech of the teachers has revealed other very interesting L1 occurrences, such as humor/personal statement, instructions/clarifications, and cultural explanations. These will be discussed in a subsequent study.

- Delayed translations: the teacher uses the L1 to give the translation of a word or expression, using a prompt which first asks students for the meaning or answering students' inquiries of meaning. This mainly focuses on lexical forms.
- Feedback: the teacher uses the L1 in order to correct students' errors or to focus on grammatical forms.

4.3.3 Immediate and delayed translations

Immediate translations differ from delayed translations in that immediate translations are done immediately following the L2 words or expressions, without a pause. The teacher uses the L1 without asking students for the meaning or taking time to check students' comprehension. A list of some of those occurrences follows (examples 56-68).

Example 56:
Monique: Ça ressemble à quelle ville? *It looks like what?*
[It looks like what city?]

Example 57:
Thierry: C'est presque comme une laitue, *it's almost like a lettuce*, mais c'est plus amer, *it's more bitter*.

Example 58:
Thierry: Vous avez fait cette erreur, *you made that mistake before*.

Example 59:
Julie: Très abstrait, *very, very abstract*.

Example 60:
Aurélie: Mon interprétation, c'est qu'il parle de l'aube, *dawn*.
[My interpretation, it is that he talks of dawn, dawn.]

Example 61:
Emilie: Amer, c'est *like bitter*.
[Bitter, it's like bitter.]

Example 62:
Emilie: Quelques images de la campagne, *country*.
[A few pictures of the country, country.]

Example 63:
Emilie: C'est une course, *it's a race, a car race* avec voitures, motos, camions.
*[It's a race, it's a race, a car race with cars, motos, trucks.]*

Example 64:
Danielle: Vous n'êtes pas obligés de copier. *You don't have to copy everything.*

Example 65:
Danielle: Et je vous aide, *okay, I can help you*, je peux vous aider.

Example 66:
Nicole: ...Les tribus, *the tribes*, et la langue officielle est le français.
*[... and the official language is French.]*

Example 67:
Marie: Des champs très différents, *fields*, des champs très différents qu'ici, en Illinois.
*[Some very different fields, fields, some fields very different than here, in Illinois.]*

Example 68:
Alice: S'il y a des mots que vous ne comprenez pas ou si vous êtes perdus avec ce que je dis, arrêtez-moi, okay? *If at some point you are lost or don't understand what I am talking about, just stop me, okay?*

Some of the immediate translation L1 episodes are done almost as if the L1 was part of the L2 discourse. However, they are used to give the immediate meaning of a word, probably due to a fear of lack of comprehension on the students' part. We do not have any evidence of students' comprehension before and after the occurrences, but it is possible students might have understood just by listening to the French version, (especially in the case of examples 58, 59, 64, 65, 66 and 68), as the level of French was basic for their levels of proficiency, or as cognates were used (e.g., 'erreur', 'abstrait', 'obligés de copier').

Episodes of delayed translation occurred more frequently. The L1 episodes mainly appeared after a prompt, such as "qu'est-ce que ça veut dire...?" (*what does ... mean?*"), "qu'est-ce que c'est ...?" (*what is ...?*), "ça veut dire" (*it means...*), "vous comprenez" (*do you understand...?*) or "ça se traduit..." (*it is translated..*), or were also given in response to a student's questions on meaning (examples 69-85). The prompts are underlined in the examples below.

Example 69:
Monique:   L'horloge de Bruges, vous savez ce que ca veut dire 'horloge'?
           *[The Bruges bell tower, do you know what it means 'bell tower'?]*
Students negotiate some meaning but not understandable
Monique:   Oui, *bell tower.*

Example 70:
Monique:   Que veut dire 'ne me quitte pas'?
           *[What does 'don't leave me" mean?]*
Student:   Don't leave me.
Monique:   Oui, *don't leave me.*

Example 71:
Monique:   Sans souci, ça veut dire '*without worries*' quand on ne s'inquiète pas.
           *[Without worries, it means 'without worries', when we don't worry.]*

Example 72:
Thierry:   Le roi n'a pas tous les pouvoirs, vous comprenez pouvoirs? En réalité c'est le Premier Ministre, c'est comme en Angleterre.
           *[The king does not have all the powers, do you understand 'powers'? In reality, it is the Prime Minister, it is like in England.]*
Student:   Pouvoirs?
           *[Powers?]*
Thierry:   Quoi?
           *[What?]*
Student:   Pouvoirs?
           *[Powers?]*
Thierry:   C'est quoi 'pouvoirs'? C'est lui qui dit qu'il a tout le pouvoir, vous comprenez? *Power.*
           *[What is 'powers'? It is he that says he has all the power, do you understand? Power.]*

Example 73:
Thierry:   Mon nain de jardin se traduit *garden gnome.*
           *[My garden gnome is translated garden gnome.]*

Example 74:
Julie:     Qu'est-ce que c'est une pirogue?
           *[What is a pirogue ?]*
Student:   Boat.
Julie:     Oui, *a bark, a boat.*

Example 75:
Julie:     Le sable, qu'est-ce que c'est?

|  |  | *[Sand, what is it ?]* |
|---|---|---|
| Student: | Sand |
| Julie: | Oui, *sand*. |

Example 76:
Julie:    Echo, *it means echo, echoing.*

Example 77:
Julie :   Qu'est-ce que c'est la sève? *Sap, right?*
          *[What is sap ?]*

Example 78:
A student asks how to say "near".
Julie:    *Near*, près de.

Example 79:
Aurélie:  Vous comprenez 'amer'? (*silence*) *bitter*, ça veut dire que le thé est amer.
          *[Do you undersand 'bitter' ? Bitter, it means that the tea is bitter.]*

Example 80:
Aurélie:  Qu'est-ce que c'est que le mouton? *Sheep.*
          *[What is mutton ?]*

Example 81:
Aurélie:  Est-ce que vous comprenez 'amer'? *Bitter.*
          *[Do you understand 'bitter' ? Bitter.]*

Example 82:
A student asks about the word "superficie".
Blanche : *The surface, the area.*

Example 83:
Emilie :  'Champs', qu'est-ce que c'est en anglais? *Like fields*.
          *['Fields, what is it in English ?]*

Example 84:
Student : Qu'est-ce que ça veut dire 'amer'?
          *[What does 'bitter' mean ?]*
Emilie:   Amer? *Bitter.*

Example 85:
Emilie:   'Camion', qu'est-ce que c'est?
          *['Truck', what is it ?]*
Student:  *Truck.*

Emilie :   *Truck*, oui, camion.

The examples above were always announced by some type of prompt. The teachers wanted the students to notice the forms and answered their questions when they came up. It is important to point out that in all cases, the focus was either onlexical forms (in the case of the planned focus-on-form group) or on meaning (when the general goal was to convey the cultural message) and not on grammatical forms. The goal was not

The difference between both types of translations might be explained by the fact that in delayed translation, the teachers believe their students might not already know the words, and they apply a more pedagogical approach to induce learners to notice those new and more difficult words. The motivation for L1 use was to ease comprehension, while still encouraging the learners to use some translation strategies that would lead them to think of the L1 equivalence. Because lexis has been brought to attention, students have an opportunity to notice it. In immediate translation, the teachers probably just did not think of the students' lexical knowledge. They had a spontaneous intuition that the words were problematic. However, when one thinks of the pedagogical implications of this strategy, if translation is used to focus on words, the manner in which it is presented should matter: if only a brief amount of time is spent on new words, it is not as likely that learners will notice them. However, if they are led, by a prompt or other strategies, to notice the forms, they will be more prone to do so. In the questionnaires teachers completed, they mentioned that they were aware they used the L1 to translate a word or expression they thought their students did not understand. These types of L1 occurrences were also found in previous research. To take an example, in Polio and Duff (1994), lack of vocabulary is one function mentioned by teachers for L1 use.

### 4.3.4 Feedback

This category represents the times teachers used their L1 in order to correct or to focus on grammatical forms by explaining them (examples 86-94).

<u>Example 86:</u>
Jeanne:    *The most, more*, le plus, plus que

Example 87:
Jeanne: L'architecture est la plus élaborée que nous avons vu. *You need to use a definite article.*
[*The architecture is the most elaborated that we have see.*]

Example 88:
Students asks about how to say a sentence for their activity.
Aurélie : Nous avons fait un voyage en bateau *in which* nous…
[*We took a boat trip in which we…*]

Example 89:
Students asks about how to say a sentence for their activity.
Aurélie: Nous avons loué un bateau avec lequel nous avons pêché, *with which, from which.*
[*We rented a boat with which we fished.*]

Example 90:
Emilie : La capitale dans laquelle se trouve le centre est Dakar. Ici par exemple, vous voyez pronom relatif 'dans laquelle' c'est parce que la capitale, c'est un nom féminin, *it's a place so* on utilise dans, dans laquelle. Alors on va voir plus d'exemples.
[*The capital in which the center is found is Dakar. Here, for example, you see the relative pronoun 'in which', it is because the capital is a feminine noun, it's a place so we use 'in, in which'. So we will see more examples.*]

Example 91:
Emilie: Les Sénégalais, c'est masculin pluriel alors on fait l'accord, parmi lesquels, *among whom.*
[*Senegalese people, it is masculine plural, so we agree, among which, among which.*]

Example 92:
Emilie: 'République' est un nom féminin et puis singulier alors, donc on utilise dans laquelle *or in which or at which.*
[*'Republic' is a feminine noun and then singular, so, so we use in which or in which or at which.*]

Example 93:
Emilie : Ses oeuvres parmi lesquelles…ici oeuvres, ça veut dire *works, literary works* parmi lesquelles parce que oeuvres, c'est féminin pluriel parmi lesquelles, *like among which so these are the titles of his works.*
[*His works among which, here, works, it means works, literary works, among which because works, it is feminine plural, among which, like among, which so these are the titles of his works.*]

Example 94:
Nicole: Cette structure, on va voir plusieurs fois, nous avons lequel, laquelle, lesquels comme pronom interrogatif pour demander *which one*. Ici on l'utilise comme pronom relatif comme que, qui, dont, avec une preposition. Donc dans laquelle, qu'est-ce que ça veut dire?
*[This structure, we will see several times, we have 'which (masculine singular), which (feminine singular), which' (masculine plural) as an interrogative pronoun to ask 'which one'. Here, we use it as a relative pronoun as, that, who, of which, with a preposition. So 'in which" what does it mean?]*
Student: *In which*

Looking at this type of feedback, it is actually grammatical forms that are in focus, using the L1 as a tool. Jeanne and Aurélie were not part of the planned focus-on-form treatment: Jeanne belonged to the incidental focus-on-form treatment and Aurélie to the focus-on-meaning treatment. During the group activity students had to accomplish at the end of the class, they answered their students' questions with brief grammar indications. The other teachers who focused on grammar and made use of the L1 to support their explanations were part of the planned focus-on-form group, which was instructed to explicitly explain the enhanced grammar and vocabulary.

All the teachers who were not part of the planned focus-on-form group used the L1, except in four instances (examples 86-89), and then solely for vocabulary clarification. Most of the teachers who used French to give feedback were just translating. Emilie and Nicole used metalinguistic references, but did so in French, while the L1 was used to give the translation of an example of the form (examples 90-94). The questionnaires showed that the teachers recognized using the L1 in order to give grammar explanations. Because of the instructions they received for the experiment, some were not aware of the targeted grammatical and lexical forms, and therefore did not see their presence as an important comprehension obstacle.

Previous research also supports these findings, as Castelloti (2001), Duff and Polio (1990), Franklin (1990), Levine (2003), Liebscher and Dailer-O'Cain (2004), Moore (2002), Nzwanga (2000), Polio and Duff (1994), Rolin-Ianziti and Brownlie (2002) and Thompson (2006), all observed that grammar explanation and feedback was a common function of the L1 in the classroom.

### 4.3.5 Conclusion

The three functions presented are important to consider, as the use of L1 by teachers is a topic that does not seem to be satisfactorily answered. One of the most active promoters of the presence of the L1 in the classroom is Vivian Cook. In his 1999 article, he claims that the field of language learning has misinterpreted the real essence of a language learner. The learner has been compared to the native speaker, which gave him an inaccessible goal to reach, and therefore implies some degree of failure right from the beginning stages of L2 acquisition. In Cook's view, L2 users should not be compared to native speakers, but should be looked at as "genuine L2 users" (p. 195). Therefore, once we consider the L2 user as such, we can look at his or her L1 use, not as a failure but as a tool for success. Cook (2001) claims that "the two languages are interwoven in the L2 user's mind" lexically, syntactically, phonologically, and pragmatically. In an immersion education context, Swain and Lapkin (2000) support the use of the L1 as a beneficial vehicle for L2 acquisition. They say "research examining the relationship between first language (L1) and second language use (…) makes it clear that the development and maintenance of the L1 supports the development of the second language" (p. 251). They add that the L1 helps students: "to understand and make sense of the requirements and content of the task; to focus attention on language form, vocabulary use, and overall organization; and to establish the tone and nature of their collaboration" (p. 268).

In my study, one positive aspect that needs to be presented concerns the quick return to the L2, shortly after using the L1. All teachers would concentrate on using the L2 as much as possible, and their L1 usages were minimal and brief. Teachers always went back to the L2 and encouraged students to do so by answering them in the L2. Levine (2003) also noticed that teachers are less likely than their students to speak the L1 when the latter asked them a question in the L1. This fact is encouraging for the language methodology teacher: With monitoring of language use, teachers seem to use the L1 for practical functions, such as facilitating comprehension, overcoming grammatical obstacles and saving time in some situations when an explanation in the L2 would be too time consuming. In an observational study (forthcoming), Levine distinguished between structured and unstructured communication. Structured communication was planned, through organized tasks, while unstructured communication happened spontaneously. He found that in the context of unstructured communication, it was the L1 that was used more than the L2 when the content was the component of focus. The L1 served important communicative, cognitive and social functions. This also means that teachers are more likely to use the L1 when spontaneous situations arise. If they think ahead of time, they might be more prone to stick to the L2 by using a certain number of strategies.

In contrast to the beliefs held in some quarters, it does not appear that the L1 is detrimental to the learning of the L2. In my study, it seems that it was in fact mainly used for easing comprehension in difficult situations.

**4.4 Summary**

This chapter has provided this thesis with a qualitative analysis of teachers' behaviors in a foreign language classroom. This analysis is primordial for the field of language teaching, as little is understood about teachers themselves. In this particular case, it has shown two aspects or two choices teachers have to make: the manner they apply instructions given to them and the language use (L1 and L2) they will have to present their lesson. Overall, it was shown that most teachers applied the instructions the researcher had provided, supporting the validity of the quantitative analysis of this study. Even though personal styles allowed for diversity in the teaching of the cultural lessons, the message and, for some groups, the focus-on-form, were given out to the learners. The two teachers who did not follow my instructions provided grounds for switching them to a different treatment group for the quantitative analysis.

Concerning the use of French and English while teaching, the vast majority of the time, French was logically the language of choice. However, a few occurrences of English were used by the teachers to either focus on form (grammatical or lexical forms) or to focus on meaning. Three main categories emerged: immediate translation, delayed translation and feedback. The L1 seemed to play a supportive role in the teaching of culture and language.

CHAPTER FIVE

Quantitative results of

The Integration of Focus-on-form Instruction

within Content-enriched instruction or Culture-Based Lessons

## 5.1 Introduction

This chapter presents the results of the quantitative data analysis of the integration of focus-on-form within a content-enriched lesson, the core of this investigation. The first research question asked if the integration of focus-on-form in content-enriched lessons facilitated the acquisition of grammar and vocabulary in intermediate French L2 classes; assuming that integrating focus-on-form in content-enriched lessons did facilitate short-term acquisition, the second research question addressed which type of focus-on-form instruction was more effective at promoting the acquisition and production of grammar and vocabulary in intermediate French L2 classes; finally, for the third research question, the study looked at the effect, if any, that focus-on-form instruction might have on learners' acquisition of content. In this chapter, each level of instruction (second and third semester) will be presented with their respective descriptive data, their within-groups effect (i.e., change over time) and finally the between-group effect (i.e., effectiveness of treatment conditions). The level of instruction (second and third semester) was analyzed separately, as the content and forms of the cultural lessons for those levels were different.

## 5.2 Second-semester learners

### 5.2.1 Descriptive statistics for vocabulary and grammar

Below are the results of the scores of the participants, presenting the total number of participants (n) in each group, the mean scores, and the standard deviations (SD). It is important to remember that depending on the component (vocabulary, focused-grammar and production-grammar), the number of participants varies, due to the fact that if the participants had scored over 90% on an individual component on the pre-test, they were removed from the analysis for that component.

Table 5.1 displays the descriptive data for the vocabulary section of the tests for the second-semester students. The maximum possible score obtainable was 7.

Table 5.1 Descriptive data for each 2nd-semester group on each test on Vocabulary

| Group | Pre-test | | Post-test 1 | | Post-test 2 | |
|---|---|---|---|---|---|---|
| | Mean | SD | Mean | SD | Mean | SD |
| Focus on meaning (n=31) | 1.44 | .95 | 2.21 | 1.12 | 2.02 | 1.16 |
| Planned focus-on-form (n=21) | 1.36 | .93 | 3.23 | 1.31 | 2.77 | 1.56 |
| Incidental focus-on-form (n=8) | .88 | .95 | 2 | 1.33 | 1.72 | 1.22 |

These results show an increase of the mean scores between the time of the pre-test and the post-tests: the focus-on-meaning group had a mean score of 1.44 (SD = 0.95) on the pre-test, 2.21 (SD = 1.12) on post-test 1, and 2.02 (SD = 1.16) on post-test 2. As for the planned focus-on-form group, it received a mean score of 1.36 (SD = 0.92) on the pre-test, 3.23 (SD = 1.31) on post-test 1 and 2.77 (SD = 1.56) on post-test 2. The incidental focus-on-form group had a mean score of 0.88 (SD = 0.95) on the pre-test, 2 (SD = 1.33) on post-test 1 and 1.72 (SD = 1.22) on post-test 2.

Figure 5.1 is the bar chart representing the scores for the vocabulary component.

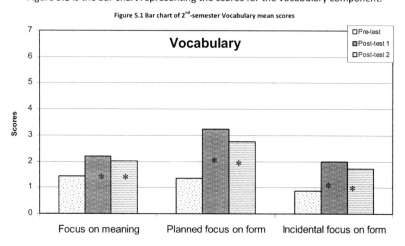

Figure 5.1 Bar chart of 2nd-semester Vocabulary mean scores

Table 5.2 provides the descriptive data for the focused-grammar component of the pre-test, post-test 1, and post-test 2. In this case, the maximum possible score obtainable was 28 points.

Table 5.2 Descriptive data for each 2$^{nd}$-semester group on each test on Focused-grammar

| Group | Pre-test | | Post-test 1 | | Post-test 2 | |
|---|---|---|---|---|---|---|
| | Mean | SD | Mean | SD | Mean | SD |
| Focus on meaning (n=30) | 7.47 | 7.53 | 13.9 | 8.09 | 12.62 | 8.89 |
| Planned focus-on-form (n=20) | 9.05 | 7.61 | 17.63 | 7.8 | 18.33 | 7.95 |
| Incidental focus-on-form (n=8) | 5.94 | 6.96 | 9.37 | 8.73 | 10.33 | 6.1 |

Table 5.2 reveals a similar pattern of score increase from the pre-test to both post-tests. Indeed, the focus-on-meaning group had a mean score of 7.47 (SD = 7.53) on the pre-test, 13.9 (SD = 8.08) on post-test 1 and 12.62 (SD = 8.89) on post-test 2. Learners on the planned focus-on-form group had a mean score of 9.05 (SD = 7.61) on the pre-test, 17.63 (SD = 7.8) on post-test 1 and 18.33 (SD = 7.95) on post-test 2. Finally, learners in the incidental focus-on-form group received a mean score of 5.94 (SD = 6.96) on the pre-test, 9.37 (SD = 8.73) on post-test 1 and 10.33 (SD = 6.1) on post-test 2. All groups show some improvements throughout the course of the experiment. The bar chart (Figure 5.2) for focused-grammar depicts the means on all three tests for the three treatment conditions.

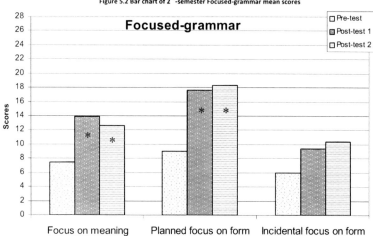

Figure 5.2 Bar chart of 2$^{nd}$-semester Focused-grammar mean scores

Finally, in Table 5.3, the descriptive data for production-grammar is displayed. In this case, the maximum possible score obtainable was 16 points.

Table 5.3 Descriptive data for each 2$^{nd}$-semester group on each test on Production-grammar

| Group | Pre-test | | Post-test 1 | | Post-test 2 | |
|---|---|---|---|---|---|---|
| | Mean | SD | Mean | SD | Mean | SD |
| Focus on meaning (n=29) | 2.83 | 4.2 | 6.26 | 6.03 | 5.33 | 4.9 |
| Planned focus-on-form (n=20) | 2.15 | 4.25 | 9.78 | 4.99 | 6.4 | 5.42 |
| Incidental focus-on-form (n=8) | 3.13 | 4.82 | 2.88 | 3.77 | 4.13 | 5.51 |

For the production-grammar component, the focus-on-meaning group received a mean score of 2.83 (SD = 4.2) on the pre-test, 6.26 (SD = 6.03) on post-test 1 and 5.33 (SD = 4.9) on post-test 2. The planned focus-on-form group's mean scores were 2.15 (SD = 4.25) on the pre-test, 9.78 (SD = 4.99) on post-test 1 and 6.4 (SD = 5.42) on post-test 2. The learners of the incidental focus-on-form group had 3.13 (SD = 4.82) on the pre-test, decreased to 2.88 (SD = 3.77) on post-test 1 and increased to 4.13 (SD = 5.51) on post-test 2. Overall, the mean scores show that there was some progress between the pre-test and the post-tests, yet not nearly as much as with the previous sections.

Figure 5.3 below charts the means for the production-grammar component.

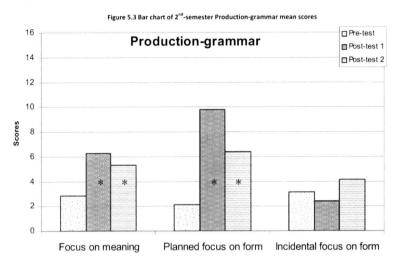

In the next section, the statistical tests performed to determine significance of learners' gains from pre-test to post-tests are presented.

5.2.2 Change over time (second-semester)

This section will answer the first research question: Does the integration of focus-on-form in content-enriched lessons facilitate the acquisition of grammar and vocabulary in intermediate French L2 classes? The analysis of the change in test scores over time for second-semester learners is based on a Mixed Model Linear Analysis (alpha level = .05), as it allows an analysis of consecutive tests and over a period of time. In this study, there is a pre-test, a post-test 1 and a delayed post-test 2 (by two weeks). The analysis of each treatment group appears in the following tables.

*5.2.2.1 Vocabulary component*

In Table 5.4, between-groups tests results are given for all groups on the vocabulary component.

Table 5.4 Mixed Model Linear Analysis among tests for Vocabulary of 2nd-semester participants

| | Tests (I) | Tests (J) | Mean Difference (I-J) | Std. Error | df | Sig.(a) |
|---|---|---|---|---|---|---|
| FonMeaning | Pre-test | Post-test 1 | -0.766 | 0.160 | 25 | 0.000* |
| | | Post-test 2 | -0.573 | 0.157 | 25 | 0.001* |
| Planned FonF | Pre-test | Post-test 1 | -1.869 | 0.252 | 20 | 0.000* |
| | | Post-test 2 | -1.417 | 0.315 | 20 | 0.000* |
| Incidental FonF | Pre-test | Post-test 1 | -1.125 | 0.334 | 7 | 0.012* |
| | | Post-test 2 | -0.844 | 0.344 | 7 | 0.044* |

* Significance at alpha level = .05

Table 5.4 shows that all groups show significant gains between the pre-test and both post-tests. As for the post-tests, the differences between the pre-test and that of post-test 2 was not as significant as for the pre-test score versus the score of post-test 1, but students still had significantly higher scores on post-test 2 than on the pre-test.

### 5.2.2.2 Focused-grammar component

Table 5.5 presents the data analyzed for the focused-grammar part for second-semester learners.

Table 5.5 Mixed Model Linear Analysis among tests for Focused-grammar of 2nd-semester participants

| | Tests (I) | Tests (J) | Mean Difference (I-J) | Std. Error | df | Sig.(a) |
|---|---|---|---|---|---|---|
| FonMeaning | Pre-test | Post-test 1 | -6.433 | 1.262 | 29 | 0.000* |
| | | Post-test 2 | -5.150 | 1.629 | 29 | 0.004* |
| Planned FonF | Pre-test | Post-test 1 | -8.575 | 1.845 | 19 | 0.000* |
| | | Post-test 2 | -9.275 | 1.654 | 19 | 0.000* |
| Incidental FonF | Pre-test | Post-test 1 | -3.438 | 3.822 | 7 | 0.398 |
| | | Post-test 2 | -4.388 | 2.505 | 7 | 0.123 |

* Significance at alpha level = .05

In Table 5.5, we see that, except for the incidental focus-on-form group, there is a significant difference between the means of the pre-test and both post-tests. This again tells us that there is progress from before the experiment to after for most groups. However, the incidental focus-on-form group does not show any significant gain on the focused-grammar component over time.

#### 5.2.2.3 Production-grammar component

Table 5.6 presents the data analyzed for the production-grammar section.

Table 5.6 Mixed Model Linear Analysis among tests for Production-grammar of $2^{nd}$-semester participants

|  | Tests (I) | Tests (J) | Mean Difference (I-J) | Std. Error | df | Sig.(a) |
|---|---|---|---|---|---|---|
| FonMeaning | Pre-test | Post-test 1 | -3.431 | 1.068 | 28 | 0.003* |
|  |  | Post-test 2 | -2.500 | 1.154 | 28 | 0.039* |
| Planned FonF | Pre-test | Post-test 1 | -7.625 | 1.041 | 19 | 0.000* |
|  |  | Post-test 2 | -4.25 | 1.140 | 19 | 0.001* |
| Incidental FonF | Pre-test | Post-test 1 | 0.750 | 2.610 | 7 | 0.782 |
|  |  | Post-test 2 | -1.000 | 1.637 | 7 | 0.561 |

* Significance at alpha level = .05

In this section, the groups performed significantly better between the pre-test and post-test 1, except for the incidental focus-on-form group that does not show any significant progress from the pre-test to both post-tests. As for the effects between the pre-test and post-test 2, there are significant differences for both the planned focus-on-form and the focus-on-meaning groups.

#### 5.2.2.4 Summary

Over time, significant differences are found for all second-semester groups on the vocabulary component. On the focused-grammar and production-grammar components, the planned focus-on-form and the focus-on-meaning groups significance difference between the pre-test results and both post-tests'. These results show positive effects of the treatments over the testing period.

### 5.2.3 Effectiveness of treatment conditions (second-semester)

This section attempts to answer question 2: If integrating focus-on-form in content-enriched lessons does facilitate acquisition, which type of focus-on-form instruction is more effective at promoting the acquisition and production of grammar and vocabulary in intermediate (second-semester) French L2 classes?

The results of the effects of different types of instruction (focus on meaning, planned focus-on-form, incidental focus-on-form) are reported within each component of the tests (vocabulary, focused-grammar, production-grammar) and over time. Therefore, in order to compare the effect of the different types of instruction on acquisition, the data was analyzed using a series of post hocs tests (alpha level = .05). As with the previous analyses, each component will be examined and the development throughout each test will be described. Because the types of instruction are the focus of the analysis, the categories will be based on the following groups: focus on meaning, planned focus-on-form, incidental focus-on-form.

### 5.2.3.1 Vocabulary component

Tables 5.7 through 5.9 present the data for the acquisition of lexis.

Table 5.7 Multivariate General Linear Model Analysis for Vocabulary pre-test of $2^{nd}$-semester participants

| Dependent Variable | | Treatment (I) | Treatment (J) | Mean Difference (I-J) | Std. Error | Sig. |
|---|---|---|---|---|---|---|
| Pre-test | Tukey HSD | FonMeaning | Planned FonF | 0.086 | 0.266 | 0.944 |
| | | | Incidental FonF | 0.569 | 0.374 | 0.289 |
| | | Planned FonF | FonMeaning | -0.086 | 0.266 | 0.944 |
| | | | Incidental FonF | 0.482 | 0.392 | 0.440 |
| | | Incidental FonF | FonMeaning | -0.569 | 0.374 | 0.289 |
| | | | Planned FonF | -0.482 | 0.392 | 0.440 |

None of the analyses were significant at alpha level = .05

All of the second-semester groups performed similarly in the pre-test (Table 5.7), meaning that the participants were the same on the vocabulary section prior to the treatment.

Table 5.8 Multivariate General Linear Model Analysis for Vocabulary post-test 1 of 2nd-semester participants

| Dependent Variable | | Treatment (I) | Treatment (J) | Mean Difference (I-J) | Std. Error | Sig. |
|---|---|---|---|---|---|---|
| Post-test 1 | Tukey HSD | FonMeaning | Planned FonF | -1.017 | 0.344 | 0.012* |
| | | | Incidental FonF | 0.210 | 0.482 | 0.901 |
| | | Planned FonF | FonMeaning | 1.017 | 0.344 | 0.012* |
| | | | Incidental FonF | 1.226 | 0.505 | 0.048* |
| | | Incidental FonF | FonMeaning | -0.210 | 0.482 | 0.901 |
| | | | Planned FonF | -1.226 | 0.505 | 0.048* |

\* Significance at alpha level = .05

As shown in Table 5.8, there were significant differences between the mean scores everywhere, except for between focus on meaning and incidental focus-on-form.

Table 5.9 Multivariate General Linear Model Analysis for Vocabulary post-test 2 of 2nd-semester participants

| Dependent Variable | | Treatment (I) | Treatment (J) | Mean Difference (I-J) | Std. Error | Sig. |
|---|---|---|---|---|---|---|
| Post-test 2 | Tukey HSD | FonMeaning | Planned FonF | -0.758 | 0.373 | 0.113 |
| | | | Incidental FonF | 0.297 | 0.523 | 0.837 |
| | | Planned FonF | FonMeaning | 0.758 | 0.373 | 0.113 |
| | | | Incidental FonF | 1.055 | 0.548 | 0.141 |
| | | Incidental FonF | FonMeaning | -0.297 | 0.523 | 0.837 |
| | | | Planned FonF | -1.055 | 0.548 | 0.141 |

None of the analyses were significant at alpha level = .05

As seen in Table 5.9, by post-test 2, all of the significant differences observed at post-test 1 have disappeared for the second-semester learners.

### 5.2.3.2 Focused-grammar component

Tables 5.10 through 5.12 present the data analyzed for the focused-grammar part.

Table 5.10 Multivariate General Linear Model Analysis for Focused-grammar pre-test of 2nd-semester participants

| Dependent Variable | | Treatment (I) | Treatment (J) | Mean Difference (I-J) | Std. Error | Sig. |
|---|---|---|---|---|---|---|
| Pre-test | Tukey HSD | FonMeaning | Planned FonF | -1.583 | 2.155 | 0.744 |
| | | | Incidental FonF | 1.529 | 2.970 | 0.864 |
| | | Planned FonF | FonMeaning | 1.583 | 2.155 | 0.744 |
| | | | Incidental FonF | 3.113 | 3.122 | 0.582 |
| | | Incidental FonF | FonMeaning | -1.529 | 2.970 | 0.864 |
| | | | Planned FonF | -3.113 | 3.122 | 0.582 |

None of the analyses were significant at alpha level = .05

All second-semester groups have statistically similar results, implying that they are not different in their knowledge of the focused-grammar at the time of the pre-test.

Table 5.11 Multivariate General Linear Model Analysis for Focused-grammar post-test 1 of 2$^{nd}$-semester participants

| Dependent Variable | | Treatment (I) | Treatment (J) | Mean Difference (I-J) | Std. Error | Sig. |
|---|---|---|---|---|---|---|
| Post-test 1 | Tukey HSD | FonMeaning | Planned FonF | -3.725 | 2.332 | 0.255 |
| | | | Incidental FonF | 4.525 | 3.215 | 0.344 |
| | | Planned FonF | FonMeaning | 3.725 | 2.332 | 0.255 |
| | | | Incidental FonF | 8.250 | 3.380 | 0.046* |
| | | Incidental FonF | FonMeaning | -4.525 | 3.215 | 0.344 |
| | | | Planned FonF | -8.250 | 3.380 | 0.046* |

* Significance at alpha level = .05

On post-test 1, the only significant mean difference occurred between the planned focus-on-form group and the incidental focus-on-form group, where the planned focus-on-form group performed significantly better. No differences were found among the other groups.

Table 5.12 Multivariate General Linear Model Analysis for Focused-grammar post-test 2 of 2$^{nd}$-semester participants

| Dependent Variable | | Treatment (I) | Treatment (J) | Mean Difference (I-J) | Std. Error | Sig. |
|---|---|---|---|---|---|---|
| Post-test 2 | Tukey HSD | FonMeaning | Planned FonF | -5.708 | 2.401 | 0.054 |
| | | | Incidental FonF | 2.292 | 3.310 | 0.769 |
| | | Planned FonF | FonMeaning | 5.708 | 2.401 | 0.054 |
| | | | Incidental FonF | 8.000 | 3.479 | 0.064 |
| | | Incidental FonF | FonMeaning | -2.292 | 3.310 | 0.769 |
| | | | Planned FonF | -8.000 | 3.479 | 0.064 |

None of the analyses were significant at alpha level = .05

However, after post-test 2, no significant difference is perceived among any of the second-semester groups on the focused-grammar component.

### 5.2.3.3 Production-grammar component

The data for the production-grammar component for second-semester students is displayed in tables 5.13 through 5.15.

Table 5.13 Multivariate General Linear Model Analysis for Production-grammar pre-test of 2nd-semester participants

| Dependent Variable | | Treatment (I) | Treatment (J) | Mean Difference (I-J) | Std. Error | Sig. |
|---|---|---|---|---|---|---|
| Pre-test | Tukey HSD | FonMeaning | Planned FonF | 0.678 | 1.251 | 0.851 |
| | | | Incidental FonF | -0.297 | 1.718 | 0.984 |
| | | Planned FonF | FonMeaning | -0.678 | 1.251 | 0.851 |
| | | | Incidental FonF | -0.975 | 1.800 | 0.851 |
| | | Incidental FonF | FonMeaning | 0.297 | 1.718 | 0.984 |
| | | | Planned FonF | 0.975 | 1.800 | 0.851 |

None of the analyses were significant at alpha level = .05

Once more, all participants scored similarly on the pre-test. Thus, on the pre-test, the level of production-grammar ability was not significantly different between groups.

Table 5.14 Multivariate General Linear Model Analysis for Production-grammar post-test 1 of 2nd-semester participants

| Dependent Variable | | Treatment (I) | Treatment (J) | Mean Difference (I-J) | Std. Error | Sig. |
|---|---|---|---|---|---|---|
| Post-test 1 | Tukey HSD | FonMeaning | Planned FonF | -3.516 | 1.577 | 0.075 |
| | | | Incidental FonF | 3.884 | 2.167 | 0.182 |
| | | Planned FonF | FonMeaning | 3.516 | 1.577 | 0.075 |
| | | | Incidental FonF | 7.400 | 2.270 | 0.005* |
| | | Incidental FonF | FonMeaning | -3.884 | 2.167 | 0.182 |
| | | | Planned FonF | -7.400 | 2.270 | 0.005* |

* Significance at alpha level = .05

After post-test 1, a significant difference between the planned focus-on-form group and the incidental focus-on-form group emerged. No significant difference is seen between the other groups.

Table 5.15 Multivariate General Linear Model Analysis for Production-grammar post-test 2 of 2nd-semester participants

| Dependent Variable | | Treatment (I) | Treatment (J) | Mean Difference (I-J) | Std. Error | Sig. |
|---|---|---|---|---|---|---|
| Post-test 2 | Tukey HSD | FonMeaning | Planned FonF | -1.072 | 1.502 | 0.756 |
| | | | Incidental FonF | 1.203 | 2.064 | 0.830 |
| | | Planned FonF | FonMeaning | 1.072 | 1.502 | 0.756 |
| | | | Incidental FonF | 2.275 | 2.162 | 0.547 |
| | | Incidental FonF | FonMeaning | -1.203 | 2.064 | 0.830 |
| | | | Planned FonF | -2.275 | 2.162 | 0.547 |

None of the analyses were significant at alpha level = .05

Table 5.15 shows that that the significantly higher scores of the planned focus-on-form group did not persist: none of the differences in group means were significant in post-test 2.

*5.2.3.4 Summary*

In summary, on the pre-test, no significant difference are found between the means of the second-semester groups, meaning that all groups were at a comparable level at the start of the experiment. On post-test 1, the planned focus-on-form group performed significantly better than the focus-on-meaning group on vocabulary and production-grammar; the planned focus-on-form group also performed significantly better than the incidental focus-on-form group on vocabulary, focused-grammar and production-grammar. On post-test 2, no significant differences in scores between treatments are retained and all groups are comparable.

### 5.2.4 Effects of focus-on-form instruction on content learning (second-semester)

In order to answer the last research question, 'what effect, if any, does focus-on-form instruction have on learners' acquisition of content?', it is necessary to examine the effects that focus-on-form instruction has on the learning of culture. It is important to understand if learning of culture occurs when instruction focus is oriented towards vocabulary and grammar.

Table 5.16 depicts the descriptive data for the culture part of the experiment for second-semester learners. In this case, the maximum possible score obtainable was 9 points.

Table 5.16 Descriptive data for each $2^{nd}$-semester group on each test on Culture

| Group | Pre-test | | Post-test 1 | | Post-test 2 | |
|---|---|---|---|---|---|---|
| | Mean | SD | Mean | SD | Mean | SD |
| Focus on meaning (n=31) | 1.66 | 1.07 | 5.58 | 1.77 | 5.15 | 2.96 |
| Planned focus-on-form (n=21) | 1.33 | .91 | 6.71 | 1.55 | 6.2 | 1.48 |
| Incidental focus-on-form (n=8) | 1.5 | 1.07 | 5.22 | 1.26 | 4.81 | 1.13 |

As illustrated in Table 5.16, learners in the focus-on-meaning group had a mean score of 1.66 (SD = 1.07) at the pre-test, which increased to 5.58 (SD = 1.77) at post-test 1 and 5.15 (SD = 2.96) at post-test 2. Similarly, learners in the planned focus-on-form group had a mean score of 1.33 (SD = 0.91) at the pre-test, 6.71 (SD = 1.55) at post-test 1 and 6.2 at post-test 2. Finally, the mean score for learners in the incidental focus-on-form group at the pre-test was 1.5 (SD = 1.07), at post-test 1 5.22 (SD = 1.26), and post-test 2 4.81 (SD = 1.13). This reveals that for all three groups the mean scores increased from the pre-test to post-tests 1 and 2 at the second-semester level.

Figure 5.4 presents the mean scores for the culture component of the tests by treatment group.

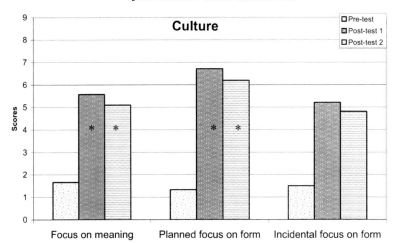

Figure 5.4 Bar chart of 2$^{nd}$-semester Culture mean scores

The following table (Table 5.17) reports a Mixed Model Linear Analysis of scores on the cultural component for all groups and between the pre-test and both post-tests.

Table 5.17 Mixed Model Linear Analysis among tests for Culture of 2$^{nd}$-semester participants

|  | Tests (I) | Tests (J) | Mean Difference (I-J) | Std. Error | df | Sig.(a) |
|---|---|---|---|---|---|---|
| FonMeaning | Pre-test | Post-test 1 | -3.431 | 1.068 | 28 | 0.003* |
|  |  | Post-test 2 | -2.500 | 1.154 | 28 | 0.039* |
| Planned FonF | Pre-test | Post-test 1 | -5.381 | 0.316 | 20 | 0.000* |
|  |  | Post-test 2 | -4.869 | 0.301 | 20 | 0.000* |
| Incidental FonF | Pre-test | Post-test 1 | 0.750 | 2.610 | 7 | 0.782 |
|  |  | Post-test 2 | -1.000 | 1.637 | 7 | 0.561 |

* Significance at alpha level = .05

Table 5.17 shows significant differences between the pre-test means and those of both post-tests in the focus-on-meaning and the planned focus-on-form groups. This means that in both groups, learners show significant increases between the pre-test and both post-tests. However, for the incidental focus-on-form group, differences in score between the pre-test and both post-tests did not reach significance, implying that learners did not learn more between the pre-test and post-tests.

Finally, the following tables (5.18-5.20) correspond to the statistical results for the comparison of the three treatment conditions related to the acquisition of culture over time.

Table 5.18 Multivariate General Linear Model Analysis for Culture pre-test of $2^{nd}$-semester participants

| Dependent Variable | | Treatment (I) | Treatment (J) | Mean Difference (I-J) | Std. Error | Sig. |
|---|---|---|---|---|---|---|
| Pre-test | Tukey HSD | FonMeaning | Planned FonF | 0.328 | 0.287 | 0.493 |
| | | | Incidental FonF | 0.161 | 0.403 | 0.916 |
| | | Planned FonF | FonMeaning | -0.328 | 0.287 | 0.493 |
| | | | Incidental FonF | -0.167 | 0.422 | 0.918 |
| | | Incidental FonF | FonMeaning | -0.161 | 0.403 | 0.916 |
| | | | Planned FonF | 0.167 | 0.422 | 0.918 |

None of the analyses were significant at alpha level = .05

Table 5.18 shows that there are no significant differences between the three groups, meaning that all groups had similar scores on the pretest.

Table 5.19 Multivariate General Linear Model Analysis for Culture post-test 1 of $2^{nd}$-semester participants

| Dependent Variable | | Treatment (I) | Treatment (J) | Mean Difference (I-J) | Std. Error | Sig. |
|---|---|---|---|---|---|---|
| Post-test 1 | Tukey HSD | FonMeaning | Planned FonF | -1.126 | 0.453 | 0.041* |
| | | | Incidental FonF | 0.370 | 0.635 | 0.830 |
| | | Planned FonF | FonMeaning | 1.126 | 0.453 | 0.041* |
| | | | Incidental FonF | 1.496 | 0.665 | 0.072 |
| | | Incidental FonF | FonMeaning | -0.370 | 0.635 | 0.830 |
| | | | Planned FonF | -1.496 | 0.665 | 0.072 |

* Significance at alpha level = .05

On post-test 1, the planned focus-on-form group scored significantly higher than the focus-on-meaning group (p = .041). However, there were no significant differences between the incidental focus-on-form group and the focus-on-meaning group, or between the two focus-on-form groups.

Table 5.20 Multivariate General Linear Model Analysis for Culture post-test 2 of 2nd-semester participants

| Dependent Variable | | Treatment (I) | Treatment (J) | Mean Difference (I-J) | Std. Error | Sig. |
|---|---|---|---|---|---|---|
| Post-test 2 | Tukey HSD | FonMeaning | Planned FonF | -1.098 | 0.486 | 0.070 |
| | | | Incidental FonF | 0.292 | 0.681 | 0.904 |
| | | Planned FonF | FonMeaning | 1.098 | 0.486 | 0.070 |
| | | | Incidental FonF | 1.390 | 0.714 | 0.135 |
| | | Incidental FonF | FonMeaning | -0.292 | 0.681 | 0.904 |
| | | | Planned FonF | -1.390 | 0.714 | 0.135 |

None of the analyses were significant at alpha level = .05

With post-test 2, the only slight observable trend is between planned focus-on-form and focus on meaning, with the former presenting slightly higher scores. However, the effect is weak and does not represent evidence for any gains.

To summarize the results of this third question, except for the incidental focus-on-form, there is significant gain for the focus-on-meaning and planned focus-on-form groups between the pre-test and both post-tests. The incidental focus-on-form group does not show any significant gains. As for the effect of the treatment, the planned focus-on-form group performed better than the focus-on-meaning group, while the other groups performed similarly.

5.2.5 Summary for second-semester groups

To sum up the results of the second semester groups, the first research question is answered positively as significant differences are found for all groups, over the testing period (post-test 1 and post-test 2), on vocabulary component, and for planned focus-on-form and the focus-on-meaning groups on focused-grammar and production-grammar components. To answer the second question, when significant differences occurred, it is the planned focus-on-form that performed significantly better than other groups. On post-test 1, the planned focus-on-form group performed significantly better than the focus-on-meaning group on vocabulary and production-grammar; the planned focus-on-form group also performed significantly better than the incidental focus-on-form group on vocabulary, focused-grammar and production-grammar. On post-test 2, no significant differences in scores between treatments are retained. On the third research question, there is significant gain for the focus-on-meaning and planned focus-on-form groups between the pre-test and both post-tests on culture. Comparing the treatments, the planned focus-on-form group performed better than the focus-on-meaning group, while the other groups performed similarly.

### 5.3 Third-semester learners

#### 5.3.1 Descriptive statistics

The following tables represent the descriptive data (total number of participants, mean, standard deviation, minimum and maximum ranges) of the third-semester groups.

Table 5.21 displays the descriptive data for the vocabulary section of the tests. The maximum obtainable score was 7.

Table 5.21 Descriptive data for each $3^{rd}$-semester group on each test on Vocabulary

| Group | Pre-test | | Post-test 1 | | Post-test 2 | |
|---|---|---|---|---|---|---|
| | Mean | SD | Mean | SD | Mean | SD |
| Focus on meaning (n=26) | .43 | .62 | 1.14 | 1.14 | .91 | 1.06 |
| Planned focus-on-form (n=25) | .6 | .81 | 2.04 | 1.47 | 1.68 | 1.43 |
| Incidental focus-on-form (n=42) | .7 | .75 | 1.24 | 1.2 | 1 | 1.13 |

On the vocabulary section of the tests, the focus-on-meaning participants obtained a mean score of 0.43 (SD = 0.62) on the pre-test, 1.14 (SD = 1.14) on post-test 1 and 0.91 (SD = 1.06) on post-test 2. The planned focus-on-form group had 0.6 as a mean score (SD = 0.81) on the pre-test, 2.04 (SD = 1.47) on post-test 1 and 1.68 (SD = 1.43) on post-test 2. Finally, the incidental focus-on-form group received 0.7 (SD = 0.75) on the pre-test, 1.24 (SD = 1.2) on post-test 1, and 1 (SD = 1.13) on post-test 2. The scores also improved in the vocabulary section of the test for third-semester learners; however, the differences between the pre-test, post-test 1, and post-test 2 do not appear to be as strong as for the second-semester participants (Table 5.21). The tests for significance will follow when I present the effects of the different treatments.

Figure 5.5 represents the mean scores of the vocabulary part of the test.

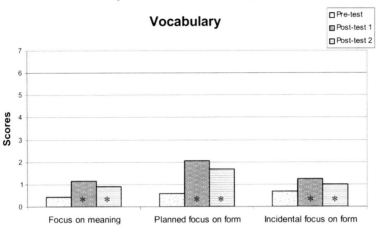

Figure 5.5 Bar chart of 3rd-semester Vocabulary mean scores

Table 5.22 provides the descriptive data for the focused-grammar component of the pre-test, post-test 1, and post-test 2. The maximum score for this section was 28 points.

Table 5.22 Descriptive data for each 3rd-semester group on each test on Focused-grammar

| Group | Pre-test | | Post-test 1 | | Post-test 2 | |
|---|---|---|---|---|---|---|
| | Mean | SD | Mean | SD | Mean | SD |
| Focus on meaning (n=25) | 18.06 | 5.52 | 17.28 | 7.4 | 15.44 | 6.43 |
| Planned focus-on-form (n=18) | 18.52 | 6.95 | 18.25 | 8.92 | 14.14 | 7.73 |
| Incidental focus-on-form (n=39) | 16.22 | 8.73 | 17.49 | 7.16 | 16.01 | 6.11 |

On these tests, the focus-on-meaning group scored 18.06 as a mean (SD = 5.52) on the pre-test, 17.28 (SD = 7.4) on post-test 1, 15.44 (SD = 6.43). The planned focus-on-form learners had 18.52 as a mean (SD = 6.95) on the pre-test, 18.25 (SD = 8.92) on post-test 1 and 14.14 (SD = 7.73) on post-test 2. As for the incidental focus-on-form, the mean scores were 16.22 (SD = 8.73) on the pre-test, 17.49 (SD = 7.16) on post-test 1 and 16.01 (SD = 6.11) on post-test 2. Unlike the other test components, a decrease in the mean scores is noticeable from the pre-test to post-test 1, and also from the pre-test to post-test 2 for the focus-on-meaning and planned focus-on-form groups; while the increase of the incidental focus-on-form groups appears to be very small.

Figure 5.6 is the bar chart for the Focused-grammar mean scores.

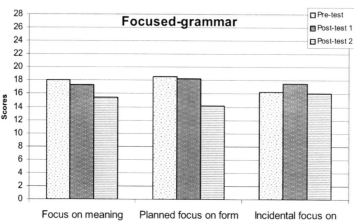

Figure 5.6 Bar chart of 3rd-semester Focused-grammar mean scores

Finally, in Table 5.23, the descriptive data for production-grammar is displayed. For this test item, the maximum obtainable score was 16 points.

Table 5.23 Descriptive data for each 3rd-semester group on each test on Production-grammar

| Group | Pre-test | | Post-test 1 | | Post-test 2 | |
|---|---|---|---|---|---|---|
| | Mean | SD | Mean | SD | Mean | SD |
| Focus on meaning (n=25) | 4.94 | 4.84 | 7.08 | 6.06 | 6.64 | 5.27 |
| Planned focus-on-form (n=21) | 5.33 | 4.9 | 8.19 | 5.91 | 8.02 | 5.28 |
| Incidental focus-on-form (n=43) | 4.63 | 4.18 | 7.38 | 5.4 | 7.5 | 4.78 |

Table 5.23 shows the mean scores show that the focus-on-meaning learners had a mean score of 4.94 (SD = 4.84) on the pre-test, which increased to 7.08 (SD = 6.06) on post-test 1 and 6.64 (SD = 5.27). Similarly, the planned focus-on-form learners had 5.33 (SD = 4.9) on the pre-test, 8.19 (SD = 5.91) on post-test 1, 8.02 (SD = 5.28) on post-test 2. Finally, the mean scores for learners in the incidental focus-on-form group at the pre-test were 4.63 (SD = 4.18) on the pre-test, 7.38 (SD = 5.4) on post-test 1 and 7.5 (SD = 4.78) on post-test 2. All groups show increases in their scores from the pre-test to the post-tests.

Figure 5.7 is the bar chart of the mean scores for production-grammar.

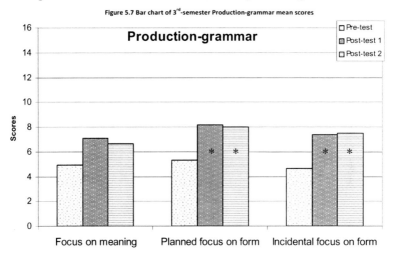

Vocabulary and production-grammar increased from the pre-test to post-test 1 and post-test 2.

5.3.2 Change over time (third-semester)

To answer the first research question "does the integration of focus-on-form in content-enriched lessons facilitate the acquisition of grammar and vocabulary in intermediate third-semester French L2 classes?", I ran a Mixed Model Linear Analysis, alpha level set at .05 in order to compare the pre-test and both post-tests overtime.

*5.3.2.1 Vocabulary component*

Table 5.24 depicts the data analyzed for the vocabulary part.

Table 5.24 Mixed Model Linear Analysis among tests for Vocabulary of 3rd-semester participants

|  | Tests (I) | Tests (J) | Mean Difference (I-J) | Std. Error | df | Sig.(a) |
|---|---|---|---|---|---|---|
| FonMeaning | | | | | | |
| | Pre-test | Post-test 1 | -0.712 | 0.172 | 25 | 0.000* |
| | | Post-test 2 | -0.481 | 0.181 | 25 | 0.014* |
| Planned FonF | | | | | | |
| | Pre-test | Post-test 1 | -1.44 | 0.245 | 24 | 0.000* |
| | | Post-test 2 | -1.08 | 0.240 | 24 | 0.000* |
| Incidental FonF | | | | | | |
| | Pre-test | Post-test 1 | -0.542 | 0.130 | 41 | 0.000* |
| | | Post-test 2 | -0.298 | 0.121 | 41 | 0.019* |

* Significance at alpha level = .05

In this case, again, there are significant differences between the pre-test and both post-tests for all three groups, showing that learners performed significantly better on post-test 1 and post-test 2 than on the pre-test.

### 5.3.2.2 Focused-grammar component

Table 5.25 shows the data analyzed for the focused-grammar part.

Table 5.25 Mixed Model Linear Analysis among tests for Focused-grammar of 3rd-semester participants

|  | Tests (I) | Tests (J) | Mean Difference (I-J) | Std. Error | df | Sig.(a) |
|---|---|---|---|---|---|---|
| FonMeaning | | | | | | |
| | Pre-test | Post-test 1 | 0.78 | 1.837 | 24 | 0.675 |
| | | Post-test 2 | 2.62 | 1.432 | 24 | 0.080 |
| Planned FonF | | | | | | |
| | Pre-test | Post-test 1 | 0.278 | 2.853 | 17 | 0.924 |
| | | Post-test 2 | 4.389 | 2.400 | 17 | 0.085 |
| Incidental FonF | | | | | | |
| | Pre-test | Post-test 1 | -1.269 | 1.279 | 38 | 0.327 |
| | | Post-test 2 | 0.205 | 1.327 | 38 | 0.878 |

None of the analyses were significant at alpha level = .05

As illustrated in Table 5.25, the focused-grammar component of the tests did not reveal any significant differences between pre-test and post-test scores. The pre-test looks to have no significant difference with post-test 1 and to be significantly better than post-test 2. This is most likely linked to the initial design of the pre-test and to the change to the consecutive tests[8].

In order to see if the addition of the prepositions in the post-tests had an effect on the scores, I recalculated the scores of the focused-grammar portion of the post-tests by scoring the tests without counting the prepositions. Then I submitted the results to another Mixed Linear Analysis. Table 5.26 displays the results.

Table 5.26 Mixed Model Linear Analysis among tests for Focused-grammar of 3rd-semester participants WITHOUT prepositions

| | (I) Tests | (J) Tests | Mean Difference (I-J) | Std. Error | df | Sig.(a) |
|---|---|---|---|---|---|---|
| FonMeaning | Pre-test | Post-test 1 | 1.84 | 2.120 | 24.000 | 0.394 |
| | | Post-test 2 | 4.98 | 1.662 | 24.000 | 0.006* |
| Planned FonF | Pre-test | Post-test 1 | 0.667 | 2.887 | 17.000 | 0.820 |
| | | Post-test 2 | 4.972 | 2.414 | 17.000 | 0.055 |
| Incidental FonF | Pre-test | Post-test 1 | 0.974 | 1.498 | 38.000 | 0.519 |
| | | Post-test 2 | 4.513 | 1.616 | 38.000 | 0.008* |

* Significance at alpha level = .05

Interestingly, the scores are modified: the pre-test is significantly better than post-test 2 for the focus-on-meaning and the incidental focus-on-form groups, and does not show any difference for the planned focus-on-form group. However, the pre-test and post-test 1 are not statistically different. This means that there was not no gain after the experimental cultural lesson, and even loss was shown to be significant for two of the groups.

*5.3.2.3 Production-grammar component*

The data analyzed for the production-grammar component are in Table 5.27.

---

[8] The design of the post-tests was slightly changed from the pre-test, on the focused-grammar section, in order to encourage learners to produce more complete features. Instead of just writing a form of the comparative or superlative (for second-semester groups) and a form of relative pronoun 'lequel' (for third-semester groups), learners had to also translate the preceding prepositions, in order to complete the task.

Table 5.27 Mixed Model Linear Analysis among tests for Production-grammar of 3rd-semester participants

| | Tests (I) | Tests (J) | Mean Difference (I-J) | Std. Error | df | Sig.(a) |
|---|---|---|---|---|---|---|
| FonMeaning | | | | | | |
| | Pre-test | Post-test 1 | -2.14 | 1.360 | 24 | 0.129 |
| | | Post-test 2 | -1.7 | 1.164 | 24 | 0.157 |
| Planned FonF | | | | | | |
| | Pre-test | Post-test 1 | -2.857 | 0.999 | 20 | 0.010* |
| | | Post-test 2 | -2.690 | 1.153 | 20 | 0.030* |
| Incidental FonF | | | | | | |
| | Pre-test | Post-test 1 | -2.756 | 0.729 | 42 | 0.000* |
| | | Post-test 2 | -2.872 | 0.734 | 42 | 0.000* |

* Significance at alpha level = .05

This final table displays similar results on production-grammar to what was previously observed in the culture and vocabulary components for the planned focus-on-form and the incidental focus-on-form groups: the pre-test vs. post-tests difference is significant on both post-tests. As for the focus-on-meaning group, when compared with the pre-test the learners did not perform significantly better on either post-test.

*5.3.2.4 Summary*

Overall, regardless of the group, on vocabulary the third-semester participants progressed from the pre-test to post-test 1 and from pre-test to post-test 2. On focused-grammar, none of the groups performed better between the pre-test and the post-tests. On production-grammar, the planned focus-on-form and incidental focus-on-form groups received significantly higher scores on the post-tests, while the focus-on-meaning group did not.

5.3.3 Effectiveness of treatment conditions (third-semester)

This section will answer research question 2: If integrating focus-on-form in content-enriched lessons does facilitate acquisition, which type of focus-on-form instruction is more effective at promoting the acquisition and production of grammar and vocabulary in intermediate third-semester French L2 classes?

Similarly to the second-semester classes, the data was analyzed using a series of post hocs tests (alpha level = .05) in order to compare the effects of the different types of instruction.

### 5.3.3.1 Vocabulary component

The following three tables (5.28-5.30) display the data analyzed for the vocabulary part on the three tests.

Table 5.28 Multivariate General Linear Model Analysis for Vocabulary pre-test of $3^{rd}$-semester participants

| Dependent Variable | | Treatment (I) | Treatment (J) | Mean Difference (I-J) | Std. Error | Sig. |
|---|---|---|---|---|---|---|
| Pre-test | Tukey HSD | FonMeaning | Planned FonF | -0.167 | 0.205 | 0.695 |
| | | | Incidental FonF | -0.270 | 0.183 | 0.308 |
| | | Planned FonF | FonMeaning | 0.167 | 0.205 | 0.695 |
| | | | Incidental FonF | -0.102 | 0.185 | 0.845 |
| | | Incidental FonF | FonMeaning | 0.270 | 0.183 | 0.308 |
| | | | Planned FonF | 0.102 | 0.185 | 0.845 |

None of the analyses were significant at alpha level = .05

At the time of the pre-test, all participants performed similarly and there were no significant differences between the groups.

Table 5.29 Multivariate General Linear Model Analysis for Vocabulary post-test 1 of $3^{rd}$-semester participants

| Dependent Variable | | Treatment (I) | Treatment (J) | Mean Difference (I-J) | Std. Error | Sig. |
|---|---|---|---|---|---|---|
| Post-test 1 | Tukey HSD | FonMeaning | Planned FonF | -0.896 | 0.355 | 0.035* |
| | | | Incidental FonF | -0.100 | 0.316 | 0.947 |
| | | Planned FonF | FonMeaning | 0.896 | 0.355 | 0.035* |
| | | | Incidental FonF | 0.796 | 0.320 | 0.039* |
| | | Incidental FonF | Incidental FonF | 0.100 | 0.316 | 0.947 |
| | | | Planned FonF | -0.796 | 0.320 | 0.039* |

* Significance at alpha level = .05

The above results show that vocabulary was significantly better assimilated in the planned focus-on-form group, as the scores of the planned focus-on-form group were significantly higher than those of the focus-on-meaning group and the incidental focus-on-form group.

Table 5.30 Multivariate General Linear Model Analysis for Vocabulary post-test 2 of 3rd-semester participants

| Dependent Variable | | Treatment (I) | Treatment (J) | Mean Difference (I-J) | Std. Error | Sig. |
|---|---|---|---|---|---|---|
| Post-test 2 | Tukey HSD | FonMeaning | Planned FonF | -0.767 | 0.337 | 0.064 |
| | | | Incidental FonF | -0.087 | 0.300 | 0.955 |
| | | Planned FonF | FonMeaning | 0.767 | 0.337 | 0.064 |
| | | | Incidental FonF | 0.680 | 0.304 | 0.070 |
| | | Incidental FonF | FonMeaning | 0.087 | 0.300 | 0.955 |
| | | | Planned FonF | -0.680 | 0.304 | 0.070 |

None of the analyses were significant at alpha level = .05

Looking at post-test 2 results for vocabulary, the significant difference which had emerged in post-test 1 (between the planned focus-on-form and the focus-on-meaning group, and between the planned focus-on-form and the incidental focus-on-form group) has now disappeared; however, a trend for significance was still present. I will interpret this result as evidence that the effect was still slightly noticeable after two weeks delay.

### 5.3.3.2 Focused-grammar component

Tables 5.31 through 5.33 present the data analyzed for the focused-grammar part.

Table 5.31 Multivariate General Linear Model Analysis for Focused-grammar pre-test of 3rd-semester participants

| Dependent Variable | | Treatment (I) | Treatment (J) | Mean Difference (I-J) | Std. Error | Sig. |
|---|---|---|---|---|---|---|
| Pre-test Focused-grammar | Tukey HSD | FonMeaning | Planned FonF | -0.468 | 2.319 | 0.978 |
| | | | Incidental FonF | 1.842 | 1.922 | 0.605 |
| | | Planned FonF | FonMeaning | 0.468 | 2.319 | 0.978 |
| | | | Incidental FonF | 2.310 | 2.138 | 0.529 |
| | | Incidental FonF | FonMeaning | -1.842 | 1.922 | 0.605 |
| | | | Planned FonF | -2.310 | 2.138 | 0.529 |

None of the analyses were significant at alpha level = .05

No significant differences in scores can be seen between the groups with the pre-test on the focused-grammar component. Therefore, all learners had a similar level of grammatical knowledge at the outset.

**Table 5.32 Multivariate General Linear Model Analysis for Focused-grammar post-test 1 of 3rd-semester participants**

| Dependent Variable | | Treatment (I) | Treatment (J) | Mean Difference (I-J) | Std. Error | Sig. |
|---|---|---|---|---|---|---|
| Post-test 1 | Tukey HSD | FonMeaning | Planned FonF | -0.970 | 2.363 | 0.911 |
| | | | Incidental FonF | -0.207 | 1.958 | 0.994 |
| | | Planned FonF | FonMeaning | 0.970 | 2.363 | 0.911 |
| | | | Incidental FonF | 0.763 | 2.178 | 0.935 |
| | | Incidental FonF | FonMeaning | 0.207 | 1.958 | 0.994 |
| | | | Planned FonF | -0.763 | 2.178 | 0.935 |

None of the analyses were significant at alpha level = .05

Table 5.32 reveals that the types of instruction seemed to have no differential effect on the focused-grammar scores, as none of the groups performed significantly better than the other ones.

**Table 5.33 Multivariate General Linear Model Analysis for Focused-grammar post-test 2 of 3rd-semester participants**

| Dependent Variable | | Treatment (I) | Treatment (J) | Mean Difference (I-J) | Std. Error | Sig. |
|---|---|---|---|---|---|---|
| Post-test 2 | Tukey HSD | FonMeaning | Planned FonF | 1.301 | 2.037 | 0.799 |
| | | | Incidental FonF | -0.573 | 1.688 | 0.939 |
| | | Planned FonF | FonMeaning | -1.301 | 2.037 | 0.799 |
| | | | Incidental FonF | -1.874 | 1.877 | 0.580 |
| | | Incidental FonF | FonMeaning | 0.573 | 1.688 | 0.939 |
| | | | Planned FonF | 1.874 | 1.877 | 0.580 |

None of the analyses were significant at alpha level = .05

As with post-test 1, no statistically significant differences emerge between any of the groups on post-test 2.

### 5.3.3.3 Production-grammar component

These last three tables (5.34-5.36) give the results for the production-grammar component for third-semester learners.

Table 5.34 Multivariate General Linear Model Analysis for Production-grammar pre-test of 3rd-semester participants

| Dependent Variable | | Treatment (I) | Treatment (J) | Mean Difference (I-J) | Std. Error | Sig. |
|---|---|---|---|---|---|---|
| Pre-test | Tukey HSD | FonMeaning | Planned FonF | -0.393 | 1.345 | 0.954 |
| | | | Incidental FonF | 0.312 | 1.143 | 0.960 |
| | | Planned FonF | FonMeaning | 0.393 | 1.345 | 0.954 |
| | | | Incidental FonF | 0.705 | 1.210 | 0.830 |
| | | Incidental FonF | FonMeaning | -0.312 | 1.143 | 0.960 |
| | | | Planned FonF | -0.705 | 1.210 | 0.830 |

None of the analyses were significant at alpha level = .05

The scores in table 5.34 above indicate that all the participants completed the production-grammar task with similar results. This implies that they all had a comparable level on this measure before the experimental lesson.

Table 5.35 Multivariate General Linear Model Analysis for Production-grammar post-test 1 of 3rd-semester participants

| Dependent Variable | | Treatment (I) | Treatment (J) | Mean Difference (I-J) | Std. Error | Sig. |
|---|---|---|---|---|---|---|
| Post-test 1 | Tukey HSD | FonMeaning | Planned FonF | -1.110 | 1.690 | 0.789 |
| | | | Incidental FonF | -0.304 | 1.436 | 0.976 |
| | | Planned FonF | FonMeaning | 1.110 | 1.690 | 0.789 |
| | | | Incidental FonF | 0.807 | 1.520 | 0.856 |
| | | Incidental FonF | FonMeaning | 0.304 | 1.436 | 0.976 |
| | | | Planned FonF | -0.807 | 1.520 | 0.856 |

None of the analyses were significant at alpha level = .05

Table 5.35 reveals that the difference between the groups is not statistically significant. Thus, the production-grammar task involved in the test does not seem to be influenced by the type of instruction for third-semester learners, as all groups performed similarly.

Table 5.36 Multivariate General Linear Model Analysis for Production-grammar post-test 2 of 3rd-semester participants

| Dependent Variable | | Treatment (I) | Treatment (J) | Mean Difference (I-J) | Std. Error | Sig. |
|---|---|---|---|---|---|---|
| Post-test 2 | Tukey HSD | FonMeaning | Planned FonF | -1.384 | 1.492 | 0.624 |
| | | | Incidental FonF | -0.860 | 1.267 | 0.777 |
| | | Planned FonF | FonMeaning | 1.384 | 1.492 | 0.624 |
| | | | Incidental FonF | 0.524 | 1.342 | 0.919 |
| | | Incidental FonF | FonMeaning | 0.860 | 1.267 | 0.777 |
| | | | Planned FonF | -0.524 | 1.342 | 0.919 |

None of the analyses were significant at alpha level = .05

As shown in Table 5.36, for post-test 2, no significant differences are observed on the delayed post-test. The learners' production-grammar performance is comparable.

### 5.3.3.4 Summary

While looking at the differences between the three treatment groups at the third-semester level, only one instance of significance comes up: the planned focus-on-form group performed better than the other two groups on the vocabulary component of post-test 1. The incidental focus-on-form and the focus-on-meaning groups did not show any significant difference for the vocabulary part. No significant difference was found among the focused-grammar and production-grammar components.

### 5.3.4 Effects of focus-on-form instruction on content learning (third-semester)

The third research question was: what effect, if any, does focus-on-form instruction have on learners' acquisition of content? In order to answer it with the third-semester participants, the following analyses were conducted.

Table 5.37 charts the descriptive data for the culture part of the experiment are displayed. The maximum possible score for this test is 9 points.

Table 5.37 Descriptive data for each 3$^{rd}$-semester group on each test on Culture

| Group | Pre-test | | Post-test 1 | | Post-test 2 | |
|---|---|---|---|---|---|---|
| | Mean | SD | Mean | SD | Mean | SD |
| Focus on meaning (n=25) | .8 | .58 | 3.02 | 1.36 | 3 | 1.53 |
| Planned focus-on-form (n=25) | 1.04 | .88 | 3.22 | 1.81 | 2.9 | 1.42 |
| Incidental focus-on-form (n=42) | 2.45 | 1.6 | 2.88 | 1.8 | 2.45 | 1.6 |

Table 5.37 shows that the mean scores for the focus-on-meaning group were 0.8 (SD = 0.58) on the pre-test, 3.02 (SD = 1.36) on post-test 1 and 3 on post-test 2 (SD = 1.53). Likewise, learners in the planned focus-on-form group had a mean score of 1.04 (SD = 0.88) on the pre-test, increased to 3.22 (SD = 1.81) on post-test 1 and had 2.9 (SD = 1.42) on post-test 2. As for the incidental focus-on-form group, on the pre-test, its mean score was of 2.45 (SD = 1.6), on post-test 1 2.88 (SD = 1.8) and on post-test 2 2.45 (SD = 1.6). This shows an increase of scores

for all groups but the incidental focus-on-form group, from the pre-test to both post-tests. The significance of this increase will be analyzed below.

Figure 5.8 represents the mean scores of all treatment groups for the culture component.

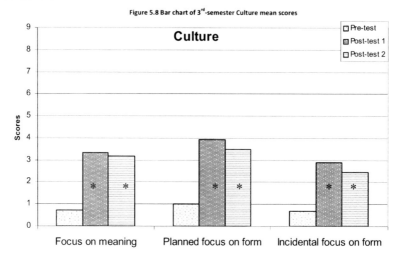

Figure 5.8 Bar chart of 3rd-semester Culture mean scores

To see if each individual treatment group has shown statistical differences over the period of the three tests, Table 5.38 presents the data analyzed for the culture component.

Table 5.38 Mixed Model Linear Analysis among tests for Culture of 3rd-semester participants

|  | Tests (I) | Tests (J) | Mean Difference (I-J) | Std. Error | df | Sig.(a) |
|---|---|---|---|---|---|---|
| FonMeaning | | | | | | |
| | Pre-test | Post-test 1 | -2.22 | 0.289 | 24 | 0.000* |
| | | Post-test 2 | -2.2 | 0.337 | 24 | 0.000* |
| Planned FonF | | | | | | |
| | Pre-test | Post-test 1 | -2.18 | 0.397 | 24 | 0.000* |
| | | Post-test 2 | -1.86 | 0.327 | 24 | 0.000* |
| Incidental FonF | | | | | | |
| | Pre-test | Post-test 1 | -2.18 | 0.397 | 24 | 0.000* |
| | | Post-test 2 | -1.86 | 0.327 | 24 | 0.000* |

* Significance at alpha level = .05

The experiment seems to have allowed learning as post-test 1 ($p = 0$) and post-test 2 ($p = 0$) are showing significantly higher scores for all groups, when compared to the pre-test.

Finally, the following tables (5.39-5.41) are the results of the treatment effects on the acquisition of culture over the period of the three tests.

Table 5.39 Multivariate General Linear Model Analysis for Culture pre-test of $3^{rd}$-semester participants

| Dependent Variable | | Treatment (I) | Treatment (J) | Mean Difference (I-J) | Std. Error | Sig. |
|---|---|---|---|---|---|---|
| Pre-test | Tukey HSD | FonMeaning | Planned FonF | -0.270 | 0.230 | 0.469 |
| | | | Incidental FonF | 0.066 | 0.205 | 0.943 |
| | | Planned FonF | FonMeaning | 0.270 | 0.230 | 0.469 |
| | | | Incidental FonF | 0.337 | 0.207 | 0.239 |
| | | Incidental FonF | FonMeaning | -0.066 | 0.205 | 0.943 |
| | | | Planned FonF | -0.337 | 0.207 | 0.239 |

None of the analyses were significant at alpha level = .05

The third-semester learners all performed similarly, as their pre-test scores were not significantly different. This also implies that before the experimental lesson, all learners had common knowledge about Senegal.

Table 5.40 Multivariate General Linear Model Analysis for Culture post-test 1 of $3^{rd}$-semester participants

| Dependent Variable | | Treatment (I) | Treatment (J) | Mean Difference (I-J) | Std. Error | Sig. |
|---|---|---|---|---|---|---|
| Post-test 1 | Tukey HSD | FonMeaning | Planned FonF | -0.085 | 0.481 | 0.983 |
| | | | Incidental FonF | 0.253 | 0.428 | 0.825 |
| | | Planned FonF | FonMeaning | 0.085 | 0.481 | 0.983 |
| | | | Incidental FonF | 0.339 | 0.433 | 0.715 |
| | | Incidental FonF | FonMeaning | -0.253 | 0.428 | 0.825 |
| | | | Planned FonF | -0.339 | 0.433 | 0.715 |

None of the analyses were significant at alpha level = .05

From Table 5.40, it can be seen that after the lesson, the groups did not perform significantly differently. The fact that one group received more focus on other components such as grammatical and lexical forms, did not seem to positively or negatively influence their scores.

Table 5.41 Multivariate General Linear Model Analysis for Culture post-test 2 of 3rd-semester participants

| Dependent Variable | | Treatment (I) | Treatment (J) | Mean Difference (I-J) | Std. Error | Sig. |
|---|---|---|---|---|---|---|
| Post-test 2 | Tukey HSD | FonMeaning | Planned FonF | 0.138 | 0.429 | 0.944 |
| | | | Incidental FonF | 0.586 | 0.382 | 0.280 |
| | | Planned FonF | FonMeaning | -0.138 | 0.429 | 0.944 |
| | | | Incidental FonF | 0.447 | 0.387 | 0.482 |
| | | Incidental FonF | FonMeaning | -0.586 | 0.382 | 0.280 |
| | | | Planned FonF | -0.447 | 0.387 | 0.482 |

None of the analyses were significant at alpha level = .05

As seen in Table 5.41, the delayed test did not show any sign of significant difference between the treatments, meaning that they all had similar effects on the learners when tested two weeks after the experimental lesson.

In sum, the third research question is answered by positive results: all groups show significantly better scores from the pre-test to both post-tests. Furthermore, no specific group performed better than the other ones, meaning that all groups gained content knowledge similarly.

### 5.3.5 Summary for third-semester groups

Across all groups, participants show significant progress on vocabulary from the pre-test to post-test 1 and from pre-test to post-test 2. However, no significance is found for any groups on focused-grammar. On production-grammar, the planned focus-on-form and incidental focus-on-form groups performed significantly better on their post-tests' scores. Answering the second research question, only one instance of significance comes up: the planned focus-on-form group performed better than the other two groups only on the vocabulary component of post-test 1. No significant difference was found among the focused-grammar and production-grammar components. Finally, the culture was statistically significant for all groups, and all groups gained content knowledge similarly.

## 5.4 Summary of the findings

As summarized in Figure 5.9 (see on next page), these analyses illustrate that the experiments in second-semester and third-semester groups have an overall positive effect on immediate improvement. Except for the second-semester incidental focus-on-form group, all groups show an overall mean significant difference between pre-test and post-tests scores. Research question 1 asks: does the integration of focus-on-form in content-enriched lessons facilitate the acquisition of grammar and vocabulary in intermediate French L2 classes? The answer seems to be yes. There are a large number of significant differences showing that progress occurs between the pre-test and the post-tests. These constitute evidence that when focused-grammar and vocabulary are integrated into a content-enriched lesson, learners do acquire a certain number of the grammatical and lexical forms. However, with this particular analysis, the second research question cannot be answered, as it is not possible to view which specific treatment benefits their acquisition the most.

The second research question asks: if integrating focus-on-form in content-enriched lessons does facilitate acquisition, which type of focus-on-form instruction is more effective at promoting the acquisition and production of grammar and vocabulary in intermediate French L2 classes? For the second-semester learners, even though the results do not show gains in every single component of the tests, the treatment that leads to predominantly higher scores on the majority of the tests for vocabulary, focused-grammar and production-grammar is the planned focus-on-form treatment. This treatment explicitly focused attention on the grammatical and lexical items, and the planned focus-on-form learners appear to have learned these items better than the learners in the other treatment groups. However, when looking at the focus-on-meaning treatment and the incidental focus-on-form treatment, they do not show any significant difference between each other, meaning that both treatments produced statistically similar scores. Those results do not show up for the third-semester participants. For them, the only instance of significance is with the planned focus-on-form group that performed significantly better on the vocabulary component of post-test 1. In the other components of the tests, no significant differences between or among treatments appear. It is also important to recall that all groups performed similarly on the pre-tests, showing that before the cultural lesson, all groups started the experiment with relatively equal knowledge.

Finally, the third research question asks: what effect, if any, does focus-on-form instruction have on learners' acquisition of content? At the second-semester level, the planned focus-on-form group performed better than the focus-on-meaning group, while not performing better than the incidental group (though the difference approached significance). The focus-on-meaning and incidental groups were similar. At the third-semester level, the culture component did not show any significant difference among all the treatments. This means that despite the presence or absence of focus-on-form on grammatical and lexical items, culture was learned for all participants, and in the case of second-semester students, the planned focus-on-form group did even better on the cultural learning component. This also suggests that the focus-on-form techniques did not interfere with the acquisition of content knowledge, and therefore did not interfere with culture. There were no perceptible negative effects on content learning.

Figure 5.9 Summary of the results

| | $2^{nd}$ semester | $3^{rd}$ semester |
|---|---|---|
| **Research question 1:** Does the integration of focus on form in content-enriched lessons facilitate the acquisition of grammar and vocabulary in intermediate French L2 classes? | Yes ⇨ Vocabulary for **all** treatments<br>Yes ⇨ Focused-grammar for FonMeaning Planned FonF<br>Yes ⇨ Production-grammar for FonMeaning Planned FonF | Yes for **all** treatments ⇨ Vocabulary<br>Yes ⇨ Production-grammar for Incidental FonF Planned FonF |
| **Research question 2:** Which type of focus on form instruction is more effective at promoting the acquisition and production of grammar and vocabulary in intermediate French L2 classes? | - Planned FonF > Incidental FonF<br>- Planned FonF > FonMeaning<br>- Incidental FonF = FonMeaning<br>⇨ Vocabulary, focused-grammar, production-grammar | - Planned FonF > Incidental FonF<br>- Planned FonF > FonMeaning<br>- Incidental FonF = FonMeaning<br>⇨ Vocabulary only |
| **Research question 3:** What effect, if any, does focus on form instruction have on learners' acquisition of content? | - Culture is learned for Planned Focus on Form and Focus on Meaning, while not for Incidental Focus on Form<br>- As for the treatments:<br>⇨ Planned FonF > FonMeaning<br>⇨ Planned FonF = Incidental FonF<br>⇨ Incidental FonF = FonMeaning | - Culture is learned similarly for all focus groups<br>⇨ Planned FonF = Incidental FonF = FonMeaning |

## CHAPTER SIX
## Discussion and conclusion

### 6.1 Introduction

This study explored the effectiveness of integrating focus-on-form and content-enriched instruction for second- and third-semester learners of French. The second-semester learners participated in a culture-based lesson about Belgium, and they showed gains in cultural knowledge, vocabulary and grammar. The third-semester learners, who had a culture-based lesson about Senegal, showed gains in cultural knowledge and vocabulary. The lessons that provided planned focus-on-form were consistently more effective than the lessons that provided incidental focus-on-form or focus-on-meaning. This chapter discusses these findings in terms of their implications for L2 teachers, L2 teacher educators, and second language acquisition theory and research. Finally, the chapter concludes by presenting the limitations of the study.

### 6.2 The effectiveness of CEI at lower-level of foreign language teaching

Researchers have argued for the use of content-based instruction in language courses in order to integrate the language into a meaningful context and to address problems with learners' production (Cook, 2001; Musumeci, 1993; Snow & Brinton, 1997; Swain, 1985, 1991, 1996, 2001). Because no previous research has targeted novice- or intermediate-level adult L2 learners through content-enriched instruction, this study focused on the effects of CEI at a lower level of adult learner proficiency. CEI was provided through a lesson based on cultural content that targeted lexical and grammatical forms in order to encourage the learning of content, vocabulary, and grammar. The following discussion addresses the issues that were raised from the findings.

### 6.2.1 The positive effects of CEI

The integration of focus-on-form in a content-enriched lesson seemed to yield measurable positive effects. Regardless of the treatment types, most second-semester learners showed evidence of learning with regard to culture, vocabulary, and grammar. For the third-semester groups, positive evidence for learning was found with culture, vocabulary, and grammar production. The effectiveness of the lessons for vocabulary learning may have been due to the association there is between culture and the need to understand the vocabulary, in order to comprehend the message (i.e., culture). For example, the second-semester groups heard and read the sentence: "*Le roi n'a pas tous les **pouvoirs***" [9] (enhanced version) or "*Le roi n'a pas tous les pouvoirs*" (non-enhanced version). The third-semester participants heard and read "*les hommes ont le premier thé, fait d'une manière très forte et **amère***"[10] (enhanced version) or "*les hommes ont le premier thé, fait d'une manière très forte et amère*" (non-enhanced version). Those two examples show that in both enhanced and non-enhanced versions, it was necessary to understand the words "pouvoirs" and "amère" in order to comprehend the sentence. The teachers probably also felt that those words would not be familiar to their students; therefore, in most cases they chose to point them out. Instances can illustrate this statement. In those two examples, teachers negotiated on vocabulary:

Example 95:
Thierry:  Le roi n'a pas tous les pouvoirs, vous comprenez 'pouvoirs'? En réalité c'est le Premier Ministre, c'est comme en Angleterre.
*[The king does not have all the powers, you understand 'powers'? In reality, it is the Prime Minister, it is like in England.]*

Example 96:
Aurélie:  Vous comprenez 'amer'? (*silence*) bitter, ça veut dire que le thé est amer.
*[Do you undersand 'bitter' ? Bitter, it means that the tea is bitter.]*

Because vocabulary knowledge is clearly fundamental to the comprehension of meaning, this hypothesis might explain why students at both the second- and third-semester levels did learn the vocabulary. With or without input enhancement, the comprehension of the message was the main objective to reach. Furthermore, the facts about the content (i.e.

---

[9] Translated in English as: The king does not have all powers.
[10] Translated in English as: The men drink the first tea, which is made very strong and bitter.

culture) were also recalled for all groups at all levels, showing the main goal of the culture-based lesson was reached. Thus, despite the presence of input enhancement on lexical items, and explicit explanations on the part of the instructors of the planned focus-on-form group, the cultural content and the vocabulary were noticed by all groups at the second- and third-semester levels. As the counts of focus-on-form was illustrated in Tables 4.1 through 4.3 (p. 95-96), all teachers pointed out some of the targeted lexical items. Furthermore, the results in Chapter V show that all learners seemed to have applied a focus on meaning, they showed progress between the pre-test and both post-tests with the cultural and lexical content. In section 6.2.3, the effectiveness of the types of treatments will be presented, in order to examine if one treatment performed significant better than the others. Even if all groups learned culture and vocabulary, one treatment group might be shown an even more positive effect.

An interesting positive effect emerged with the grammar production task of the tests. For both levels, the students' scores on the grammar production task part improved significantly between the pre-test to post-test 1 and/or post-test 2. Even though the third-semester students did not show any positive evidence of learning the focused-grammatical items (due to possible test design problems, as discussed in the next subsection), all treatment groups showed some evidence of learning for the grammar production task. For the second-semester learners, significant progress was noticed for the planned focus-on-form and the focus-on-meaning groups. This suggests that when the learners are put in a more communicative situation, they might be able to apply what they have learned (Brown, 1994, 2000; Cook, 1996, 2001; Doughty & Williams, 1998; Doughty & Varela, 1998; Hymes, 1972; Long, 1991, Long & Robinson, 1998; Omaggio, 1983; Omaggio Hadley, 2001; Savignon, 1972, 1983, 1991, 1997; VanPatten, 1985, 2003b). In the present study, because students were given an open-ended topic that involved their personal life (past or best vacations), they seem to have been able to better integrate the grammatical targeted forms with their production.

Overall, CEI shows that the integration of vocabulary and grammar within content has positive initial effects. As it will be discussed in section 6.2.3, some instructional treatments might be more effective than others.

### 6.2.2 Differences of instructional levels

One observation that can be made is that the two levels (i.e., second- and third-semester French) targeted in this experiment have shown slightly different results in their outcomes. The second-semester learners performed better on the vocabulary, the fill-in-the-blanks grammar task and the grammar production task, while the third-semester learners showed positive evidence of improvement on vocabulary and grammar production only. The main reason that could explain this difference, particularly on the fill-in-the-blanks grammar tasks, resides in test design. As mentioned in the methodology chapter, a change of the fill-in-the-blanks grammar task on the post-tests had been necessary, due to high scores on the pre-test. After scoring the pre-test, it became obvious that the format of the fill-in-the-blanks grammar task component of the test was not conducive to eliciting production on the part of the learners. The second-semester participants only had to produce the form of the comparative or superlative, without the adjective, while the third-semester learners had to produce the form of *lequel*, according to the agreement of the noun. Recall that this was the reason for changing the test format on the fill-in-the-blanks grammar task for both levels: it was in order to have learners produce more language on the post-tests (Appendices K, L, U, V). Before the experiment, the scores for both second and third-semester learners on the fill-in-the-blanks grammar task were high. After the experiment, and with a more demanding task, learners had either significantly higher scores for the case of the planned focus-on-form and focus-on-meaning groups of the second-semester learners, or, in the case of the third-semester learners, had scores with very small increases and even decreases. The test changes could explain these losses or minimal gains, as more was expected of the learners, and as the scoring did not attribute points with the same intensity on the relative pronouns for the third-semester groups. The additional analysis, done in Chapter V (Table 5.26, p. 134) shows that, if the post-tests had focused only on the relative pronouns, instead of adding a preposition into the item, the scores would have actually accentuated the lack of gain from the cultural lesson. The pre-test's scores either showed no significant difference with post-test 1, or significant differences between the pre-test and post-test 2, where the pre-tests scores were more significant for two of the groups (i.e., incidental focus-on-form and focus-on-meaning). Again, it is the planned focus-on-form treatment that showed more significantly different results than the other two groups. Therefore, learners did not progress on the relative pronouns and did not perform significantly better on the post-tests, when only the relative pronoun is taken into consideration, as in the pre-test.

Furthermore, considering the fact that the second-semester participants did seem to have learned from exposure to the forms, enhanced or not, the choice of grammatical targeted forms for the third-semester groups might have been relatively more difficult to process. For the second-semester groups, the forms were the comparative and superlative of adjectives, which might have been easier in terms of requisite cognitive processes, as it might have been a form that the instructors might have commonly used in their everyday speech, therefore providing some preliminary input of the form for learners. In the video recordings, most of the second-semester teachers used the comparative and/or superlative, not only as the transparencies were presenting, but also to talk about other points (examples 97-101).

Example 97:
Jeanne: La France est beaucoup plus grande que la Belgique.
[France is much bigger than Belgium.]

Example 98:
Jeanne: On dit qu'on mange aussi bien que les Français, mais qu'on mange autant que les Allemands.
[It is said that they eat as well as Frenchmen, but that they eat as much as Germans.]

Example 99:
Annabelle: Le plus important personage, c'est pas le roi. C'est le Premier Ministre.
[The most important character is not the king. It is the Prime Minister.]

Example 100:
Danielle: Je crois qu'il y a beaucoup plus de variétés de bières en Belgique qu'en France. La France a moins de variétés de bières que la Belgique.
[I think there are many more varieties of beer in Belgium than in France. France has less varieties of beer than Belgium.]

Example 101:
Alexandra: Des températures plus tempérées.

*[More temperate temperatures.]*

The comparative and the superlative generate forms that limit possibilities for misunderstanding. If, for instance, the words *Bruxelles* (Brussels), *plus* (more), *petite* (small), *ville* (town), *Chicago* are given, the learners may quickly understand that *Brussels is smaller than Chicago*. The word order and meaning accompanying the comparative and superlative structures do not demand as much effort in terms of comprehension strategies when one is exposed to them. According to the Processability Theory (Pienemann, 1998; VanPatten, 2003a), language acquisition is based on an implicational hierarchy. Certain procedures occur only after others are acquired. In the case of the comparative and superlative forms, they belong to earlier procedures, as they are part of what is called 'simplified S-procedure', which happens before the 'subordinate clause procedure', as used in the third-semester material.

The third-semester learners were introduced to the relative pronoun *lequel* preceded by a preposition. For example, *un rituel sénégalais* **pendant lequel** *on boit le thé attaya (à la sénéglaise) peut durer des heures* implies that the learners understand the preposition *pendant* and that *lequel* has to agree with *rituel*. Because the learners had been exposed to the similar interrogative pronoun *lequel* in a previous chapter, they were already familiar with its agreement in gender and number. The objective for using this form as a relative pronoun was to observe if the learners could associate it, in a meaningful and logical way, with the prepositions and the nouns that had to agree with *lequel*. Despite the design problem, the choice of this grammatical form for the third-semester groups might have been more difficult to process than the comparative and superlative forms used for the second-semester groups. The learners had to know the gender of the nouns and understand the meaning of the prepositions in order to produce the correct form. Even though meaning was involved, the prepositions might have been too abstract making them too demanding at the processing level. In the video recordings, the teachers, who were not prompted to present forms (i.e., the incidental focus-on-form and focus-on-meaning teachers), did not highlight those prepositions. They presented the cultural information, with some focus on vocabulary items, as if students already knew the grammatical structures, or as if their meaning was not obstructive to comprehension. However, it is very important to point out that when looking at the grammar production task results, the planned focus-on-form and incidental focus-on-form treatments of the third-semester group show progress on post-test 1, implying that retention of the grammar items was present when applied to a productive task. For the second-semester participants, two of the treatment conditions (planned focus-on-form and focus-on-meaning) also showed improvement on the grammar production task. These results need to be compared with the teachers' behavior. Looking at Tables 4.1 through 4.3 (p. 95-96) in Chapter 4, it was noted that teachers focused on the lexical and grammatical forms differently. The data in Tables 4.1 through 4.3 shows that the second-semester and third-semester teachers of the incidental focus-on-form treatment produced as much focus on grammatical items as the focus-on-meaning treatment (i.e., 0 episodes). However, in the case of the second-semester teachers, they produced a lot more episodes of focus on meaning (i.e., vocabulary). This fact is difficult to explain from the data. Beside the fact that much more lexical foci was done by incidental focus-on-form teachers, it seems that, qualitatively, the treatments of incidental focus-on-form and focus-on-meaning might not really be different, as teacher behave very similarly. Quantitatively, both the focus-on-meaning and incidental focus-on-form groups performed similarly (i.e., they did not show any statistical treatment difference). If they are not told many directions, their natural instinct is to want to make sure their students understand what is presented to them, therefore focus on meaning, usually by looking at vocabulary with the goal to convey the cultural message. The quantity of the lexical foci did not seem to make a statistical difference between the focus-on-meaning group and the incidental focus-on-form group. As for the planned focus-on-form group, the instances of focus on vocabulary were as numerous as the incidental focus-on-form group's, but since they were more targeted on the enhanced vocabulary, the learners were able to notice and better learn those specific lexical forms.

From the discussion in section 6.2.1 and section 6.2.2, the first research question can be answered positively, as the data show that focus-on-form might facilitate the acquisition of lexical and grammatical forms. However, since improvement from pre-test to post-tests was shown, in general, for all the treatments, including the focus on meaning treatment, it is not possible to draw any conclusions concerning the efficacy of focus-on-form. CEI has positive effects on content learning and positive effects on the learning of grammar and vocabulary. Yet, the type of instruction might give further support to the model that CEI should adopt in order to make content, vocabulary and grammar more salient. The next issue looks at the effectiveness of the focus-on-form treatments that were designed for the study.

### 6.2.3 The effectiveness of focus-on-form: planned or incidental?

The second research question asked: Which type of focus-on-form instruction is more effective at promoting the acquisition and production of grammar and vocabulary in intermediate French L2 classes? The results analyzing the efficiency of the treatment are clear. Any significant differences in the data occur with the planned focus-on-form group being more effective than the other two groups. This is true of both the second- and the third-semester participants. However, due to probable test design differences, the number of occurrences of significant results varies with the level of the learners, as seen in the previous subsection. As shown in the previous chapter, the second-semester planned focus-on-form learners outperformed on the post-test 1 the incidental focus-on-form group on the fill-in-the-blanks grammar task and production grammar, and both groups (incidental focus-on-form and focus on meaning) for vocabulary and culture. No significance of instruction types was retained on the post-test 2 for the second-semester learners. As for the third-semester treatments, the planned focus-on-form group performed better on the vocabulary component of the post-test 1, as compared to the other groups. No other significance between groups was noticed.

This brings up the efficiency of input enhancement and explicit teaching of the instructors. In the case of the second-semester learners, when the written input (on the transparencies) was enhanced on the lexical and grammar forms, the learners seemed to have noticed the lexical and grammatical items. However, for the third-semester learners, the planned focus-on-form group, that received enhanced materials, only shows learning on the vocabulary items. The point that recognizing vocabulary is necessary for comprehending meaning is essential to explain the fact that the planned focus-on-form treatment of both second and third-semester learners outperformed the other treatments, including incidental focus-on-form. Norris and Ortega (2000) mention that explicit teaching appears to make a positive difference for noticing forms. Their meta-analysis shows that treatments that include a focus-on-form are more effective than treatments that do not, and that the explicitness of the focus-on-form is an important factor for positive results. In addition, when looking at which group performed better on the grammar-production task among the second-semester learners, a significant difference appears at this level: the planned focus-on-form group had higher mean scores than the two other groups. Their opportunity to notice the targeted forms seem to have increased the likelihood of integrating those forms in the context of a communicative productive task. Again, this is supported by Norris and Ortega's study (2000), in which the planned focus-on-form group was able to notice not only the vocabulary but, in the case of the second-semester learners, also the fill-in-the-blanks grammar task. One possibility to explain the lack of stronger gain for the third-semester planned focus-on-form group on grammar is through the change in the test design. Another reason could be explained by the overloading of input processes (VanPatten, 1993, 1996, 2003a). Due to an additional focus on the grammar and vocabulary, unlike the focus-on-meaning and the incidental focus-on-form groups, the planned focus-on form group might have received an overwhelming amount of information for learning to happen. It is important to remind the reader that learning occurred on production grammar for all groups, but not one specific group outperformed the others.

Because vocabulary was also textually enhanced and because it was also closely linked to the meaning of the presentation, the learners in the planned focus-on-form acquired the vocabulary better than the other two groups. The planned focus-on-form teachers who saw the enhanced forms made sure to cover them by asking if students knew what each word meant and by giving a synonym, a translation, a paraphrase, or by stressing them with their voice. For example, Emilie translated the word *amère* (bitter) and *course* (race). Thierry paraphrased the word *pouvoirs* (powers). Several of the teachers stressed some of the targeted words with their voice. In this case, the input enhancement does have a positive effect on teaching, and possibly learning. Researchers (VanPatten, 1993, 1996, 2003a; Sharwood-Smith, 1993; Wong, 2004) who have studied the effect of input enhancement have encouraged its use in order to help learners distinguish between meaning and form, as meaning might attract the most attention. The participants of this study have noticed the vocabulary, bringing support to input enhancement in the case of lexical items.

It could also be argued that the success of input enhancement, in the case of this study, is based on teachers' noticing the forms to focus on due to the bolding and coloring of target forms. It might have helped them remembering better what the focused forms were. Incidental focus-on-form did not show differences from focus on meaning. This might have been caused by a lack of input enhancement and explicit instruction. This last remark needs more investigation.

Part of my initial hypothesis on learning stated that the incidental focus-on-form instruction the teacher would provide would still foster learning. I also hypothesized that when the enhanced forms were removed, and the focus-on-form became incidental, noticing would measurably decrease. If the incidental focus-on-form was also taken away from instruction, it was hypothesized that the learners would have little chance to notice the forms at all, as the meaning would become the sole focus of instruction. As seen previously, all treatments showed learning, and the group that outperformed the other ones was the planned focus-on-form group. However, when comparing incidental focus-on-form and the focus on meaning, differences in the learning did not seem to be statistically significant in any part of the tests. Therefore, this section of my initial hypothesis is not supported. Responding to learners' questions or focusing some attention on form immediately, without planning, does not seem to make a difference from just focusing on the meaning. Importantly, the videos revealed that teachers' feedback in the incidental focus-on-form and focus-on-meaning groups was very similar: in each case, teachers focused attention on lexical forms they apparently thought would be difficult in both conditions. As Tables 4.1 through 4.3 have shown (p. 95-96), the count of focus-on-form instances was quite similar for both groups and at both levels of instruction. The main difference is the encouragement which incidental focus-on-form teachers made when they told their students to ask questions if they had any. This was the case with Annabelle, Blanche, Julie, Eddy, and Danielle. So apparently, when no attention to form is planned, the teachers act in very similar manners in an incidental focus-on-form context or in a focus-on-meaning one: if no specific grammatical problems are raised, then no incidental grammatical focus-on-form is made. Teachers who are in a focus on meaning context might also focus on forms that they want their students to notice, or they might give feedback in response to an error. Planned focus-on-form, with the help of input enhancement, allows the teachers to remember to bring students' attention to particular grammatical and lexical forms, while still presenting a meaningful content. This might explain the findings of this study, supporting the planned focus-on-form treatment.

Another characteristic that is essential to point out is that even though cultural learning was not being enhanced in the text (although there were pictures illustrating the cultural content), the second-semester planned focus-on-form group performed better on the cultural component, meaning they retained more information than the other two groups. One possible reason for this might be due to the fact that learners realized that they had to concentrate on different aspects of the language (culture, vocabulary and grammar). It can be hypothesized that input enhancement of vocabulary and grammar might help learners concentrate more on the general meaning of the lesson as well as vocabulary and grammar.

For the third-semester groups, significant differences between groups are not as frequent. The only instance where one of the three groups performed better than the other groups in post-test 1 was on the vocabulary component. Again, it was the planned focus-on-form group that scored higher. In this study, input enhancement did appear to help the lexical forms be noticed and acquired. One reason why there appears to be a strong difference in acquisition between the second- and the third-semester planned focus-on-form participants could be based on the difficulty of the content and of the forms. The perception that learners might have of Belgium might have been more related to their cultural experience in the United States or in Europe. However, Senegal is a very different country from the United States and France, being non-western, and has more unique traditions and words related to its culture (e.g., Wolof, Pular, Léopold Sédar Sanghor, Youssou) when compared to American and French ones. As mentioned earlier, the grammatical features might also have been more complex to understand, due to the need to comprehend not only the relative pronoun, but also the preceded preposition. According to the Processability Theory, the implicational hierarchy shows that subordinate clauses are the last aspect learned by an L2 learner (Pienemann, 1998;

VanPatten, 2003a). Williams (2001) stated that "proficiency is clearly a factor that needs to be investigated further as it relates to the effectiveness of focus-on-form" (p. 311). She further suggests that the higher the proficiency of the learners is, the more effective the focus-on-form might be. However, in this case, the opposite seems to have happened. The choice of form and meaning could possibly be a factor explaining the better success of focus-on-form for second-semester learners in this study.

In conclusion, my hypothesis has been supported, as the *planned focus-on-form* type of instruction, especially at the second-semester level, is the most effective at promoting the acquisition and production of grammar and vocabulary. Some positive effects are also found for the third-semester planned focus-on-form group, though not as frequently.

### 6.2.4 Lack of long-term effect between treatment effects

When looking at the differences between treatment types, post-test 2 raises an important issue for both levels. The significant differences between the planned focus-on-form treatment and the other two groups, noted on post-test 1, disappeared after two weeks. Among treatments, the knowledge of the vocabulary and grammatical components was still retained; however, the advantage of the planned focus-on-form group on post-test 1 did not persist. Previously mentioned, Norris and Ortega (2000) found that explicit teaching of focus-on-form is more effective than other less explicit treatments. However, the lack of sustained advantage for the planned focus-on-form group in this present study may have been related to the short exposure to the target forms. Looking at the length of exposure, Norris and Ortega (2000) noticed that instruction seems to have a long-term effect. In the 78 studies Norris and Ortega reviewed, the more explicit treatments had an average length of exposure of at least three hours. My study provided a short period of exposure to content and form with a small number of form instances, which may not have been sufficient for the planned focus-on-form group to sustain its initial advantage. It is important to remember that most textbooks allow for longer exposure of grammatical and lexical form within each chapter and throughout the textbook. Furthermore, the explicitness of teaching might make a difference and often depends on the style of the textbooks used. The textbook authors' beliefs have an influence on how the teachers are expected to present language instruction.

Despite a loss of advantages of the planned focus-on-form treatment, it is important to point out that long-term retention (after 2 weeks) was noticeable on post-test 2, when looking at each treatment group individually (within test analyses). For the second-semester learners, all groups showed long-term retention for vocabulary. The focus-on-meaning and planned focus-on-form treatments showed retention for the fill-in-the-blanks grammar task and the grammar production task. For the third-semester, all groups retained their lexical knowledge and were able to perform significantly better than on the pre-test on the grammar production task. Despite not spending much time on the cultural presentation, a certain degree of retention remains and brings support to the integration of forms in content-enriched instruction. The only caveat is that the effect of treatment types does not seem to last, as the planned focus-on-form does not show significant differences, when compared to the other two groups, on post-test 2.

### 6.2.5 Does prompting on tasks matter?

The grammar production task of this study shows that learners can apply and integrate the small amount of grammar they have learned visually and audibly into a written paragraph. The results are not strong but there are significant effects that prove that the learners, at the second- and third semester and in most groups (planned focus-on-form and focus-on-meaning for second-semester learners; all three treatments for third-semester learners), do perform better on the written component of the tests after the cultural presentation. This could be partially explained by the instructions accompanying the writing component. Because they were explicitly asking the participants to use the targeted grammatical forms, they were probably more aware of what they were asked to do.

Instruction for second-semester: Make sure you use the **comparative** (i.e. ***more...than, less...than, as...as***), or the **superlative** (i.e. ***the most, the least***).

Instruction for third-semester: Give detailed descriptions using **four (4) relative pronouns** "**lequel**" (and its variations: *laquelle, lesquels, lesquelles*) with a preceding preposition such as: **avec, pour, sans, dans, pendant**, etc. (e.g. *dans lequel*).... ?

Even the groups that focused on meaning seem to do better on the grammar production task. The only group that did not perform better after the cultural lesson was the second-semester incidental focus-on-form group. The instructions might have cued the learners, by textually enhancing the targeted items to use. The learners were prompted to use specific items, even though learners, belonging to the focus-on-meaning and incidental focus-on-form conditions, had not been directed to them during the cultural lessons. This is giving support to the value of instructions given to a task. Making it successful does not seem to depend just on the acquisition of form, but also on the way the learners are led to it. Explicitness can help a learner notice the objective of the task and be successful at performing it.

The effect of focus-on-form, planned or incidental, does not only depend on the learners, but also depends on the teachers themselves. As shown in chapter IV, the interpretation of the instructions given to the teachers varies greatly and even caused the change of teachers from the group they were originally placed in. This could mean that focus-on-form instruction might have different effects on learners' acquisition depending on the wording of those instructions and of the way the teachers present them compared to other teachers. The focus might be more explicit or more concentrated on one specific item if the teachers have realized the presence of a problematic form, or if they were explicitly instructed to do it. In most cases of incidental focus-on-form, the focus on the form came from teachers' questions (for example, asking for the meaning of a word to check learners' comprehension). In a few instances, a student asked a question on meaning or on culture, but this was rare. One example was when one of Emilie's students asked her *"qu'est-ce que ça veut dire 'amer'?"*[11], Emilie answered by saying *"amer?* Bitter". Those few student-generated questions might explain why incidental focus-on-form was not as efficient as predicted. Since in the focus-on-meaning groups, some teachers also brought some lexical forms to students' attention, even though this was not as frequent, the difference between the two groups was reduced (see

---

[11] Translated in English as: What does "amer" mean?

Table ... for count of episodes). Furthermore, teaching style and training might have a strong influence on the way instructions are carried out. In this study, there were teachers who had particular interests in language learning and were more knowledgeable of the theories and techniques of the field of second language teaching. Eddy and Blanche, for instance, have had more coursework in SLA, and they were more focused on the meaning than the form, as they were more aware of possible learning through implicit teaching. Therefore, as in the case of Blanche, instructions might have been interpreted based on personal beliefs of language acquisition. However, not only pedagogical beliefs, but also personal beliefs based on past experience might influence teacher practices, and eventually student learning outcomes. Research (Borg, 1998a, 1998b, 1999b, 2003, Johnston & Goettsch, 2000) has shown that teachers often believe that students do not like grammar or do not find it important in language teaching. In the study, the majority of the teachers actually say that students do not generally like grammar. Students' questionnaires show that when they ranked the components of grammar, culture, vocabulary, and speaking, grammar on a scale of 1 to 4 (1 being the most important and 4 the least important), grammar was ranked as a 3 or 4 by more than 60% of the students. Speaking and vocabulary received the most appreciation. Culture was ranked as a 3 or 4 on the scale by over 80% of the students, which makes the findings of this study interesting, especially as the participants significantly learned the cultural content regardless of the treatment groups. So, the results on the fill-in-the-blanks grammar task, especially at the third-semester level, could have been partially justified by the expressed interest students have for grammar; however, the results for culture are not characterized by students' beliefs. Despite their apparently lower interest in culture, they do learn it. Personal beliefs on teachers' and students' parts might play a role, but learning still seems to occur. In summary, instructions to teachers need to be clear if a specific goal is sought by the initiator of those instructions. However, it is important to take personal interests of teachers and students into account.

### 6.2.6 Does content-enriched instruction work?

Because no empirical research had been previously carried out in the context of content-enriched instruction, the goal for this present study was well motivated. It has shown that during content-enriched instruction, linguistic forms can be noticed and learned without hindering the learning of content. In this experiment, all groups showed significantly improvement on culture on the post-tests than on the pre-tests, implying that despite the presence of focus-on-form for some of the groups, the attention to content was not hindered. So does content-enriched instruction work? My answer is yes, as at the end of the lessons (and two weeks later with some of the components), learners heard about content related to the foreign language and in many cases, gained on vocabulary and grammar. Furthermore, with the planned focus-on-form instructions, the gains were significantly better than for the other treatment conditions at post-test 1. More work on the design of a content-enriched instruction lesson is needed, but the present results do suggest that content-enriched instruction can be successful in lower-level French courses.

### 6.3 Implications

This study sheds some light on how content-enriched instruction could be beneficial at lower levels of instruction. Some implications for L2 teachers are first given, followed by some for L2 teacher educators, and for second language theory, and finally for further research for content-enriched instruction and focus-on-form applications.

#### 6.3.1 Implications for L2 teachers

This study has shown that input enhancement provoked some favorable results; this technique may therefore be useful when presenting new content or new form to learners. In this particular study, positive effects of learning were found on vocabulary, grammar and culture. Yet, as VanPatten (1993, 1996, 2003b) believes, if form is first enhanced through an already familiar content, it might be noticed more easily. Also, even though form might not always be noticed when content is new, it might still be helpful to present enhanced forms for a future and deeper noticing. By this logic, grammar is worth presenting as it offers to the learners a first contact with the language forms. Previous research on the acquisition of linguistic form suggests the notion that forms have to be presented within a meaningful message to be noticed and learned; this is what focus-on-form is about (e.g. Doughty & Varela,

1998; Doughty & Williams, 1998a; Ellis, 2001; Ellis et al, 2001, 2002; Long, 1991; Spada, 1997; Williams & Evans, 1998). In order to increase the probability of noticing the form through content, so that the flow of attention is not as disturbed, enhancing forms is encouraged (Doughty & Williams, 1998a; Sharwood-Smith, 1991, 1993, Wong, 2004). It can be done in many different ways (textual, visual, physical) and teachers can expand their imagination in many directions in order to help learners notice meaning and form. Furthermore, if input enhancement causes the teachers to focus on form, this might be a good technique to use in order to guide them in a specific teaching style.

This study also gives support for focus-on-form when explicit explanations are given to the learners. Nowadays, communicative language teaching is endorsed by both researchers and teachers for the way that it provides learners with meaningful ways to use the linguistic structures they have acquired. As for content-based instruction, content-enriched instruction provides this integration of content and form, as both are part of the same module (Ballman, 1997; Freeman & Freeman, 1997; Grabe & Stoller, 1997; Kowal & Swain, 1997; Musumeci, 1993). There are numerous possible choices for content, as a language is related to countries and the cultural wealth associated with them (literature, music, food, history, geography, economy, cultural facts such as school systems, driving laws, etc.), while the quantity of form is unlimited; however, the appropriate choice of forms with a specific content can be somewhat problematic. In order to make the form more noticeable, it is important to keep in mind that content needs to promote the form in a more communicative setting (Davison & Williams, 2001; Pica, 2002; Snow & Brinton, 1997; Swain, 1985, 1991, 1996, 2001; Swain & Lapkin, 2000). A first step would be to familiarize learners with the content through various tasks. Then, forms could be added, through the already known content.

In order to bring diversity to content-enriched instruction, a variation of content is suggested. Content in CEI does not have to be only about a francophone country, but can be about cinema (drama, comedies, cartoons), literature (novels, short stories, plays, poetry), cultural elements specific to a country (school system, driving laws, sports, cuisine, etc.), history, geography, etc. All these possible types of content can be of great value for the learners, as they not only can learn language through them, but can also learn about the countries' cultures. The biggest difference with a content-based instruction course is that the instructors might still decide to introduce the linguistic forms in a more explicit manner, such as using through input enhancement. It is also suggested that the grammatical forms should vary as well. Matching the appropriate forms with a specific content might be a difficult task, but it is also necessary to find a link between content and form in order to ease the acquisition of both. The language form could be introduced with different contents in order to give a variety of learning contexts. This would also allow for longer exposure, which is necessary for acquisition. Diverse activities, using the different learning skills, can be created to help learners develop those skills. Because communicative language teaching is the focus of teaching, the content and the activities should help learners to have opportunities to develop their communicative abilities.

The design of a syllabus, with the integration of CEI, can be done at different levels, even at lower levels of college language classes. Often, a textbook is the major source for pedagogical material in such classes. However, on a regular basis, the presence of a content-enhanced lesson, using culture, literature, cinema, etc. can also be included. Ballman (1997) offers a four-step model that can serve as a foundation for creating such types of lessons. The four steps include a *setting of the stage, providing input,* offering *guided participation,* and having an *extension activity*. This suggestion is in keeping with a very communicative approach to teaching, as it allows for a brief introduction (also called a warm-up), a large amount of input vital for acquisition, a time of creation with guidance, and finally an activity that allows learners to freely practice what they have learned. Ballman encourages the use of CEI at the beginning level of language teaching, as CBI might be too overwhelming for beginning learners. Recently, I had the privilege to meet a professor at Colorado State University, who explained to me that in her first-semester class, she integrates the reading and performance of a play, besides the regular use of a textbook. Specific linguistic forms are carefully chosen and highlighted for students. They also learn about the context and the culture of the play. At the end of the semester, students perform the play in front of an audience. This instance is a good example of how CEI could be adopted in a communicative language classroom. Using ideas from Ballman's (1997) article, teachers should carefully plan their CEI lessons, making sure there is a smooth continuity between sections of the lesson, in order to clearly convey the message and bringing the forms to learners' attention.

### 6.3.2 Implications for L2 teacher educators

From my observations, I was able to point out how teachers' teaching styles and beliefs might influence the outcome of teaching experience and, presumably, of student learning. Research has also shown that personal and common beliefs influence the style of teaching and need to be considered (Borg, 2003; Breen at al, 2001; Richards, 1994; Schulz, 1996, 2001; Shulman, 1987). If the goal of educators is to present a specific method of teaching, they should advise their student teachers to carefully look at instructions when preparing their lesson plans. If the educators have more global beliefs on language methods, they should remember that teachers might include their personal experiences and beliefs when reading instructions and interpret directives in their own way. Encouraging teachers to consider the principles behind teaching might be an essential step to take when planning their lesson. If teachers are well aware of the consequences of some methodologies and techniques, they might be more careful in preparing their lessons. Personal experience is useful but cannot be the sole foundation for practice, as it can be distorted by biases a culture might have induced. For example, if I were to use my own experience in learning English, German or Dutch, I would ask my students to always stay in their seats, fill in the blanks, and recite dialogues or irregular verbs memorized at home (very much like the traditional methods). I have learned that decontextualized L2 learning is not successful, especially when you travel abroad and are asked to converse. However, researchers, practitioners and teachers have not found a single true method. It is important for teacher educators to listen to their teachers' ideas on teaching and to propose additional ones. It is also essential to make teachers aware of their own teaching practices, in order for them to carefully plan and build their teaching experiences.

This study also suggests that the use of the first and second language has to be considered as a topic of discussion in teacher training. Research has shown that the question of the role of the L1 has not yet found a satisfactory answer (Cook, 2001; Levine, 2003; Macaro, 2001; Turnbull & Arnett, 2002); however, this research points out different instances when the

L1 was used in order to emphasize lexical and grammatical forms. Two of the L1 episode codes used in this study were immediate translations and delayed translations. The immediate translations were intertwined into the discourse, as if the L1 word was part of the L2. The delayed translations were introduced by a prompt or by a student's question. It appears that in the case of the delayed translations, the teachers were giving their students an opportunity to use comprehension and translation strategies. In the case of the immediate translations, no time was allowed for the use of such strategies. It might be important and more efficient for helping students to notice forms if teacher educators point out to their teachers to listen to their own L1 use, and to make sure they do lead their students to strategies by giving them time to do so. In this study, I did not always see the point in using a immediate translation, as either the L2 would have been sufficient, or time spent on the work was too short to have a significant impact on student comprehension. Time helps students to process the context of the words. Nevertheless, teachers do not seem to continue in the L1; instead, they very rapidly return to using the L2. This fact is an encouragement for educators: the presence of the L1, when carefully used, seems to serve practical functions that will ease some comprehension problems and that save time in some situations when an explanation in the L2 would be too time consuming.

For educators who are attracted by content-based teaching, the model of CEI that Ballman (1997) proposes is a good example of communicative language teaching as it is able to integrate forms within content at the lower level of adult L2 instruction. Educators might help student teachers to exploit this method by brainstorming content ideas and adequate forms to suit the content. Materials need to be created for the specific use of CEI in lower-level language classrooms. Even though the content is not always static, as some cultural facts for example are very dynamic, suggestions can be made, or lesson plans can be designed for using literature, cinema, culture, arts, history and many other topics. With the help of teachers, educators could work towards that goal so that the scope of materials can be theoretically based, while being practical for language classrooms.

### 6.3.3 Implications for Second Language Acquisition Theory

Regarding second language theory, an issue that this research has raised is the role that focus-on-form plays in language learning. Long (1991) and Ellis (2001) claim that focus-on-form is the notion that refers to a combination of form and meaning, as opposed to focus on meaning and focus-on-forms. It can happen incidentally, as in the original definition, or it can be planned. However, one issue has been raised by my results. My conclusions cannot be generalized as this study is the first one of its kind and needs improvement in the design; still, this study appropriately looks at the balance between meaning and form in focus-on-form. Specifically, how much weight should meaning take as compared to form? And how present should form be not to hinder meaning? This is a challenge that theory has not particularly examined. Focus-on-form has had positive support from many researchers; however, a model for its application in a diversity of contexts (e.g. college L2 classes, immersion classes, content-based courses, etc.) might be an important initiative in the understanding of focus-on-form and its applications in language learning.

VanPatten (2003a, 2003b) believes that input is primordial for second language learning, and that without input, learning cannot occur. He furthermore points out that input is not always successful, especially depending on the manner in which it is introduced. Through one of the language principles he lists, he says that learners attend to meaning before attending to forms. If the input presents too much information, input processing may be overloaded and learners will give priority to meaning. This belief is weakly supported by the present study. A large amount of new input was given at the time of the experiment, and only one group (i.e., second-semester incidental) of learners' working memory seem to have been overloaded and grammatical forms did not get processed as intake. However, furthering our understanding of learners' input processing will be necessary if we are to increase the likelihood of learning in the presence of meaning and form. The qualitative chapter observed in part the language choice teachers made to highlight, incidentally or via previous planning, the targeted forms. The teachers of the planned focus-on-form treatment identified some of the targeted grammatical structures mainly by using the L1. Generally, all teachers also used the L1 to clarify difficulties in meaning, which occurred much more frequently. Therefore, a solution which teachers in this particular study, but also in others (Cook, 1999; Duff & Polio, 1990: Levine, 2003, forthcoming; Polio & Duff, 1994), have opted for is to switch to the L1 to present the meaning and the lexicon, and from time to time, the grammatical forms. Despite teachers' practices and beliefs, language switching might not be the answer to a lack of noticing lexical and grammatical forms and to an overloaded input processing. Theoretical work is still needed regarding the impact of the L1 in the mind of a learner. Does the L1 ease input processing? Or does it, rather, distract the learners from the target language? This area of research has yet to be explored by psycholinguists.

### 6.3.4 Implication for further research for CEI and FonF applications

This study suggests many opportunities for further research, as it is a new area of investigation. Due to lack of evidence, empirical research is strongly needed to bring more understanding to content-enriched instruction at the college level, but also at other levels, such as the secondary-school level. Content-based instruction appears to have been adopted by many upper-level programs, as it attracts more advanced learners who are majoring in specific areas. Therefore, if content-enriched instruction appears to have positive overall effects on language acquisition (i.e., on the acquisition of both meaning and form) at the lower levels of instruction, it could be a motivating method for beginning language learners and their teachers. They could learn some content related to the foreign language, while still learning specific vocabulary and grammar points. However, in my search of the literature, no other empirical studies on content-enriched instruction were found, which strongly suggests the need for more research in this area.

Research in the area of focus-on-form is also recommended from this study. Even though focus-on-form is a well-investigated method, its implementation in subject-matter courses has not yet been well applied. In most cases, content takes precedence over form, and neither teachers nor learners focus on accuracy. Increasing studies that would strive to look at forms within content are necessary. Small- and large-scale studies would be beneficial, as the small ones could focus more on techniques for including content and form in a content-enriched instruction environment, while the large ones could focus on the quantitative results of acquisition. Focus-on-form can either be presented incidentally when errors from students occur, or it can be planned ahead through a specific lesson that will bring learner attention to the forms. This study has given stronger support for planned focus-on-form. Research on how to better present grammatical forms, while still attending to content, is necessary to substantiate the positive effects of focus-on-form. Furthermore, the implementation of the input enhancement technique might be considered for guiding learners and teachers in the process to follow in noticing or teaching the targeted forms. Further research is necessary to observe the impact input enhancement might have in a CEI environment.

### 6.4 Limitations of the present study

Because this study was one of the first empirical ones in the area of content-enriched instruction, a few limitations warrant discussion, when looking back at the design. First of all, the results probably cannot be generalized, as it was the first one of its kind to look at the implementation of content-enriched instruction in an empirical research study. Replications are definitely necessary in order to lend support to the new findings. New content and forms need to be tested before any type of definitive conclusions can be drawn.

Another major limitation is based on the fact that the cultural, lexical and grammatical presentation was carried out over a 50-minute period. Normal instruction of particular linguistic items is often presented to the learners and practiced over several days. In order to make the grammatical and lexical forms of the present study more salient, it might have been more efficient to present the treatments over several days. However, due to syllabus constraints, the time for this experiment was limited, and therefore could not entirely show how students would have learned in a normal context. However, positive results were still observed; this is an encouraging sign both for this study and for future research projects.

Another limitation concerns the test design. Because of problems observed by the outcome of the pre-test on the fill-in-the-blanks grammar task component for third-semester participants, the decision was made to have participants produce more for that particular component. This was a necessary choice, which unfortunately did not allow for strong comparisons between the pre-test and the post-tests for the fill-in-the-blanks grammar task in the third-semester groups. In the future, the tests will need to stay consistent and involve questions allowing for more production from the pre-test. The grammar production task gave some support to CEI, as the learners performed significantly better on the post-test1 in most groups at both levels, when compared with the pre-test.

One argument one might raise is the format of the tests. The goal of CEI is to be communicative and focused on meaning, while integrating form. However, some of the tests used for verifying learning were quite focused and lacked communicative objectives. Except for the grammar production task, all the items were discrete point. The content knowledge constituted only half the test (culture and grammar were both based on content), while the rest of the test was on lexis recognition and recollection of a past event. Another limiting test-related factor concerns the technical problem of implementation of the tests within a fixed syllabus. Due to the scope of the language program, it was not possible to take more time to administer longer and complete tests. Despite this limitation, the tests used for this experiment provided reliable data with which to analyze the research questions.

The choice of using a quantitative analysis to study the effects of a CEI lesson on learners' knowledge of grammar, vocabulary and culture could have been a limitation in trying to fully understand learners' progress. A qualitative analysis, through learners' interactions with teachers or other peers, might have helped to get a better perspective on learners' cognitive processing. However, it was felt that the research questions were better answered through the present analysis. Further qualitative research is to be considered for a better comprehension of L2 acquisition in the classroom setting.

Watching the videos of the cultural presentations, I observed that instructors had their particular and personal styles of teaching. Even though the lessons were similar within each treatment group, the outcome of the presentations differed. Some of the instructors gave more feedback than others, even though students did not particularly ask for more clarifications; some used the L1 more frequently; others, in the planned focus-on-form group, gave more detailed explanations of the grammatical forms, than their peers in the same group. Overall, it was pointed out in chapter IV that some of the teachers did not always clearly follow the instructions I had provided for their treatment group. This resulted in moving the scores of their class to a different treatment group. However, does it mean that more specific instructions should have been given? I do not believe so, as the goal of this study was to observe what happened in the language classroom, not in a laboratory setting. I wanted to be able to analyze the natural reaction of teachers when they were faced with particular instructions. The fact that they already were asked to participate in this study was artificial for them, so decreasing the level of anxiety was necessary to put them feel at ease. Furthermore, authors who write language textbooks with instructions to the teachers might expect specific results with the method they promote in their book. It is important to keep in mind that individual interpretations can change the anticipated outcome. The background and personality that different teachers have, the way they learned a foreign language, their beliefs about and attitudes toward foreign language teaching methodology, etc., can alter teacher practice. If the objectives of instructions have to be closely followed, it is important to anticipate how teachers might interpret what is asked of them. Authors have to keep this in mind when they design the object of their textbooks. If specific results are expected, then specific instructions should be given. My objective is to understand teachers in their natural setting, not in an artificial environment.

A final shortcoming to mention in this section is the format of the presentation the teachers and the learners were exposed to. A normal class session involves the use of the book that presents the language structures and applies them through a variety of whole class, pair or individual activities. Based on a communicative language teaching style, the rhythm between the teaching of the language and its communicative application is very dynamic. Thus, the style of the cultural presentation that was needed for this study was different from what teachers and learners were accustomed to. The cultural presentation contained a 20-minute lecture, which learners could interrupt with questions; this was followed by a listening and reading whole class activity. Finally, learners were paired and had to write a paragraph, imagining a vacation in the country they had just learned about. Even though the cultural presentation involved the four skills, its unusual format might have been a drawback.

**6.5 Conclusions**

Learning or teaching a foreign language is not an easy task. A long-standing preoccupation in the field of second language acquisition concerns the search for methodologies that can lead to success in either endeavor. As described in this study, content-enriched instruction might allow the integration of meaning and form within the single module. This combines a communicative environment and a focus-on-form approach within the same curriculum.

From this research project, I have learned much about different aspects of language teaching and learning. When a method, such as content-enriched instruction is exploited, it is important to think of both sides of the classroom: the teacher and the learner. Teachers need to be able to clearly understand the techniques designed for CEI. Presenting form while still focusing on meaning might not be a natural skill, and teachers may need further instruction. Comprehending how learners process forms in a communicative context is also essential if we are ever to know the amount of planning necessary for an efficient CEI lesson. Since in this study focus-on-form, with the support of input enhancement, was shown to help learning, developing material that would promote content and form with the purpose of fulfilling CEI objectives seems warranted. From the conclusions I have drawn from the results, I realize many areas remain to be investigated, in regards to teachers' behavior and learners' language processing. I am hoping to continue examining those subjects, as they will build my personal L2 teaching experience and hopefully help others in their own language experience.

# REFERENCES

ACTFL Proficiency Guidelines – Speaking (1999). Yonkers, NY: American Council on the Teaching of Foreign Languages.

Andrews, S. (1994). The grammatical knowledge/awareness of native-speaker EFL teachers: What the trainers say. In M. Bygate, A. Tonkyn and E. Williams (Eds.) *Grammar and the Language Teacher.* London: Prentice Hall International.

Andrews, S. (1999). 'All these like little name things': A comparative study of language teachers' explicit knowledge of grammar and grammatical terminology. *Language Awareness, 8,* 143-159.

Asher, J. (1972). Children's first language as a model for second language learning. *The Modern Language Journal, 56,* 3, 133-139.

Atkinson, D. (1987). The mother tongue in the classroom: A neglected resource? *ELT Journal, 41,* 4, 241-247.

Atkinson, D. (1993). Teaching in the target language: A problem in the current orthodoxy. *Language Learning Journal, 8,* 2-5.

Bachman, L. (1990). *Fundamental considerations in language testing.* Oxford: Oxford University Press.

Ballman, T. (1997). Enhancing beginning language courses through content-enriched instruction. *Foreign Language Annals, 30,* 2, 173-186.

Basturkmen, H., Loewen, S. & Ellis, R. (2002). Metalanguage in focus on form in the communicative classroom. *Language Awareness, 11,* 1, 1-13.

Borg, S. (1998a). Talking about grammar in the foreign language classroom. *Language Awareness, 7,* 159-175.

Borg, S. (1998b). Teachers' pedagogical systems and grammar teaching: A qualitative study. *TESOL Quarterly, 32,* 1, 9-38.

Borg, S. (1999a). Studying teacher cognition in second language grammar teaching. *System, 27,* 19-31.

Borg, S. (1999b). Teachers' theories in grammar teaching. *ELT Journal 53,* 157-167.

Borg, S. (2003). Teacher cognition in grammar teaching: A literature review. *Language Awareness, 12*, 2, 96-108.

Breen, M. (2002). From a language policy to classroom practice: The intervention of identity and relationships. *Language and Education, 16*, 4, 260-283.

Breen, M., Hird, B., Milton, M., Oliver, R. & Thwaite, A. (2001). Making sense of language teaching: Teachers' principles and classroom practices. *Applied Linguistics, 22*, 4, 470-501.

Brinton, D., Snow, M., & Wesche, M. (1989). *Content-based language instruction.* Philadelphia, PA: Newbury House.

Brown, H. D. (1994). *Principles of language learning and teaching.* 3$^{rd}$ edition. Englewood Cliffs, NJ: Prentice Hall. 1$^{st}$ edition: 1980. 2$^{nd}$ edition: 1987.

Brown, H. D. (2000). *Principles of language learning and teaching.* 4$^{th}$ edition. White Plains, NY: Addison-Wesley Longman.

Burger, S. & Chrétien, M. (2001). The development of oral production in content-based second language courses at the university of Ottawa. *The Canadian Modern Language Review, 58*, 1, 84-102.

Bialystok, E. (1994). Analysis and Control in the Development of Second Language Proficiency. *Studies in Second Language Acquisition, 16*, 2, 157-168.

Byrnes, H. & Kord. S. (2002). Developing literacy and literary competence: Challenges for Foreign Language Departments. In V. Scott and H. Tucker (Eds), *SLA and Literature Classroom: Fostering Dialogues* (pp.35-73). Heinle & Heinle-Thomson Learning.

Cammarata, L. (2007). Understanding and implementing content-based instruction: An exploration of foreign language teachers' lived experience. Dissertation Abstracts International, A: The Humanities and Social Sciences, 67, 07, Jan, 2443.

Canale, M. (1983). From communicative competence to communicative language pedagogy. In J. Richards and R. Schmidt (Eds.) *Language and Communication.* London: Longman.

Canale, M. and Swain, M. (1980). Theoretical bases of communicative approaches to second language teaching and testing. *Applied Linguistics, 1*, 1, 1-47.

Carr, T. & Curran, T. (1994). Cognitive factors in learning about structured sequences: Applications to syntax. *Studies in Second Language Acquisition, 16,* 205-230.

Castellotti, V. (2001). *La langue maternelle en classe de langue étrangère.* CLE International.

Chandler, P., Robinson, W.P. & Noyes, P. (1988). The level of linguistic knowledge and awareness among students training to be primary teachers. *Language and Education, 2,* 161-173.

Colombo, J. (1982). The critical period concept: Research, methodology, and theoretical issues. *Psychological Bulletin, 1,* 260-275.

Cook, V. (1999). Going beyond the native speaker in language teaching. *TESOL Quarterly, 33,* 2, 185-209.

Cook, V. (2001). *Second Language Learning and Language Teaching.* 3rd edition. London: Arnold. 2nd edition: 1996.

Crandall, J. (1987). *ESL through content-area instruction.* Englewood Cliffs, NJ: Prentice-Hall Regents.

Curran, C. (1976). *Councelling-learning in second languages.* Apple River, IL: Apple River Press.

Curran, T & Keele, W. (1993). Attentional and nonattentional forms of sequence learning. *Journal of Experimental Psychology, 19,* 189-202.

Davidson, F. & Lynch, B. (2002). *Testcraft: A teacher's guide to writing and using language test specifications.* New Haven and London: Yale University Press.

Davison, C., & Williams, A. (2001). Integrating language and content: Unresolved issues. In B. Mohan, C. Leung, & C. Davison (Eds.), *English as a second language in the mainstream* (pp. 51-70). New York: Longman/Pearson.

Doughty, C. (1991). Second language instruction does make a difference. *Studies in Second Language Acquisition, 13,* 431-469.

Doughty, C. & Pica, T. (1986). "Information gap" tasks: Do they faciliatate second language acquisition? *TESOL Quarterly, 20,* 2, 305-325

Doughty, C. & Varela, E. (1998). Communicative focus on form. In C. Doughty & J. Williams (Eds.), *Focus on form in classroom second language acquisition* (pp. 114-138). Cambridge, UK: Cambridge University Press.

Doughty, C. & Williams, J. (1998a). *Focus on Form in classroom second language acquisition.* Cambridge, UK: Cambridge University Press.

Doughty, C. & Williams, J. (1998b). Issues and terminology. In C. Doughty & J. Williams (Eds.), *Focus on Form in classroom second language acquisition* (pp. 1-11). Cambridge, UK: Cambridge University Press.

Doughty, C. & Williams, J. (1998c). Pedagogical choices in focus on form. In C. Doughty & J. Williams (Eds.), *Focus on Form in classroom second language acquisition* (pp. 197-261). Cambridge, UK: Cambridge University Press.

Duff, P. & Polio, C. (1990). How much foreign language is there in the foreign language classroom. *Modern Language Journal, 74*, 154-166.

Early, M. (1991). Using wordless picture books to promote second language learning. *ELT Journal, 45*, 3, 245-251.

Ellis, R. (1993). The structural syllabus and second language acquisition. *TESOL Quarterly, 27*, 91-113.

Ellis, R. (2001). Introduction: Investigating form-focused instruction. *Language Learning, 51* (supplement 1), 1-46.

Ellis, R., Basturkmen, H. & Loewen, L. (2001). Preemptive focus on form in the ESL classroom. *TESOL Quarterly, 35*, 3, 407-432.

Ellis, R., Basturkmen, H. & Loewen, L. (2002). Doing focus-on-form. *System, 30*, 419-432.

Fotos, S. (1993). Consciousness raising and noticing through focus on form: Grammar task performance versus formal instruction. *Applied Linguistics, 14*, 385-407.

Franklin, C. (1990). Teaching in the target language. *Language Learning Journal, 2*, 20-24.

Frantzen, D. (2002). Rethinking foreign language literature: Towards an integration of literature and language at all levels. In V. Scott and H. Tucker (Eds), *SLA and Literature Classroom: Fostering Dialogues* (pp.109-130). Heinle & Heinle-Thomson Learning.

Freeman, D. & Freeman, Y. (1997). Whole language teaching and content-based instruction: Are they compatible?. In M.A. Snow & D.M. Brinton (Eds.), *The content-based classroom* (pp. 351-354). White Plains, NY: Addison-Wesley Longman.

Gass, S. (1997). *Input, Interaction, and the Second Language Learner*. Mahwah, N.J.: Lawrence Erlbaum Associates.

Gass, S., Mackey, A. & Pica, T. (1998). The role of input and interaction in second language acquisition introduction to the special issue. *The Modern Language Journal, 82*, 3, 299-307.

Gass, S. & Varonis, E. (1985). Variation in native speaker speech modification to non-native speakers. *Studies in Second Language Acquisition, 7*, 1, 37-57.

Giauque, G. & Ely, C. (1990). Code-switching in beginning foreign language teaching. In R. Jacobson & C. Faltis (Eds.), *Language Distribution Issues in Bilingual Schooling* (p. 174-184). Clevedon, UK: Multilingual Matters.

Grabe, W. & Stoller, F.L. (1997). Content-based instruction: Research foundations. In M.A. Snow & D.M. Brinton (Eds.), *The content-based classroom* (pp. 5-21). White Plains, NY: Addison-Wesley Longman.

Grandin, J. (1993). Developing internships in Germany for International Engineering students. *Unterrichtspraxis / Teaching German, 24*, 2, 209-214.

Grim, F. (2004). Case study on the factors influencing teachers' L1 and L2 practice in the classrooms. Presentation at the Second University of California Language Consortium Conference on Theoretical and Pedagogical Perspectives, University of Santa Cruz, CA.

Harley, B. (1989). Functional Grammar in French immersion: A classroom experiment. *Applied Linguistics, 10*, 3, 331-359.

Harley, B. (1993). Instructional Strategies and SLA in Early French Immersion. *Studies in Second Language Acquisition, 15*, 2, June, 245-259.

Harley, B., Allen, P., Cummins, J. & Swain, M. (1990). *The Development of second language proficiency*. Cambridge ; New York : Cambridge University Press.

Harley, B. & Swain, M. (1978). Form and function in a second language: A close look at the verb system. *Fifth International Congress of Applied Linguistics (AILA)*.

Harper, J., Lively, M. & Williams, M. (2000). *Thèmes: French for the Global Community*. Boston, MA: Heinle & Heinle Publishers.

Hatch, E. (1978). *Second language acquisition: A book of readings.* Rowley, MA: Newbury House.

Hawkins, R. (1989). Do second language learners acquire restrictive relative clauses on the basis of relational or configurational information? The acquisition of French subject, direct object and genitive restrictive relative clauses by second language learners. *Second Language Research, 5,* 2, 156-188.

Hymes, D. (1972). On communicative competence. In J.B. Pride and J. Holmes (Eds.), *Sociolinguistics.* London: Penguin.

Jacobson, R. & Fattis, C. (1990). *Language description issues in bilingual schooling.* Clevedon, Avon: Multilingual Matters, 3-17.

Johnston, B. & Goettsch, K. (2000). In search of the knowledge base language teaching: Explanations by experienced teachers. *The Canadian Modern Language Review, 56,* 3, 437-468.

Kowal, M. & Swain, M. (1997). From semantic to syntactic processing: How can we promote it in the immersion classroom? In M. Swain & R. Johnson (Eds.), *Immersion education: International perspectives* (pp. 284-309). Cambridge: University Press.

Krashen, S. (1981). *Second language acquisition and second language learning.* Oxford: Pergamon.

Krashen, S. (1982). *Principles and practice in second language acquisition.* Oxford, NY: Pergamon.

Krashen, S. (1985). *The input hypothesis: Issues and implications.* London: Longman.

Krashen, S. (1989). We acquire vocabulary and spelling by reading: Additional evidence for the input hypothesis. *Modern Language Journal, 73,* 440-464.

Krashen, S. & Terrell, T.D. (1983). *The natural approach : Language acquisition in the classroom.* Oxford, UK : Pergamon.

Lado, R. (1964). *Language teaching : A scientific approach.* New York : McGraw-Hill.

La Pierre, D. (1994). Language output in a cooperative learning setting : Determining its effects on second language learning. MA thesis, University of Toronto (OISE).

Lee, J. & VanPatten, B. (1995). *Making communicative language teaching happen*. New York : McGraw-Hill.

Leeser, M. (2004). Learner proficiency and focus on form during collaborative dialogue. *Language Teaching Research, 8,* 1, 55-81.

Lenneberg, E. (1967). *Biological foundations of language*. New York: Wiley.

Leow, R. (1993). To simplify or not to simplify: A look at intake. *Studies in Second Language Acquisition, 15,* 333-355.

Leow, R. (1995). Modality and intake in second language acquisition. *Studies in Second Language Acquisition, 17,* 79-89.

Leow, R. (1998). Towards operationalizing the process of attention in SLA: Evidence for Tomlin and Villa's (1994) fine-grained analysis of attention. *Applied Psycholinguistics, 19,* pp. 133-159.

Leow, R. (2000). A study of the role of awareness in foreign language behavior: Aware versus unaware learners. *Studies in Second Language Acquisition, 22,* pp 557-584.

Levine, G. (2003). Student and instructors beliefs and attitudes about target language use, first language use, and anxiety: Report of a questionnaire study. *The Modern Language Journal, 87*, 3, 343-364.

Levine, G. (forthcoming). *Code Choice in the Foreign Language Classroom: the Multilingual Model*. Mahwah, NJ: Lawrence Erlbaum Associates, Inc.

Liebscher, G. and Dailer-O'Cain, J. (2004). Learner code-switching in the content-based foreign language classroom. *The Canadian Modern Language Review, 60,* 4, 501-525.

Lightbown, P. & Spada, N. (1990). Focus-on-form and corrective feedback in communicative language teaching: Effects on second language learning. *Studies in Second Language Acquisition, 12*, 4, 429-448.

Lightbown, P & Spada, N. (2003) *How languages are learned*. Oxford: Oxford Press.

Lim, J. (2001). The effects of different types of instruction: Focus-on-form study. *Pan-Pacific Association of Applied Linguistics, 5*, 2, 253-266.

Long, M. (1985). *Bibliography of research on second language classroom processes and classroom second language acquisition*. Center for Second Language Classroom Research, Social Science Research Institute, University of Hawaii at Manoa.

Long, M. (1991). Focus on form: a design feature in language teaching methodology. In K. De Mott, R. Ginsberg & C. Kramsch (Eds.), *Foreign language research in cross-cultural perspective* (pp. 39-52). Amsterdam/Philadelphia: John Benjamins.

Long, M. (1996). The role of linguistic environment in Second Language Acquisition. In W. Ritchie & T. Bhatia (Eds.), *Handbook of research on second language acquisition* (pp. 413-468). New York: Academic Press.

Long, M. (1997). Fossilization: Rigor mortis in living linguistic systems? Paper presented at EuroSLA7, Barcelona.

Long, M. & Robinson, P. (1998). Focus on form: Theory, research, and practice. In C. Doughty & J. Williams (Eds.), *Focus on form in classroom second language acquisition* (pp. 15-41). Cambridge: Cambridge University Press.

Macaro, E. (1997). *Target language, collaborative learning and autonomy*. Clevedon (England); Philadelphia, PA: Multilingual Matters.

Macaro, E. (2001). Analyzing student teachers' codeswitching in foreign language classrooms: theories and decision making. *The Modern Language Journal, 85*, 4, 531-548.

Macdonald, C. (1993). *Using the Target Language*. Cheltenham, UK: Mary Glasgow Publications.

Magnan, S. (1986). Assessing Speaking Proficiency in the Undergraduate Curriculum: Data from French. *Foreign Language Annals, 19*, 429-437.

Magnan, S., Rochette Ozello, Y, Martin-Berg, L. & Berg, W. (1998). *Paroles*. Orlando, FL: Holt, Rinehart and Winston.

Met, M. (1991). Learning language through content: Learning content through language. *Foreign Language Annals, 24*, 4, 281-295.

Metcalf, M. (1993). Foreign languages across the curriculum from a social science perspective: The Minnesota model. In M. Krueger & F. Ryan (Eds.), *Language and content: Discipline- and content-based approaches to language study* (pp.114-119). D.C. Heath and Company.

Mohan, B. (1986). *Language and content*. Reading, MA: Addison-Wesley.

Mohan, B. & Beckett, G. (2003). A functional approach to research on content-based language learning: Recasts in casual explanations. *Modern Language Journal, 87*, 3, 421-432.

Moore, D. (2002). Code-switching and learning in the classroom. *International Journal of Bilingual Education and Bilingualism, 5*, 5, 279-293.

Muranoi, H. (2000). Focus on form through interaction enhancement: integrating formal instruction into a communicative task in EFL classrooms. *Language Learning, 50*, 4, 617-173.

Musumeci, D. (1993). Second language reading and content area instruction: The role of second language reading in the development of communicative and subject matter competence. In M. Krueger & F. Ryan (Eds.), *Language and content: Discipline- and content-based approaches to language study* (pp.169-179). D.C. Heath and Company.

Musumeci, D. (1997). *Breaking tradition: An exploration of the historical relationship between theory and practice in second language teaching*. McGraw-Hill.

Muyskens, J. & Omaggio Hadley, A. (2002). *Rendez-Vous: an Invitation to French*. Sixth edition. McGraw-Hill Companies, Inc.

Nassaji, H. (1999). Towards form-focused instruction and communicative interaction in the second language classroom: some pedagogical possibilities. *The Canadian Modern Language Review, 55*, 3, 385-402.

Nissen, M. & Bullemer, P. (1987). Attentional requirements of learning: Evidence from performance measures. *Cognitive Psychology, 19*, 1-32.

Norris, J & Ortega, L. (2000). Effectiveness of L2 instruction: A research synthesis and quantitative meta-analysis. *Language Learning, 50*, 417-528.

Nunan, D. (1992). The teacher as decision maker. In J. Flowerdew, M. Brook and S. Hsia (eds), *Perspectives on Second Language Teacher Education* (pp. 135-165). Hong Kong: City of Polytechnic of Hong Kong.

Nzwanga, M. (2000). A study of French-English code-switching in a foreign language college teaching environment. Dissertation Abstracts International, A: The Humanities and Social Sciences, 2000, 61, 5, Nov, 1718-A.

Oliver, R. (1995). Negative feedback in child NS-NSS conversation. *Studies in Second Language Acquisition, 17*, 4, 459-482.

Omaggio, A. (1983). Methodology in transition: The new focus on proficiency. *The Modern Language Journal, 67*, 4, 330-341.

Omaggio Hadley, A. (2001). *Teaching language in context,* 3rd edition. Heinle & Heinle.1st edition: ; 2nd edition: .

Ortega, L. & Long, M. (1997). The effects of models and recasts on the acquisition of object topicalization and adverb placement in L2. Spanish. *Spanish Applied Linguistics, 1*, 1.

Palmer, B. (1993). Eastern Michigan University's Programs in language and international business: Disciplines with content. In In M. Krueger & F. Ryan (Eds.), *Language and content: Discipline- and content-based approaches to language study* (pp.138-147). D.C. Heath and Company.

Pessoa, S., Hendry, H., Donato, R., Tucker, G. R. and Lee, H. (2007). Content-based instruction in the foreign language classroom: A discourse perspective. *Foreign Language Annals, 40*, 1, 102-121.

Pica, T. (1994). Review article research on negotiation: What does it reveal about second-language learning conditions, processes, and outcomes? *Language Learning, 44*, 3, 493-527.

Pica, T.(2002). Subject-Matter Content: How Does It Assist the Interactional and Linguistic Needs of Classroom Language Learners? *The Modern Language Journal, 86*, I, 1-19.

Picker, R. (2005). Second language acquisition in a head start classroom: The role of play, status, gender, and teachers' language choice. Dissertation Abstracts International, A: The Humanities and Social Sciences, 66, 10, Apr, 3562.

Pienemann, M. (1998). *Sentence processing and second language development: Processability theory.* Philadelphia: Benjamins.

Polio, C. & Duff, P. (1994). Teachers' language use in university foreign language classrooms: a qualitative analysis of English and target language alternation. *The Modern Language Journal, 78*, 313-326.

Redmann, J. (2005). An interactive reading journal fro all levels of the foreign language curriculum. *Foreign Language Annals, 38*, 4, 484-493.

Rell, A. B. (2005). The role of the first language (L1) in the second language (L2) classroom. Dissertation Abstracts International, A: The Humanities and Social Sciences, 66, 5, Nov, 1744-A.

Rhodes, N., Christian, D. & Barfield, S. (1997). Innovations in immersion: The Key School two-way model. In M. Swain & R. Johnson (Eds.), *Immersion education: International perspectives* (pp. 265-283). Cambridge: University Press.

Richards, J. (1994). The sources of language teachers' instructional decisions. *City Polytechnic of Hong Kong...*

Robinson, P. (1995). Attention, memory and the "noticing" hypothesis. *Language learning, 45*, 283-331.

Rogers, D. (2006). Developing content and form: Encouraging evidence from Italian content-based instruction. *The Modern Language Journal, 90*,3, 373-386.

Rolin-Ianziti, J. & Brownlie, S. (2002). Teacher use of learners' native language in the foreign language classroom. *The Canadian Modern Language Review, 58*, 3, 402-426.

Rosa, E. & O'Neill, D. (1999). Explicitness, intake, and the issue of awareness: Another piece to the puzzle. *Studies in Second Language Acquisition, 21, 511-553.*

Samuda, V. (2001). Guiding relationships between form and meaning during taks performance: The role of the teacher. In M. Bygate, P. Skehan & M. Swain, *Researching pedagogic tasks. Second language learning, teaching and testing* (pp. 119-140). Longman.

Savignon, S. (1972). *Communicative competence: An experiment in foreign languge teaching.* Philadelphia: Center for Curriculum Development.

Savignon, S. (1983). *Communicative competence: Theory and classroom practice.* Reading, Mass.: Addison-Wesley.

Savignon, S. (1991). Communicative language teaching: The state of the art. *TESOL Quarterly, 25*, 2, 261-277.

Savignon, S. (1997). *Communicative competence: Theory and classroom practice. Texts and contexts in second language learning,* $2^{nd}$ edition: New York: McGraw-Hill.

Schmidt, R. (1990). The role of consciousness in second language learning. *Applied Linguistics, 11*, 129-158

Schmidt, R. (1995). *Attention and awareness in foreign language learning.* Honolulu: University of Hawai'i Press.

Schmidt, R. (2001). Attention. In P. Robinson (Ed.), *Cognition and second language instruction* (pp. 3-32). Cambridge: Cambridge University Press.

Schmidt, R. & Frota, S. (1986). Developing basic conversational ability in a second language: A case study of an adult learner of Portuguese. In R. Day (Ed.), *Talking to learn: Conversation in a second language* (pp. 237-326). Rowley, MA: Newbury House.

Schulz, R. (1996). Focus on form in the foreign language classroom: students' and teachers' views on error correction and the role of grammar. *Foreign Language Annals, 29*, 3, 343-364.

Schulz, R. (2001). Cultural differences in student and teacher perceptions concerning the role of grammar instruction and corrective feedback: USA-Colombia. *The Modern Language Journal, 85*, 2, 244-258.

Schwartz, B. (1993). On explicit and negative data effecting and affecting competence and linguistic behavior. *Studies in Second Language Acquisition, 15*, 147-163.

Sharwood-Smith, M. (1981). Consciousness-raising and the second language learner. *Applied Linguistics, 2,* pp. 159-168.

Sharwood Smith, M. (1991). Speaking to many minds. *Second Language Research, 7*, 118-132.

Sharwood Smith, M. (1993). Input enhancement in instructed SLA: Theoretical bases. *Studies in Second Language Acquisition, 15,* 2, 165-179.

Sharwood Smith, M. (1995). The current state of interlanguage: Studies in honor of William E. Rutherford. In L. Eubank, L. Selinker & M. Sharwood-Smith (Eds.). Amesterdam; Philadelphia, PA: J. Benjamins.

Shook, D. (1996). Foreign language literature and the beginning learner-reader. *Foreign Language Annals, 29,* 2, 201-216.

Shook, D. (1998). A touch of ... class! *Canadian Modern Language Review, 54,* 2, 286-290.

Short, D. (1999). Integrating language and content for effective sheltered instruction programs. In C. Faltis & P. Wolfe (Eds.), *So much to day: Adolescents, bilingualism, and ESL in the secondary school* (pp. 105-137). New York: Teachers College Press.

Shulman, L. (1987). Knowledge and teaching: Foundations of the new reform. *Harvard Educational Review, 57*, 1, 1-21.

Simard, D. & Wong, W. (2001). Alertness, orientation, and detection: The conceptualization of attentional functions in SLA. *Studies in Second Language Acquisition, 23*, 103-124.

Snow, M. & Brinton, D. (1997). *The content-based classroom: Perspectives on integrating language and content*. White Plains, NY: Addison-Wesley Longman.

Spada, N. (1997). Form-focused instruction and second language acquisition: a review of classroom and laboratory research. *Language Teaching, 30*, 73-87.

Spada, N. & Lightbown, P. (1993). Instruction and the development of questions in the L2 classroom. *Studies in Second Language Acquisition, 15*, 205-221.

Stoller, F.L., & Grabe, W. (1997). A six-T's approach to content-based instruction. In M.A. Snow & D.M. Brinton (Eds.), *The content-based classroom* (pp. 78-94). White Plains, NY: Addison-Wesley Longman.

Stoller, F. (2004). Content-based instruction: perspectives on curriculum planning. *Annual Review of Applied Linguistics, 24*, 261-283.

Swain, M. (1985). Communicative competence: Some roles of comprehensible input and comprehensible output in its development. In S. Gass & C. Madden (Eds.), *Input in second language acquisition* (pp. 235-253). Rowley, MA: Newburry House.

Swain, M. (1988). Manipulating and complementing content teaching to maximize second language learning. *TESL Canada Journal, 6*, 68-83.

Swain, M. (1991). French immersion and its offshoots: Getting two for one. In B. Freed (Ed.), *Foreign language acquisition research and the classroom* (pp. 91-103). Lexington, Mass.: Heath.

Swain, M. (1993). The output hypothesis: Just speaking and writing aren't enough. *Canadian Modern Language Review, Golden Anniversary Issue, 50*, 1, 158-164.

Swain, M. (1995). Three functions of output in second language learning. In G. Cook & B. Seidlhofer (Eds.), *Principle and practice in applied linguistics* (pp. 125-144). Oxford, UK: Oxford University Press.

Swain, M. (1996). Integrating language and content in the immersion classrooms: Research perspectives. *Canadian Modern Languages Review, 52,* 529-548.

Swain, M. (1998). Focus on form through conscious reflection. In C. Doughty & J. Williams (Eds.), *Focus on Form in classroom second language acquisition* (pp. 64-81). Cambridge, UK: Cambridge University Press.

Swain, M. (2001). Integrating language and content teaching through collaborative tasks. *The Canadian Modern Language Review, 58,* 1, 44-63.

Swain, M. & Johnson, R. (1997). *Immersion education: International perspectives.* Cambridge: University Press.

Swain, M. & Lapkin, S. (1995). Problems in output and the cognitive processes they generate: A step towards second language learning. *Applied Linguistics, 16,* 3, 371-391.

Swain, M. & Lapkin, S. (2000). Task-based second language learning: The uses of the first language. *Language Teaching Research, 4,* 3, 251-274.

Tarallo, F. & Myhill, G. (1983). Interference and natural language processing in second language acquisition. *Language Learning, 33,* 1, 55-76.

Terrell, T. (1977). A natural approach to second language acquisition and learning. *Modern Language Journal, 61,* 325-337.

Terrell, T. (1982). The natural approach to language learning: An update. *Modern Language Journal, 66,* 121-132.

Thompson, G. (2006). Teacher and student first language and target language use in the foreign language classroom: A qualitative and quantitative study of language choice. *Dissertation Abstracts International, A: The Humanities and Social Sciences,* 67, 4, Oct, 1316.

Tomaselli, A. & Schwartz, B. (1990). Analyzing the acquisition stages of negation in L2 German: Support for UG in adult SLA. *Second Language Research, 6,* 1, 1-38.

Tomlin, R. & Villa, V. (1994). Attention in cognitive science and second language acquisition. *Studies in Second Language Acquisition, 16,* 183-203.

Trahey, M. (1996). Positive Evidence in Second Language Acquisition: Some Long-Term Effects. *Second Language Research,12,* 2, 111-139

Turnbull, M. & Arnett, A. (2002). Teachers' uses of the target and first languages in second and foreign language classrooms. *Annual Review of Applied Linguistics, 22,* 204-218.

VanPatten, B. (1985). Communicative value and information processing in second language acquisition. In P. Larson, E. Judd & D. Messerschmidt (Eds.), *On TESOL '84: A brave new world for TESOL* (pp. 89-100). Washington, DC: TESOL.

VanPatten, B. (1990). Attending to form and content in the input: An experiment in consciousness. *Studies in Second Language Acquisition, 12,* 287-301.

VanPatten, B. (1993). Grammar teaching for the acquisition-rich classroom. *Foreign Language Annals, 26,* 4, 435-450.

VanPatten, B. (1996). *Input processing and grammar instruction.* New York: Alex.

VanPatten, B. (2003a) *From Input to Output: A Teacher's Guide to Second Language Acquisition.* McGraw-Hill.

VanPatten, B. (2003b). Input processing in SLA. In VanPatten, B. (Ed.), *Processing instruction: theory, research and commentary,* (pp. 5-31). Mahwah, NJ: Lawrence Erlbaum.

Wesche, M. (1993). Discipline-based approaches to language study. In M. Krueger and F. Ryan (eds.) *Language and content: discipline- and content-based approaches to language study* ( pp. 57-82). Lexington, MA: Heath.

White, J. (1998). Getting the learners' attention: A typographical input enhancement study. In C. Doughty & J. Williams (Eds.), *Focus on Form in classroom second language acquisition* (pp. 91-128). Cambridge, UK: Cambridge University Press.

Williams, J. (1999). Learner-generated attention to form. *Language learning, 51,* 303-346.

Williams, J. (2001). The effectiveness of spontaneous attention to form. *System, 29,* 325-340.

Williams, J. & Evans, J. (1998). What kind of focus and on which forms?. In C. Doughty & J. Williams (Eds.), *Focus on form in classroom second language acquisition* (pp. 139-155). Cambridge, UK: Cambridge University Press.

Williamson, J. & Hardman, F. (1995). Time for refilling the bath? A study of primary student-teachers' grammatical knowledge. *Language and Education, 9*, 117-134.

Wong, W. (2004) *Input Enhancement: From Theory and Research to the Classroom.* Mc-Graw-Hill.

Wray, D. (1993). Student-teachers' knowledge and beliefs about language. In N. Bennett and C. Carré (eds.) *Learning to teach.* London: Routledge.

Zobl, H. (1995). Converging evidence for the "acquisition-learning" distinction. *Applied Linguistics, 16*, 1, 35-56.

Zucker, C. (2005). Teaching grammar in the foreign language classroom: A study of teacher beliefs, teacher practices and current research. *Dissertation Abstracts International, A: The Humanities and Social Sciences, 2006, 66, 11, May, 3920*

## APPENDIX A
## CONSENT FORM

You are invited to participate in a research study being carried out by Frédérique Grim, a graduate student and teaching assistant in the French Department, under the supervision of Assistant Professor Peter Golato. The purpose of this study is to investigate the usefulness of cultural materials for teaching French culture and language at UIUC.

If you agree to participate in this study, you will be asked to complete a background questionnaire and carry out four activities during your regularly scheduled French 102 or French 103 class over a 3-week period. Three activities consist of questions about the culture of French-speaking countries, and the French language. Each one will take a maximum of 10 minutes to complete. The fourth activity is a short lesson about a Francophone country, which will take 50 minutes to complete. All of these activities will take place during your regular class time and in your regular classroom. They will be video-taped for better analysis of your teacher's teaching methodology.

Participation in this study is strictly voluntary, and you may withdraw from the study at any time by telling the researcher or your French teacher. There are no risks or discomforts expected as a result of your participation. If you wish, after the experiment you can hear more about the purposes of the study. A summary of the results can be sent to you as well.

Your decision whether or not to participate will not affect your present or future relations with the University of Illinois or with your French teacher. It will have no effect on your grades in this class.

All information that is obtained in connection with this study will remain confidential and will be disclosed only with your permission. The data from your responses will be assigned a code number to assure confidentiality. Furthermore, the records of all responses will be archived by code number and will not bear the names of any subjects. Only I, the researcher, will have the key to the code and this will be destroyed after data analysis is finished.

If you have any questions now, please ask me. If you have any questions later about this research project, or if you experience any problems related to your participation in the project, please contact me at (217) 333-2020 or via e-mail: fgrim@uiuc.edu. Also, if you have any questions regarding your rights as a research subject, please contact the UIUC Institutional Review Board, 417 Swanlund Administration Building, (217) 333-2670.

You will be given a copy of this form. Thank you very much for your participation.

YOUR FULL NAME (printed) _____ DATE _____

I have read and understood this form.

YOUR SIGNATURE _____

SIGNATURE OF EXPERIMENTER _____

## APPENDIX B
## BACKGROUND QUESTIONNAIRE

**About yourself:**
- Name                    _____
- Age                     _____
- Gender                  _____
- Nationality(ies)        _____

**About your language background:**
- How many semesters of French have you had before the present one in

    High school?     _____

    College?         _____

- Why are you studying French?
_____

- Have you learned another language in the past?
_____

If yes, which one(s)?
_____

For how long?
_____

**About your relationship with the French-speaking world:**
- Have you even been to a French-speaking country?
_____

If yes, where?                          For how long?
_____            _____

- Do you have any French-speaking friends?  _____

- Do you sometimes watch French-speaking movies, read French-speaking books or magazine, or surf on the French-speaking websites?

**Your opinion:**
- What is your favorite part of learning French?
  _____
  _____

- What particularities do you think are essential while learning a foreign language?
  _____
  _____

- What have you really enjoyed so far about your French class?
  _____

- What would have liked to see different?
  _____

- Among these four components that is part of a language, rank them from the most important (1) to the least important (4) according to your personal feelings:

  _____ Grammar      _____ Culture      _____ Vocabulary      _____ Speaking

Thank you very much for your participation in this study! ☺

APPENDIX C
LESSON PLANS
With focus-on-form
BELGIUM

Bonjour! Tout d'abord je voudrais te remercier pour bien vouloir participer à cette étude.

Ci-joint tu trouveras la leçon à couvrir pendant la présentation culturelle (Jeudi 1$^{er}$ avril).

Essaye de suivre les directions autant que possible, afin que l'instruction est (j'espère !) un effet positif. Merci! Et j'espère que ça sera intéressant pour toi et tes étudiants.

Le sujet concerne la Belgique.

1. Sur les transparents que je te donne, tu verras des informations sur ce pays, une carte et des photos. J'ai numéroté le tout afin que tu puisses montrer les documents supplémentaires aux transparents au bon moment.

Il est important que tu te familiarises avec tout le matériel avant la présentation pour que tu ne sentes pas trop perdu(e).

2. Présente les informations au fur et à mesure. Par exemple :
* Il y a des questions de « warm-up » au début de quelques sections. Utilise-les afin d'attirer l'attention des étudiants.
* Quand la géographie est présentée, montre la carte et explique sa situation par rapport aux autres pays.
* Quand on parle de Bruxelles, tu peux montrer les photos de Bruxelles et des autres villes en général.
* Quand on parle de la nourriture, tu peux montrer la photo de la gaufre.
* Quand on parle de Tintin et Milou et des Schtroumfs, montre les dessins/bandes dessinées de ces personnages.
* **Comme tu peux le remarquer, il y a des choses qui sont soulignées de différentes couleurs. Essaye d'insister dessus en pensant que certains points sont sur des informations culturelles, sur du vocabulaire ou sur de la grammaire. Essaye de tous les présenter aussi bien que tu peux, mais ne passe pas trop de temps.**
* Encourage les étudiants à poser des questions s'ils en ont.

3. Suis les directions en anglais que tu trouveras ci-dessous pour savoir exactement en quoi consiste la leçon et les activités.

    1. <u>Setting the stage</u> **(3 minutes maximum)**:
Teacher : To start up the lesson, ask general questions to your students about their knowledge of Belgium. For example :
    *Où est situé la Belgique ?*

*Quelles langues parle-t-on en Belgique ?*
*Que connaissez-vous de particulier sur ce pays ?*
*Connaissez-vous d'autres petits pays où l'on parle français ? (la Suisse, le Luxembourg, le Burkina Faso, ...)*

2. Providing input **(20 minutes maximum)**:

Teacher: Below is the information you should cover, with the help of the transparencies and the other materials (pictures and music).

Use the transparencies and other materials to make this presentation.

3. Guided participation **(12 minutes maximum)**:

**Oral activity**
* During this activity, you will replay two extracts of songs from Jacques Brel and Renaud.

* Give the words of the songs (sheets provided)

  * Play the extracts a first time, asking students to try to follow.
  * Play the extracts a second time, asking students to try to listen for the types of feelings the singers attempt to emit.
  * Ask students to give you adjectives or nouns that could describe those feelings. Write them down on the board.
* Using the answers on the board, ask students to give their opinion making comparisons between the two songs, using the vocabulary on the board (or other words they know).

*Quelle chanson préférez-vous? Pouquoi?*

*Quelles comparaisons pouvez-vous faire entre les deux chansons?*

4. Extension activity **(minimum 20 minutes)**:

**Written activity**
* Ask students to break into groups of 2 or 3. Hand out the envelops with the pictures. Ask them to follow the instructions.
* Collect their written activity at the end of class.

Thank you **very** much for being willing to help me with my study. You are **SO** kind!

## LA BELGIQUE

**La géographie :**

La Belgique se trouve au Nord-Est de la France (*cf. carte de Rendez-vous*), sur la Mer du Nord (*cf. photo 1*)

Il y a deux régions principales avec deux langues officielles :
- la Flandre où l'on parle flamand (hollandais)
- la Wallonie où l'on parle français. (*cf. carte linguistique*)

La **capitale, Bruxelles**, est bilingue.

Bruxelles est la ville la plus (+++) importante de l'Europe parce que c'est la capitale de l'Europe. (*photos 2, 2b, 2c*)

La Belgique est aussi (=) grande que l'état de **Maryland**. Donc elle est relativement petite !

La population est aussi (=) large que celle du Michigan (**environ 10 millions**).

Voici quelques photos d'une autre ville belge appelée Bruges. Bruges est une très jolie ville qui est plus (+) petite et rustique que Bruxelles. Il y a des canaux. (*Cf. photos 3, 4, 5, 6, 6b*)

**La monnaie :**

La monnaie belge est la même que la monnaie européenne, c'est-à-dire que c'est **l'Euro (€)**. (*cf. le billet en Euro*)

**La monarchie :**

Teacher : *ask your students: à votre avis, quel genre de gouvernement y a-t'il ?*

En Belgique, il y a une **monarchie** depuis 1830, donc il y a un roi. Il s'appelle **Albert II**. (*cf. photo 7*)

Le roi n'a pas tous les pouvoirs. En réalité, c'est le **Premier Ministre**, Guy Verhofstadt, qui est la personne politique la plus (+++) importante.

**Les religions :**

Les religions en Belgique sont le **christianisme, l'islam, le judaïsme**, et d'autres religions moins populaires. La religion la plus (+++) répandue est le christianisme, en particulier le **catholicisme** (95%).

**Le climat :**

En général, en Belgique, il fait plus (+) chaud en hiver que dans le Midwest.
Mais il fait moins (-) chaud en été que dans le Midwest.

**La cuisine :**

**Teacher :** *ask your students: quel genre de cuisine trouve-t-on en Belgique ?*

Les Belges aiment la bonne cuisine (comme les français !), mais ils aiment aussi beaucoup manger (comme les Allemands !). (*cf. photo 8*)

Un plat typique de la Belgique est les moules-frites. Attention, les frites sont d'origine belge, pas française ! (*cf. photo 9*)

Les endives sont d'origine belge et font partie de nombreuses recettes.

Une autre spécialité belge : les gaufres... avec de la crème Chantilly.(*cf. photo 10*)

Il y a une grande variété de fromages mais elle est moins (+) grande qu' en France.

La bière belge est aussi très populaire.

**La musique belge :**
**Teacher:** *ask your students: Est-ce que vous connaissez des chanteurs belges ?*

Il y a aussi des célébrités francophones originaires de la Belgique.

En musique, par exemple, il y a Jacques Brel qui était très populaire dans les années 50.

Renaud est aussi un chanteur très populaire et il est plus (+) contemporain que Jacques Brel. (*cf. extraits de chansons*)

En général, les jeunes préfèrent Renaud parce qu'il chante sur les problèmes de la société.

Les chansons d'amour de Jacques Brel sont parmi les plus (+++) populaires dans la musique de langue française.

**Les personnages imaginaires :**

Il y a aussi des personnages de bandes dessinées qui sont « nés » en Belgique. (*montrer les BD*)
Par exemple, « Tintin et Milou » raconte les aventures d'un jeune homme et de son chien.
Les « Schtroumpfs » sont des célébrités internationales qui sont aussi belges.

Parmi les francophones, c'est « Tintin et Milou » qui sont les plus appréciés (+++), surtout parmi le public adulte.

**Les fêtes belges:**
En Belgique, il y a bien sûr des fêtes nationales qui sont soit religieuses, soit pieuses.

La Saint-Nicolas, qui est décembre, est plus (+) populaire que Noël.

Il y a aussi la fête nationale : le 21 juillet

APPENDIX D
LESSON PLANS
With incidental focus-on-form
BELGIUM

Bonjour! Tout d'abord je voudrais te remercier pour bien vouloir participer à cette étude.

Ci-joint tu trouveras la leçon à couvrir pendant la présentation culturelle.

Essaye de suivre les directions autant que possible, afin que l'instruction est (j'espère !) un effet positif. Merci! Et j'espère que ça sera intéressant pour toi et tes étudiants.

Le sujet concerne la Belgique.

1. Sur les transparents que je te donne, tu verras des informations sur ce pays, une carte et des photos. J'ai numéroté le tout afin que tu puisses montrer les documents supplémentaires aux transparents au bon moment.

Il est important que tu te familiarises avec tout le matériel avant la présentation pour que tu ne sentes pas trop perdu(e).

2. Présente les informations au fur et à mesure. Par exemple :
* Il y a des questions de « warm-up » au début de quelques sections. Utilise-les afin d'attirer l'attention des étudiants.
* Quand la géographie est présentée, montre la carte et explique sa situation par rapport aux autres pays.
* Quand on parle de Bruxelles, tu peux montrer les photos de Bruxelles et des autres villes en général.
* Quand on parle de la nourriture, tu peux montrer la photo de la gaufre.
* Quand on parle de Tintin et Milou et des Schtroumfs, montre les dessins/bandes dessinées de ces personnages.
**\* Comme tu peux le remarquer, il y a de la grammaire qui est répétée plusieurs fois ou du vocabulaire que les étudiants ne connaissent pas. Explique ces points seulement si tu vois que les étudiants ont des questions. Dis-leur de poser des questions s'ils ne comprennent pas. \***
Encourage les étudiants à poser des questions s'ils en ont.

3. Suis les directions en anglais que tu trouveras ci-dessous pour savoir exactement en quoi consiste la leçon et les activités.

    1. <u>Setting the stage</u> **(3 minutes maximum)**:
Teacher : To start up the lesson, ask general questions to your students about their knowledge of Belgium. For example :
    *Où est situé la Belgique ?*
    *Quelles langues parle-t-on en Belgique ?*

*Que connaissez-vous de particulier sur ce pays ?*
*Connaissez-vous d'autres petits pays où l'on parle français ? (la Suisse, le Luxembourg, le Burkina Faso, ...)*

2. Providing input **(20 minutes maximum):**
Teacher: Below is the information you should cover, with the help of the transparencies and the other materials (pictures and music).

Use the transparencies and other materials to make this presentation.

3. Guided participation **(12 minutes maximum):**
**Oral activity**
* During this activity, you will replay two extracts of songs from Jacques Brel and Renaud.
* Give the words of the songs (sheets provided)
    * Play the extracts a first time, asking students to try to follow.
    * Play the extracts a second time, asking students to try to listen for the types of feelings the singers attempt to emit.
    * Ask students to give you adjectives or nouns that could describe those feelings. Write them down on the board.
* Using the answers on the board, ask students to give their opinion making comparisons between the two songs, using the vocabulary on the board (or other words they know).

*Quelle chanson préférez-vous? Pouquoi?*

*Quelles comparaisons pouvez-vous faire entre les deux chansons?*

4. Extension activity **(minimum 20 minutes):**
**Written activity**
* Ask students to break into groups of 3. Hand out the envelops with the pictures. Ask them to follow the instructions.
* Collect their written activity at the end of class.

Thank you **very** much for being willing to help me with my study. You are **SO** kind!

## LA BELGIQUE

**La géographie :**
La Belgique se trouve au Nord-Est de la France (*cf. carte de Rendez-vous*), sur la Mer du Nord (*cf. photo 1*)

Il y a deux régions principales avec deux langues officielles:
- la Flandre où l'on parle flamand (hollandais)

- la Wallonie où l'on parle français. (*cf. carte linguistique*)

La capitale, Bruxelles, est bilingue. (*cf. photo 2*)

Bruxelles est la ville la plus importante de l'Europe parce que c'est la capitale de l'Europe.
La Belgique est aussi grande que l'état de Maryland. Donc elle est relativement petite !
La population est aussi large que celle du Michigan **(environ 10 millions)**.

Voici quelques photos d'une autre ville belge appelée Bruges. Bruges est une très jolie ville qui est plus petite et rustique que Bruxelles. Il y a des canaux. *(Cf. photos 3, 4, 5)*

**La monnaie :**

La monnaie belge est la même que la monnaie européenne, c'est-à-dire que c'est l'Euro (€). *(cf. le billet en Euro)*

**La monarchie :**

**Teacher :** *ask your students: à votre avis, quel genre de gouvernement y a-t-il ?*

En Belgique, il y a une monarchie depuis 1830, donc il y a un roi. Il s'appelle Albert II. *(cf. photo )*

Le roi n'a pas tous les pouvoirs. En réalité, c'est le Premier Ministre, Guy Verhofstadt, qui est la personne politique la plus importante.

**Les religions :**

Les religions en Belgique sont le christianisme, l'islam, le judaïsme, et d'autres religions moins populaires. La religion la plus répandue est le christianisme, en particulier le catholicisme (95%).

**Le climat :**

En général, en Belgique, il fait plus chaud en hiver que dans le Midwest.
Mais il fait moins chaud en été que dans le Midwest.

**La cuisine :**

**Teacher :** *ask your students: quel genre de cuisine trouve-t-on en Belgique ?*

Les Belges aiment la bonne cuisine (comme les Français !), mais ils aiment aussi beaucoup manger (comme les Allemands !).

Un plat typique de la Belgique est les moules-frites. Attention, les frites sont d'origine belge, pas française ! *(photo 9)*

Les endives sont d'origine belge et font partie de nombreuses recettes.

Une autre spécialité belge : les gaufres... avec de la crème Chantilly. (*cf. photo 6*)

Il y a une grande variété de fromages mais elle est moins grande qu'en France.

La bière belge est aussi très populaire.

**La musique belge :**
**Teacher:** *ask your students: Est-ce que vous connaissez des chanteurs belges ?*

Il y a aussi des célébrités francophones originaires de la Belgique.

En musique, par exemple, il y a Jacques Brel qui était très populaire dans les années 50.

Renaud est aussi un chanteur très populaire et il est plus contemporain que Jacques Brel. (cf. extraits de chansons sur K7)

En général, les jeunes préfèrent Renaud parce qu'il chante sur les problèmes de la société.

Les chansons d'amour de Jacques Brel sont parmi les plus populaires dans la musique de langue française.

**Les personnages imaginaires :**

Il y a aussi des personnages de bandes dessinées qui sont « nés » en Belgique. (*montrer les BD*)
Par exemple, « Tintin et Milou » raconte les aventures d'un jeune homme et de son chien. Les « Schtroumpfs » sont des célébrités internationales qui sont aussi belges.

Parmi les francophones, c'est « Tintin et Milou » qui sont les plus appréciés, surtout parmi le public adulte.

**Les fêtes belges:**
En Belgique, il y a bien sûr des fêtes nationales qui sont soit religieuses, soit pieuses.

La Saint-Nicolas, qui est décembre, est plus populaire que Noël.

Il y a aussi la fête nationale : le 21 juillet

APPENDIX E
LESSON PLANS
With focus-on-meaning
BELGIUM

Bonjour! Tout d'abord je voudrais te remercier pour bien vouloir participer à cette étude.

Ci-joint tu trouveras la leçon à couvrir pendant la présentation culturelle.

Essaye de suivre les directions autant que possible, afin que l'instruction est (j'espère !) un effet positif. Merci! Et j'espère que ça sera intéressant pour toi et tes étudiants.

Le sujet concerne la Belgique.

1. Sur les transparents que je te donne, tu verras des informations sur ce pays, une carte et des photos. J'ai numéroté le tout afin que tu puisses montrer les documents supplémentaires aux transparents au bon moment.

Il est important que tu te familiarises avec tout le matériel avant la présentation pour que tu ne sentes pas trop perdu(e).

2. Présente les informations au fur et à mesure. Par exemple :
* Il y a des questions de « warm-up » au début de quelques sections. Utilise-les afin d'attirer l'attention des étudiants.
* Quand la géographie est présentée, montre la carte et explique sa situation par rapport aux autres pays.
* Quand on parle de Bruxelles, tu peux montrer les photos de Bruxelles et des autres villes en général.
* Quand on parle de la nourriture, tu peux montrer la photo de la gaufre.
* Quand on parle de Tintin et Milou et des Schtroumfs, montre les dessins/bandes dessinées de ces personnages.
* Encourage les étudiants à poser des questions s'ils en ont.

3. Suis les directions en anglais que tu trouveras ci-dessous pour savoir exactement en quoi consiste la leçon et les activités.

    1. <u>Setting the stage</u> **(3 minutes maximum)**:
Teacher : To start up the lesson, ask general questions to your students about their knowledge of Belgium. For example :
    *Où est situé la Belgique ?*
    *Quelles langues parle-t-on en Belgique ?*
    *Que connaissez-vous de particulier sur ce pays ?*

*Connaissez-vous d'autres petits pays où l'on parle français ? (la Suisse, le Luxembourg, le Burkina Faso, ...)*

2. Providing input **(15 minutes maximum):**
Teacher: Below is the information you should cover, with the help of the transparencies and the other materials (pictures and music).

Use the transparencies and other materials to make this presentation.

3. Guided participation **(12 minutes maximum):**
**Oral activity**
* During this activity, you will replay two extracts of songs from Jacques Brel and Renaud.

* Give the words of the songs (sheets provided)

   * Play the extracts a first time, asking students to try to follow.
   * Play the extracts a second time, asking students to try to listen for the types of feelings the singers attempt to emit.
   * Ask students to give you adjectives or nouns that could describe those feelings. Write them down on the board.
* Using the answers on the board, ask students to give their opinion making comparisons between the two songs, using the vocabulary on the board (or other words they know).

*Quelle chanson préférez-vous? Pouquoi?*

*Quelles comparaisons pouvez-vous faire entre les deux chansons?*

4. Extension activity **(minimum 20 minutes):**
**Written activity**
* Ask students to break into groups of 2 or 3. Hand out the envelops with the pictures. Ask them to follow the instructions.
* Collect their written activity at the end of class.

Thank you **very** much for being willing to help me with my study. You are **SO** kind!

## LA BELGIQUE

**La géographie :**
La Belgique se trouve au Nord-Est de la France (*cf. carte de Rendez-vous*), sur la Mer du Nord (*cf. photo 1*)

Il y a deux régions principales avec deux langues officielles:
- la Flandre où l'on parle flamand (hollandais)
- la Wallonie où l'on parle français. (*cf. carte linguistique*)

La capitale, Bruxelles, est bilingue. (*cf. photo 2*)

Bruxelles est la ville la plus importante de l'Europe parce que c'est la capitale de l'Europe. (*photos ?*)
La Belgique est aussi grande que l'état de Maryland. Donc elle est relativement petite !
La population est aussi large que celle du Michigan (environ 10 millions).

Voici quelques photos d'une autre ville belge appelée Bruges. Bruges est une très jolie ville qui est plus petite et rustique que Bruxelles. Il y a des canaux. *(Cf. photos 3, 4, 5)*

**La monnaie :**
La monnaie belge est la même que la monnaie européenne, c'est-à-dire que c'est l'Euro (€). *(cf. le billet en Euro)*

**La monarchie :**

**Teacher** : *ask your students: à votre avis, quel genre de gouvernement y a-t-il ?*

En Belgique, il y a une monarchie depuis 1830, donc il y a un roi. Il s'appelle Albert II. *(cf. photo )*

Le roi n'a pas tous les pouvoirs. En réalité, c'est le Premier Ministre, Guy Verhofstadt, qui est la personne politique la plus importante.

**Les religions :**
Les religions en Belgique sont le christianisme, l'islam, le judaïsme, et d'autres religions moins populaires. La religion la plus répandue est le christianisme, en particulier le catholicisme (95%).

**Le climat :**
En général, en Belgique, il fait plus chaud en hiver que dans le Midwest.
Mais il fait moins chaud en été que dans le Midwest.

**La cuisine :**

**Teacher** : *ask your students: quel genre de cuisine trouve-t-on en Belgique ?*

Les Belges aiment la bonne cuisine (comme les Français !), mais ils aiment aussi beaucoup manger (comme les Allemands !).

Un plat typique de la Belgique est les moules-frites. Attention, les frites sont d'origine belge, pas française ! *(photo 9)*

Les endives sont d'origine belge et font partie de nombreuses recettes.

Une autre spécialité belge : les gaufres... avec de la crème Chantilly. (*cf. photo 6*)

Il y a une grande variété de fromages mais elle est moins grande qu'en France.

La bière belge est aussi très populaire.

**La musique belge :**
**Teacher:** *ask your students: Est-ce que vous connaissez des chanteurs belges ?*

Il y a aussi des célébrités francophones originaires de la Belgique.

En musique, par exemple, il y a Jacques Brel qui était très populaire dans les années 50.

Renaud est aussi un chanteur très populaire et il est plus contemporain que Jacques Brel. (cf. extraits de chansons sur K7)

En général, les jeunes préfèrent Renaud parce qu'il chante sur les problèmes de la société.

Les chansons d'amour de Jacques Brel sont parmi les plus populaires dans la musique de langue française.

**Les personnages imaginaires :**

Il y a aussi des personnages de bandes dessinées qui sont « nés » en Belgique. (*montrer les BD*)
Par exemple, « Tintin et Milou » raconte les aventures d'un jeune homme et de son chien. Les « Schtroumpfs » sont des célébrités internationales qui sont aussi belges.

Parmi les francophones, c'est « Tintin et Milou » qui sont les plus appréciés, surtout parmi le public adulte.

**Les fêtes belges:**
En Belgique, il y a bien sûr des fêtes nationales qui sont soit religieuses, soit pieuses.

La Saint-Nicolas, qui est décembre, est plus populaire que Noël.

Il y a aussi la fête nationale : le 21 juillet

APPENDIX F
SONG - BELGIUM

**Ne me quitte pas**
De Jacques Brel

Ne me quitte pas, il faut oublier,
Tout peut s'oublier qui s'enfuit déjà,
Oublier le temps des malentendus,
Et le temps perdu à savoir comment,
Oublier ces heures qui tuaient parfois
À coup de pourquoi le cœur du bonheur.
Ne me quitte pas, ne me quitte pas,
Ne me quitte pas, ne me quitte pas.

Moi je t'offrirai des perles de pluie
Venues de pays où il ne pleut pas,
Je creuserai la terre jusqu'après ma mort
Pour couvrir ton corps d'or et de lumière,
Je ferai un domaine où l'amour sera roi,
Où l'amour sera loi, où tu seras reine.
Ne me quitte pas, ne me quitte pas
Ne me quitte pas, ne me quitte pas.
...

**Mon nain de jardin**
De Renaud

Déjà que j'avais pas grand' chose
Dans ma petite vie pas toujours rose
Dans mon p'tit pavillon de banlieue
Oublier des hommes et de Dieu
Entre ma petite femme et mon chien
J'avais que la télé et puis rien
A peine un p'tit carré de pelouse
d'un mètre vingt-trois sur un mètre douze
Où il trônait comme un pasha
Mon p'tit simplet qui n'est plus là.

Si je tenais l'enfant de gredin
Qui m'a volé mon nain de jardin
J'lui ferai passer le goût du pain
J'lui ferai passer le goût du pain

C'était un vrai p'tit de Blanche Neige
Pantalon rouge et polo beige
Pas une saloperie en plastique
La plus jolie des céramiques
Mettait du soleil sur la pelouse
Toutes les fleurs en étaient jalouses
Tenait compagnie aux oiseaux
... il était beau
Avec son p'tit bonnet pointu
C'était le plus joli de la rue

Si je tenais l'enfant de gredin
Qui m'a volé mon nain de jardin
J'lui ferai passer le goût du pain
J'lui ferai passer le goût du pain
...

## APPENDIX G
## GROUP ACTIVITY - BELGIUM

> Ha ! La Belgique...

Mettez-vous en groupe de 3.

Maintenant, vous allez imaginer un voyage en Belgique. Voici les photos que vous avez prises avec votre appareil photo digital. Choisissez-en 5 à 7. Et à partir de ces photos, écrivez (en discutant avec votre groupe) une description de 8 phrases minimum de votre voyage. Vous pouvez choisir le présent ou le passé (*passé composé ou imparfait*). Mais attention ! Il est important de faire **quatre (4) formes du comparatif** (*more...than, less...than, as...as*) et du **superlatif** *(the most, the least)*.

Par exemple : The visit at the museum was *less* interesting *than* the one at the sea.

En résumé : - décrivez votre voyage en Belgique en **français**
- à partir de 5 à 7 photos
- au présent ou au passé
- 8 phrases minimum
- utilisez le comparatif (*more...than, less...than, as...as*) ou le superlatif (*the most, the least*)

Vous pouvez utiliser les idées suivantes pour vous guider: villes, activités, temps (*weather*), durée (*length of trip*), nourriture, vêtements, votre opinion du voyage, différences avec les Etats-Unis

Bon voyage !

_____
_____
_____
_____
_____
_____
_____
_____
_____
_____
_____
_____
_____
_____

APPENDIX H
SPEC - BELGIUM

SPEC # 1 (Belgium)
TITLE: pre-test / post-test I / post-test II for experiments on doctoral research
LEVEL: second-semester French students

General Description: The objective of this test is to study the effect of content-enriched instruction through the integration of content and language forms (grammar and vocabulary). Beside learning about the culture(s) of the target language, the learners are exposed to grammar and lexical items that they can practice with the theme of the culture through task-based activities. In this specific testing situation, subjects will show their acquisition of cultural, lexical and grammatical knowledge, presented to them through a cultural lesson on Belgium. The test is valid for checking the cultural, grammatical and lexical knowledge presented in the lesson, as it specifically asks participants to recall items from the lesson.

Prompt Attribute 1: Subjects will be asked to answer questions concerning the culture of Belgium. On each of the tests, 7 questions, related to the content of the cultural lesson, will be asked. Subjects will have to answer in English.
The scoring will be done as follow : # 1, 3, 5, 6, 7: 1 pt right answer / ½ pt right answer with spelling errors / 0 pt wrong/no answer. # 2: 2 pts 2 right answers / 1 pt 1 right answers / ½ pt off for each spelling error. # 4: 2 pts right answer / 1 pt right month or day / 0 pt wrong/no answer

Prompt Attribute 2: Subjects will be asked to translate into French from English 7 non-or false-cognate words that were presented during the cultural lesson on Belgium. The list of words were chosen, as they did not appear earlier in the curriculum, supporting the need to be new to the participants.
The scoring will be done as follow : # 8-14 : 1 pt right answer / ½ pt right answer with spelling errors or partial answer / 0 pt wrong/no answer

Prompt Attribute 3 for pre-test: Subjects will fill in blanks with comparatives and superlatives (of adjectives), using the adjective given below the blank (when applicable). The translation in English is provided in order to give the meaning. The reason for this type of activity is to show if the learners are able to produce the targeted grammatical forms. Seven items compose this section.
The scoring will be done as follow : # 15 - 21: 4 pts right answer / 3 pts for right answer with missing preposition (plus, moins, aussi, que) / 2 pts for wrong forms but right order (take off ½ for wrong agreement or spelling) / 2 pts for right forms but wrong order (take off ½ for wrong agreement or spelling) / 0 pt all wrong answer/no answer

Prompt Attribute 3 for post-tests: Subjects will fill in blanks with comparatives and superlatives (of adjectives), using the adjective given below the blank (when applicable). The translation in English is provided in order to give the meaning. The reason for this type of activity is to show if the learners are able to produce the targeted grammatical forms. Ten items compose this section, as three distracters are integrated. Distracters are defined as ajectives preceded by a non compative or superlative adverb.

The scoring will be done as follow : # 16, 17, 18, 21, 22: 4 pts right answer / 3 pts for right answer with missing preposition (plus, moins, aussi, que) / 2 pts for wrong forms but right order (take off ½ for wrong agreement or spelling) / 2 pts for right forms but wrong order (take off ½ for wrong agreement or spelling) / 0 pt all wrong answer/no answer. # 20, 23: 4 pts right answer / 2 pts for right order but wrong agreement / 2 pts for right adjective (take off ½ for wrong agreement or spelling) / 1 pt for right preposition or adverb / 0 pt all wrong answer/no answer

Prompt Attribute 4: Subjects will have to write a paragraph of 7 sentences, using four grammatical structures targeted in the lesson (comparatives and superlatives). The topics will be related to vacations they spent.

The scoring will be done as follow : 1 pt per correct form of the comparative or superlative (take off ½ for minor errors) / 1 pt for correct agreement adjective / 1 pt for correct meaning / 1 pt for trying

### Sample Item 1:
Here are 22 questions that are divided in three categories: the first one (7 questions) concerning facts about Belgium, the second one (14 questions) concerning what you know about the French language, and the third one asking you to write a little paragraph. If you don't know the answer, simply leave it blank.

### I. Culture
**Fill in the blank with a short but clear answer in English:**
1. How many inhabitants does Belgium approximately have? _____

### Sample Item 2:
**II. Language**
  **A. Translate the following words in French:**

8. A king _____

### Sample Item 3 for pre-test:
  **B. Below are sentences comparing different facts about Belgium. Complete the sentences by filling the blanks using the words, if applicable, and the translations given below. \***

15. L'hiver belge est _____ l'hiver du Midwest.
           **chaud**
*(The Belgian winter is **warmer than** the Midwest winter.)*

**Sample Item 3 for post-test:**
B. Below are sentences comparing different facts about Belgium. Complete the sentences by filling in the blanks with an appropriate French expression. In formulating your answers, use the provided English translations.

16. L'hiver belge est _____ l'hiver du Midwest.
(*The Belgian winter is **warmer than** the Midwest winter.*)

**Sample Item 4:**
**III. Spring break.**

Spring Break was just around the corner. What did you do? In a paragraph of a minimum of seven (7) sentences, describe what you did and where you went, making at least four (4) comparisons with a previous vacation you have had. Which one was better? Why? Make sure you use the comparison forms (i.e. *plus ... que, moins ... que, autant / aussi ... que*, or superlative *(the most)*). Use the past tense (passé composé or imparfait) in your sentences.

APPENDIX I
PRE-TEST - BELGIUM

## La Belgique

Here are 22 questions that are divided in three categories: the first one (7 questions) concerning facts about Belgium, the second one (14 questions) concerning what you know about the French language, and the third one asking you to write a little paragraph. If you don't know the answer, simply leave it blank.

### I. Culture
**Fill in the blank with a short but clear answer in English:**
1. How many inhabitants does Belgium approximately have? _____
2. What are the two official languages of Belgium? _____
3. What is the name of the Belgian money? _____
4. What is the date of the Belgian national day? _____
5. What is the name of the King of Belgium? _____
6. What is the name of a famous Belgian singer (past or present)? _____
7. What is one comic book that finds its origins in Belgium? _____

### II. Language
**A. Translate the following words in French:**
8. A king _____
9. A comic book _____
10. A waffle _____
11. Mussels and French fries _____
12. Flemish _____
13. Powers _____
14. Holidays _____

B. Below are sentences comparing different facts about Belgium. Complete the sentences by filling the blanks using the words, if applicable, and the translations given below.

15. L'hiver belge est _____ l'hiver du Midwest.
             **chaud**
*(The Belgian winter is **warmer than** the Midwest winter.)*

16. Noël est _____ la Saint-Nicolas.
          **populaire**
*(Christmas is **less popular than** Saint-Nicholas.)*

17. La population de la Belgique est _____ la population du Michigan.       **nombreuse**

*(The population of Belgium is **as numerous as** the population of Michigan.)*

18. Les jeunes belges pensent que la musique moderne est _____ intéressante.

*(The young Belgians think that modern music is **the most** interesting.)*

19. La Belgique est _____ les Etats-Unis. (+)
                               **petite**
*(Belgium is **smaller than** the United States.)*

20. La bière belge est _____ la bière allemande.
                               **bonne**
*(The Belgian beer is **as good as** the German beer.)*

21. Le chocolat belge est _____ délicieux.

*(Belgian chocolate is **the most** delicious.)*

### III. Spring break.

Spring Break was just around the corner. What did you do? In a paragraph of a minimum of seven (7) sentences, describe what you did and where you went, making at least four (4) comparisons with a previous vacation you have had. Which one was better? Why? Make sure you use the comparison forms (i.e. *plus ... que, moins ... que, autant / aussi ... que*, or superlative *(the most)*). Use the past tense (passé composé or imparfait) in your sentences.[12]

In summary: 7 sentences with 4 comparisons in the past tense.

_____
_____
_____
_____
_____
_____
_____

---

[12] The scoring for this section went as follow:
4 points total per form present in the writing, divided as:
- 1 pt per correct form of the comparative or superlative
- 1 pt for correct agreement adjective
- 1 pt for correct meaning regarding the preceding preposition
- 1pt for trying

APPENDIX J
POST-TEST I - BELGIUM

### La Belgique

This activity contains 25 questions, divided in three categories: the first one (7 questions) concerns facts about Belgium, the second one (17 questions) concerns the French language, while in the third one you are asked to write a short paragraph. If in the first two categories, you do not know an answer, simply leave the answer blank.

### I. Culture
**Fill in the blanks with a short but clear answer in English:**
1. Approximately how many inhabitants does Belgium have? _____
2. What are the two official languages of Belgium? _____
3. What is the name of the Belgian currency? _____
4. What is the date of the Belgian national holiday? _____
5. What is the name of the King of Belgium? _____
6. What is the name of a famous Belgian singer (past or present)? _____
7. What is one comic book that finds its origins in Belgium? _____

### II. Language
**A. Translate the following words into French:**

8. king _____
9. comic book _____
10. waffle _____
11. Mussels and French fries _____
12. Flemish _____
13. powers _____
14. holidays _____

**B. Below are sentences comparing different facts about Belgium. Complete the sentences by filling in the blanks with an appropriate French expression. In formulating your answers, use the provided English translations.**

Example :   Les trains européens sont <u>confortables et rapides</u>.
            *(European trains are **comfortable and fast**.)*

15. Bruges est _____ et admirée par les touristes.
(*Bruges is **very beautiful** and admired by tourists.*)

16. L'hiver belge est _____ l'hiver du Midwest.
(*The Belgian winter is **warmer than** the Midwest winter.*)

17. Noël est _____ la Saint-Nicolas.
(*Christmas is **less popular than** Saint-Nicholas.*)

18. La population de la Belgique est _____ la population du Michigan.
(*The population of Belgium is **as large as** the population of Michigan.*)

19. La bonne cuisine est _____ les Belges.
(*Fine cuisine is **essential for** Belgians.*)

20. Les jeunes belges pensent que la musique moderne est _____.
(*The young Belgians think that modern music is **the most** interesting.*)

21. La Belgique est _____ les Etats-Unis.
(*Belgium is **smaller than** the United States.*)

22. La bière belge est _____ la bière allemande.
(*Belgian beer is **as good as** German beer.*)

23. Le chocolat belge est _____.
(*Belgian chocolate is **the most delicious**.*)

24. Le premier ministre est _____ politiques.
(*The Prime Minister is **central in** Politics.*)

### III. Spring break.
Spring Break was only last week. What did you do? In a paragraph of a minimum of seven (7) sentences, describe what you did and where you went, making at least **four (4) comparisons** with a previous vacation you have had (i.e. briefly state which one of the two vacations was better? why? etc.). Make sure you use the **comparative** (i.e. ***more...than, less...than, as...as***), or the **superlative** (i.e. ***the most, the least***). Use the past tense (***passé composé*** or ***imparfait***) in your sentences[13].

In summary: write at least 7 sentences, making 4 comparisons in the past tense by using the comparative and/or superlative.

_____
_____
_____
_____

---

[13] The scoring for this section went as follow:
4 points total per form present in the writing, divided as:
- 1 pt per correct form of the comparative or superlative
- 1 pt for correct agreement adjective
- 1 pt for correct meaning regarding the preceding preposition
- 1pt for trying

APPENDIX K
POST-TEST II - BELGIUM

### La Belgique

This activity contains 25 questions, divided in three categories: the first one (7 questions) concerns facts about Belgium, the second one (17 questions) concerns the French language, while in the third one you are asked to write a short paragraph. If in the first two categories, you do not know an answer, simply leave the answer blank.

### I. Culture
**Fill in the blanks with a short but clear answer in English:**
1. What are the two official languages of Belgium? _____
2. What is the name of the Belgian currency? _____
3. Approximately how many inhabitants does Belgium have? _____
4. What is one comic book that finds its origins in Belgium? _____
5. What is the date of the Belgian national holiday? _____
6. What is the name of the King of Belgium? _____
7. What is the name of a famous Belgian singer (past or present)? _____

### II. Language
**A. Translate the following words into French:**

| | | |
|---|---|---|
| 8. | king | _____ |
| 9. | comic book | _____ |
| 10. | waffle | _____ |
| 11. | Mussels and French fries | _____ |
| 12. | Flemish | _____ |
| 13. | powers | _____ |
| 14. | holidays | _____ |

**B. Below are sentences comparing different facts about Belgium. Complete the sentences by filling in the blanks with an appropriate French expression. In formulating your answers, use the provided English translations.**

Example :   Les trains européens sont <u>confortables et rapides</u>.
(European trains are **comfortable and fast**.)

15. Bruges est _____ et admirée par les touristes.
(*Bruges is **very beautiful** and admired by tourists.*)

16. L'hiver belge est _____ l'hiver du Midwest.
(*The Belgian winter is **warmer than** the Midwest winter.*)

17. Noël est _____ la Saint-Nicolas.
(*Christmas is **less popular than** Saint-Nicholas.*)

18. La population de la Belgique est _____ la population du Michigan.
(*The population of Belgium is **as large as** the population of Michigan.*)

19. La bonne cuisine est _____ les Belges.
(*Fine cuisine is **essential for** Belgians.*)

20. Les jeunes belges pensent que la musique moderne est _____.
(*The young Belgians think that modern music is **the most** interesting.*)

21. La Belgique est _____ les Etats-Unis.
(*Belgium is **smaller than** the United States.*)

22. La bière belge est _____ la bière allemande.
(*Belgian beer is **as good as** German beer.*)

23. Le chocolat belge est _____.
(*Belgian chocolate is **the most delicious**.*)

24. Le premier ministre est _____ politiques.
(*The Prime Minister is **central in** Politics.*)

## III. A past vacation.

Think of a fun vacation you have had in the past. What did you do? With whom were you? Where was it? What was the weather like? In a paragraph of a minimum of seven (7) sentences, describe your vacation, making at least **four (4) comparisons** with another vacation maybe not as fun (i.e. briefly state which one of the two vacations was better? why? etc.). Make sure you use the **comparative** (i.e. *more...than, less...than, as...as*), or the **superlative** (i.e. *the most, the least*). Use the past tense (*passé composé* or *imparfait*) in your sentences.[14]

In summary: write at least 7 sentences, making 4 comparisons in the past tense by using the comparative and/or superlative.

_____
_____
_____

---

[14] The scoring for this section went as follow:
4 points total per form present in the writing, divided as:
- 1 pt per correct form of the comparative or superlative
- 1 pt for correct agreement adjective
- 1 pt for correct meaning regarding the preceding preposition
- 1pt for trying

APPENDIX L
LESSON PLANS
For planned focus on form
SENEGAL

Bonjour! Tout d'abord je voudrais te remercier pour bien vouloir participer à cette étude.

Voici la leçon qu'il faut essayer de couvrir pendant la présentation culturelle.

Essaye de suivre les directions autant que possible. Merci! Et j'espère que ça sera intéressant pour toi et tes étudiants.

Le sujet concerne le Sénégal.

1. Sur les transparents que je te donne, tu verras des informations sur ce pays, une carte et des photos. J'ai numéroté le tout afin que tu puisses montrer les documents supplémentaires aux transparents au bon moment.

Il est important que tu te familiarises avec tout le matériel avant la présentation.

2. Présente les informations au fur et à mesure.
\* Quand la géographie est présentée, montre la carte et explique sa situation par rapport aux autres pays, par rapport au monde.
\* Quand on parle de Dakar, tu peux montrer les photos de Dakar et des autres villes en général.
\* Quand on parle de la pêche, tu peux montrer la photo des pêcheurs.
\* Quand on parle de la religion, tu peux montrer la mosquée.
\* Comme tu peux le remarquer, il y a des choses qui sont soulignées de différentes couleurs. Essaye d'insister dessus en pensant que certains points sont sur des informations culturelles, sur du vocabulaire ou sur de la grammaire. Essaye de présenter ces différents aussi bien que tu peux, mais ne passe pas trop de temps.
\* Encourage les étudiants à poser des questions s'ils en ont.

3. Suis les directions en anglais que tu trouveras ci-dessous pour savoir exactement en quoi consiste la leçon et les activités.

    1. Setting the stage **(3 minutes maximum)**:
Teacher : To start up the lesson, ask general questions to your students about their knowledge of Senegal. For example :
    *Où est situé le Sénégal ?*
    *Quelles langues parle-t-on au Sénégal ?*
    *Que connaissez-vous de particulier sur ce pays ?*
    *Connaissez-vous d'autres petits pays où l'on parle français ? (la Suisse, le Luxembourg, le Burkina Faso, ...)*

2. Providing input **(20 minutes maximum)**:

Teacher: Below is the information you should cover, with the help of the transparencies and the other materials (pictures and music).

**Use the transparencies and other materials to make this presentation**

3. Guided participation **(12 minutes maximum)**:
**Oral activity**
* During this activity, you will read with the students two poems from L. S. Senghor.
* Ask students to read them first silently.
* Ask a few volunteers to read the poems (divide the poems in two halves and have a volunteer to read each half).
- * Ask if there are words that they recognize, what images they have when they read...
    *Quel(s) mots connaissez-vous?*
    *A quoi (à quelles images) pensez-vous quand vous entendez ces mots?*
- * Go over a few of the main unknown vocabulary words.
- * Ask students what they think of the poems
    *Aimez-vous ces poèmes? Pourquoi? Ou pourquoi pas?*

4. Extension activity **(minimum 20 minutes)**:
**Written activity**
* Ask students to break into groups of 3. Hand out the activity sheet with the pictures (in the envelopes). Ask them to follow the instructions.
* Collect their written activity and the pictures at the end of class.

Thank you **very** much for being willing to help me with my study. You are **SO** kind!

## LE SENEGAL

**La géographie :**

Le Sénégal est sur la côte atlantique de **l'Afrique**, avec la Mauritanie au nord, le Mali à l'est, la Guinée et la Guinée-Bissau au sud. *(cf. carte de l'Afrique de Rendez-vous + cf. carte du Sénégal) + (Photos 1, 2, 3)*

La superficie du Sénégal est comparable à celle de l'état du **Missouri**.

La capitale dans laquelle se trouve le centre économique est **Dakar**.

**Saint-Louis**, la deuxième ville du Sénégal, était la capitale dans le passé et reste un centre culturel important.

Il y a environ **10 millions** d'habitants parmi lesquels on trouve une grande diversité ethnique :
les **Wolof** (36%), les **Sérère** (19%), les **Toucouleur** (12%),
les **Peul** (10.5%), les **Diola** (8%), les **Lébou** (un petit groupe habitant sur une île), les **Mandingue**, les **Bassari**. *(cf. photo 4)*

Et les langues sont aussi diverses : **le wolof, le pular, le sérère, le français**, et beaucoup d'autres ! Mais la **seule langue officielle** est le **français**.

**L' histoire :**

Entre 1626 à 1659, le Sénégal a été colonisé par la France puis a pris son indépendance le 4 avril 1960.

En 1960, le **premier président** est élu : **Léopold Sedar Senghor**, qui est aussi un **poète** très célèbre dans la littérature francophone.

**La politique :**

Aujourd'hui, c'est une république dans laquelle il y a un président démocratiquement élu. Depuis 2000, le président est : **Abdoulaye Wade**.

**L'économie :**

La monnaie sénégalaise s'appelle **le Franc CFA**. *(cf. le franc CFA)*

Les **sources économiques** les plus importantes au Sénégal sont **la pêche, le tourisme, l'extraction de phosphate et de fer**. *(cf. photos 5, 6, 7, 8, 9, 10, 11)*

**La religion :**
Les **religions** principales sont **l'islam** (92%), **le christianisme** (moins de 7%), et **la religion traditionnelle** (l'animisme) qui est surtout trouvée dans les campagnes. (*photos 12 et 13 : mosquée et campagne*)

**Le climat :**
En général, le climat est très constant et varie de 24°C **(75°F)** à 29°C **(84°F)** en moyenne.

Mais il y a **une saison des pluies** en **juillet, août et septembre,** pendant laquelle les agriculteurs préparent leurs champs. (*photo 14*)

**La cuisine typique :**
Le **plat typique** du Sénégal est le « **ceebujën** », **le riz au poisson**.

Pendant les fêtes, on mange **du mouton**.

Un **rituel** sénégalais pendant lequel on boit le **thé attaya** (*à la sénéglaise*) peut durer des heures.
- Tout d'abord, les hommes ont le premier thé, fait d'une manière très forte et amère.
- Le deuxième thé est adouci avec du sucre, et les femmes peuvent le boire.
- Les enfants doivent attendre le troisième thé, dans lequel on ajoute beaucoup de sucre.

**Les célébrités sénégalaises :**
\* La **littérature**, dans laquelle on trouve beaucoup de poètes, est le domaine culturel le plus riche.

**Léopold Sédar Senghor** est un poète très connu et était aussi le 1[er] président sénégalais.

Ses oeuvres parmi lesquelles on trouve : « chants d'Ombre » (1945), « Hosties Noires » (1948), « Anthologie de la nouvelle poésie nègre et malgache (1948) sont très riches en **couleurs** et **images**.

Il a développé le concept de négritude dans la littérature francophone.

\* En **musique**, il y a **Youssou**. Sa musique, dans laquelle on trouve les images de l'Afrique traditionnelle, est moderne.

Youssou chante en trois langues : **wolof, français et anglais,** avec lesquelles il touche le cœur des populations africaines. (*cf. extrait de musique sur K7*)

**Les fêtes :**

Il y a beaucoup de fêtes religieuses et traditionnelles.

Les **musulmans** célèbrent la **Tabaski** et la **Korite** (la fin du Ramadan).

Les **chrétiens** célèbrent **Noël**, le 25 décembre.

Le **31 décembre**, pendant lequel **tout le monde** fait la fête, réunit les amis et les familles.

La **fête nationale**, qui marque l'indépendance du Sénégal est **le 4 avril**.

**Le Paris-Dakar :**

Chaque année, il y a une course **de véhicules divers** (voitures, camions et motos) qui se passe **de Paris à Dakar**. (*Photos 15, 16*)

Le Paris-Dakar, très populaire en Europe, dure environ **deux semaines** et permet aux compétiteurs et aux francophones d'apprécier les différences culturelles qui se trouve en France et au Sénégal.

APPENDIX M
LESSON PLANS
For incidental focus on form
SENEGAL

Bonjour! Tout d'abord je voudrais te remercier pour bien vouloir participer à cette étude.

Voici la leçon qu'il faut essayer de couvrir pendant la présentation culturelle.

Essaye de suivre les directions autant que possible. Merci! Et j'espère que ça sera intéressant pour toi et tes étudiants.

Le sujet concerne le Sénégal.

1. Sur les transparents que je te donne, tu verras des informations sur ce pays, une carte et des photos. J'ai numéroté le tout afin que tu puisses montrer les documents supplémentaires aux transparents au bon moment.

Il est important que tu te familiarises avec tout le matériel avant la présentation.

2. Présente les informations au fur et à mesure.
* Quand la géographie est présentée, montre la carte et explique sa situation par rapport aux autres pays, par rapport au monde.
* Quand on parle de Dakar, tu peux montrer les photos de Dakar et des autres villes en général.
* Quand on parle de la pêche, tu peux montrer la photo des pêcheurs.
* Quand on parle de la religion, tu peux montrer la mosquée.
* Comme tu peux le remarquer, il y a des choses qui sont soulignées de différentes couleurs.
* Encourage les étudiants à poser des questions s'ils en ont.
* **Comme tu peux le remarquer, il y a de la grammaire qui est répétée plusieurs fois ou du vocabulaire que les étudiants ne connaissent pas. Explique ces points seulement si tu vois que les étudiants ont des questions. Dis-leur de poser des questions s'ils ne comprennent pas.**

3. Suis les directions en anglais que tu trouveras ci-dessous pour savoir exactement en quoi consiste la leçon et les activités.

     1. Setting the stage **(3 minutes maximum)**:
Teacher : To start up the lesson, ask general questions to your students about their knowledge of Senegal. For example :
    *Où est situé le Sénégal ?*
    *Quelles langues parle-t-on au Sénégal ?*
    *Que connaissez-vous de particulier sur ce pays ?*
    *Connaissez-vous d'autres petits pays où l'on parle français ? (la Suisse, le Luxembourg, le Burkina Faso, ...)*

2. Providing input **(15 minutes maximum)**:

Teacher: Below is the information you should cover, with the help of the transparencies and the other materials (pictures and music).

**Use the transparencies and other materials to make this presentation**

3. Guided participation **(12 minutes maximum)**:

**Oral activity**
* During this activity, you will read with the students two poems from L. S. Senghor.

* Ask students to read them first silently.

* Ask a few volunteers to read the poems (divide the poems in two halves and have a volunteer to read each half).

  * Ask if there are words that they recognize, what images they have when they read…
        *Quel(s) mots connaissez-vous?*
        *A quoi (à quelles images) pensez-vous quand vous entendez ces mots?*
  * Go over a few of the main unknown vocabulary words.
  * Ask students what they think of the poems
        *Aimez-vous ces poèmes? Pourquoi? Ou pourquoi pas?*

4. Extension activity **(minimum 20 minutes)**:

**Written activity**
* Ask students to break into groups of 2 or 3. Hand out the activity sheet with the pictures (in the envelopes). Ask them to follow the instructions.
* Collect their written activity and the pictures at the end of class.


Thank you **very** much for being willing to help me with my study. You are **SO** kind!

## LE SENEGAL

**La géographie :**

Le Sénégal est sur la côte atlantique de l'Afrique, avec la Mauritanie au nord, le Mali à l'est, la Guinée et la Guinée-Bissau au sud. (*cf. carte de l'Afrique de Rendez-vous + cf. carte du Sénégal) + (Photos 1, 2, 3)*

La superficie du Sénégal est comparable à celle de l'état du Missouri.

La capitale dans laquelle se trouve le centre économique est Dakar.

Saint-Louis, la deuxième ville du Sénégal, était la capitale dans le passé et reste un centre culturel important.

Il y a environ 10 millions d'habitants parmi lesquels on trouve une grande diversité ethnique :
les Wolof (36%), les Sérère (19%), les Toucouleur (12%),
les Peul (10.5%), les Diola (8%), les Lébou (un petit groupe habitant sur une île), les Mandingue, les Bassari. (*cf. photo 4*)

Et les langues sont aussi diverses : le wolof, le pular, le sérère, le français, et beaucoup d'autres ! Mais la seule langue officielle est le français.

**L' histoire :**

Entre 1626 à 1659, le Sénégal a été colonisé par la France puis a pris son indépendance le 4 avril 1960.

En 1960, le premier président est élu : Léopold Sedar Senghor, qui est aussi un poète très célèbre dans la littérature francophone.

**La politique :**

Aujourd'hui, c'est une république dans laquelle il y a un président démocratiquement élu. Depuis 2000, le président est : Abdoulaye Wade.

**L'économie :**

La monnaie sénégalaise s'appelle le Franc CFA. *(cf. le billet en Euro)*

Les sources économiques les plus importantes au Sénégal sont la pêche, le tourisme, l'extraction de phosphate et de fer. (*cf. photos 5, 6, 7, 8, 9, 10, 11*)

**La religion :**

Les religions principales sont l'islam (92%), le christianisme (moins de 7%), et la religion traditionnelle (l'animisme) qui est surtout trouvée dans les campagnes. (*photos 12 et 13 : mosquée et campagne*)

**Le climat :**

En général, le climat est très constant et varie de 24°C **(75°F)** à 29°C **(84°F)** en moyenne.

Mais il y a une saison des pluies en juillet, août et septembre, pendant laquelle les agriculteurs préparent leurs champs. (*photo 14*)

**La cuisine typique :**

Le plat typique du Sénégal est le « ceebujën », le riz au poisson.

Pendant les fêtes, on mange du mouton.

Un rituel sénégalais pendant lequel on boit le thé attaya (*à la sénéglaise*) peut durer des heures.
- Tout d'abord, les hommes ont le premier thé, fait d'une manière très forte et amère.
- Le deuxième thé est adouci avec du sucre, et les femmes peuvent le boire.
- Les enfants doivent attendre le troisième thé, dans lequel on ajoute beaucoup de sucre.

**Les célébrités sénégalaises :**

\* La littérature, dans laquelle on trouve beaucoup de poètes, est le domaine culturel le plus riche.

Léopold Sédar Senghor est un poète très connu et était aussi le 1$^{er}$ président sénégalais.

Ses oeuvres parmi lesquelles on trouve : « chants d'Ombre » (1945), « Hosties Noires » (1948), « Anthologie de la nouvelle poésie nègre et malgache (1948) sont très riches en couleurs et images.

Il a développé le concept de négritude dans la littérature francophone.

\* En musique, il y a Youssou. Sa musique, dans laquelle on trouve les images de l'Afrique traditionnelle, est moderne.

Youssou chante en trois langues : wolof, français et anglais, avec lesquelles il touche le cœur des populations africaines. (*cf. extrait de musique sur K7*)

**Les fêtes :**
Il y a beaucoup de fêtes religieuses et traditionnelles.

Les musulmans célèbrent la Tabaski et la Korite (la fin du Ramadan).

Les chrétiens célèbrent Noël, le 25 décembre.

Le 31 décembre, pendant lequel tout le monde fait la fête, réunit les amis et les familles.

La fête nationale, qui marque l'indépendance du Sénégal est le 4 avril.

**Le Paris-Dakar :**

Chaque année, il y a une course de véhicules divers (voitures, camions et motos) qui se passe de Paris à Dakar. (*Photos 15, 16*)

Le Paris-Dakar, très populaire en Europe, dure environ deux semaines et permet aux compétiteurs et aux francophones d'apprécier les différences culturelles qui se trouve en France et au Sénégal.

APPENDIX N
LESSON PLANS
For focus on meaning
SENEGAL

Bonjour! Tout d'abord je voudrais te remercier pour bien vouloir participer à cette étude.

Voici la leçon qu'il faut essayer de couvrir pendant la présentation culturelle.

Essaye de suivre les directions autant que possible. Merci! Et j'espère que ça sera intéressant pour toi et tes étudiants.

Le sujet concerne le Sénégal.

1. Sur les transparents que je te donne, tu verras des informations sur ce pays, une carte et des photos. J'ai numéroté le tout afin que tu puisses montrer les documents supplémentaires aux transparents au bon moment.

Il est important que tu te familiarises avec tout le matériel avant la présentation.

2. Présente les informations au fur et à mesure.
* Quand la géographie est présentée, montre la carte et explique sa situation par rapport aux autres pays, par rapport au monde.
* Quand on parle de Dakar, tu peux montrer les photos de Dakar et des autres villes en général.
* Quand on parle de la pêche, tu peux montrer la photo des pêcheurs.
* Quand on parle de la religion, tu peux montrer la mosquée.
* Encourage les étudiants à poser des questions s'ils en ont.

3. Suis les directions en anglais que tu trouveras ci-dessous pour savoir exactement en quoi consiste la leçon et les activités.

    1. Setting the stage **(3 minutes maximum)**:
Teacher : To start up the lesson, ask general questions to your students about their knowledge of Senegal. For example :
> *Où est situé le Sénégal ?*
> *Quelles langues parle-t-on au Sénégal ?*
> *Que connaissez-vous de particulier sur ce pays ?*
> *Connaissez-vous d'autres petits pays où l'on parle français ? (la Suisse, le Luxembourg, le Burkina Faso, …)*

    2. Providing input **(20 minutes maximum)**:

Teacher: Below is the information you should cover, with the help of the transparencies and the other materials (pictures and music).

**Use the transparencies and other materials to make this presentation**

    3. Guided participation **(12 minutes maximum)**:

**Oral activity**
   \* During this activity, you will read with the students two poems from L. S. Senghor.

   \* Ask students to read them first silently.

   \* Ask a few volunteers to read the poems (divide the poems in two halves and have a volunteer to read each half).

     \* Ask if there are words that they recognize, what images they have when they read...
         *Quel(s) mots connaissez-vous?*
         *A quoi (à quelles images) pensez-vous quand vous entendez ces mots?*
     \* Go over a few of the main unknown vocabulary words.
     \* Ask students what they think of the poems
         *Aimez-vous ces poèmes? Pourquoi? Ou pourquoi pas?*

    4. Extension activity **(minimum 20 minutes)**:

**Written activity**
   \* Ask students to break into groups of 3. Hand out the activity sheet with the pictures (in the envelopes). Ask them to follow the instructions.
   \* Collect their written activity and the pictures at the end of class.

Thank you **very** much for being willing to help me with my study. You are **SO** kind!

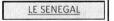

**La géographie :**
    Le Sénégal est sur la côte atlantique de l'Afrique, avec la Mauritanie au nord, le Mali à l'est, la Guinée et la Guinée-Bissau au sud. (*cf. carte de l'Afrique de Rendez-vous + cf. carte du Sénégal) + (Photos 1, 2, 3)*

    La superficie du Sénégal est comparable à celle de l'état du Missouri.

    La capitale dans laquelle se trouve le centre économique est Dakar.

    Saint-Louis, la deuxième ville du Sénégal, était la capitale dans le passé et reste un centre culturel important.

    Il y a environ 10 millions d'habitants parmi lesquels on trouve une grande diversité ethnique :

les Wolof (36%), les Sérère (19%), les Toucouleur (12%), les Peul (10.5%), les Diola (8%), les Lébou (un petit groupe habitant sur une île), les Mandingue, les Bassari. (*cf. photo 4*)

Et les langues sont aussi diverses : le wolof, le pular, le sérère, le français, et beaucoup d'autres ! Mais la seule langue officielle est le français.

**L' histoire :**
Entre 1626 à 1659, le Sénégal a été colonisé par la France puis a pris son indépendance le 4 avril 1960.

En 1960, le premier président est élu : Léopold Sedar Senghor, qui est aussi un poète très célèbre dans la littérature francophone.

**La politique :**
Aujourd'hui, c'est une république dans laquelle il y a un président démocratiquement élu. Depuis 2000, le président est : Abdoulaye Wade.

**L'économie :**
La monnaie sénégalaise s'appelle le Franc CFA. *(cf. le billet en Euro)*

Les sources économiques les plus importantes au Sénégal sont la pêche, le tourisme, l'extraction de phosphate et de fer. (*cf. photos 5, 6, 7, 8, 9, 10, 11*)

**La religion :**
Les religions principales sont l'islam (92%), le christianisme (moins de 7%), et la religion traditionnelle (l'animisme) qui est surtout trouvée dans les campagnes. (*photos 12 et 13 : mosquée et campagne*)

**Le climat :**
En général, le climat est très constant et varie de 24°C **(75°F)** à 29°C **(84°F)** en moyenne.

Mais il y a une saison des pluies en juillet, août et septembre, pendant laquelle les agriculteurs préparent leurs champs. (*photo 14*)

**La cuisine typique :**
Le plat typique du Sénégal est le « ceebujën », le riz au poisson.

Pendant les fêtes, on mange du mouton.

Un rituel sénégalais pendant lequel on boit le thé attaya (*à la sénéglaise*) peut durer des heures.

- Tout d'abord, les hommes ont le premier thé, fait d'une manière très forte et amère.
- Le deuxième thé est adouci avec du sucre, et les femmes peuvent le boire.
- Les enfants doivent attendre le troisième thé, dans lequel on ajoute beaucoup de sucre.

**Les célébrités sénégalaises :**

\* La littérature, dans laquelle on trouve beaucoup de poètes, est le domaine culturel le plus riche.

Léopold Sédar Senghor est un poète très connu et était aussi le 1$^{er}$ président sénégalais.

Ses oeuvres parmi lesquelles on trouve : « chants d'Ombre » (1945), « Hosties Noires » (1948), « Anthologie de la nouvelle poésie nègre et malgache (1948) sont très riches en couleurs et images.

Il a développé le concept de négritude dans la littérature francophone.

\* En musique, il y a Youssou. Sa musique, dans laquelle on trouve les images de l'Afrique traditionnelle, est moderne.

Youssou chante en trois langues : wolof, français et anglais, avec lesquelles il touche le cœur des populations africaines. (*cf. extrait de musique sur K7*)

**Les fêtes :**

Il y a beaucoup de fêtes religieuses et traditionnelles.

Les musulmans célèbrent la Tabaski et la Korite (la fin du Ramadan).

Les chrétiens célèbrent Noël, le 25 décembre.

Le 31 décembre, pendant lequel tout le monde fait la fête, réunit les amis et les familles.

La fête nationale, qui marque l'indépendance du Sénégal est le 4 avril.

**Le Paris-Dakar :**

Chaque année, il y a une course de véhicules divers (voitures, camions et motos) qui se passe de Paris à Dakar. (*Photos 15, 16*)

Le Paris-Dakar, très populaire en Europe, dure environ deux semaines et permet aux compétiteurs et aux francophones d'apprécier les différences culturelles qui se trouve en France et au Sénégal.

APPENDIX O
POEMS - SENEGAL

## Léopold Sedar Senghor

Votre instructeur vous a présenté des informations sur le Sénégal.

Léopold Sedar Senghor (1906-2001) a voulu, à travers ses poèmes, montré qu'être noir, qu'être africain, c'était être un humain parmi d'autres. Il a valorisé l'identité africaine. Par sa poésie et ses nombreuses oeuvres, il s'exprime par des descriptions de paysages, par des couleurs, des sons, des sentiments.

Photo Editions du Seuil

**Tout le long du jour...**

Tout le long du jour, sur les longs rails étroits
Volonté inflexible sur la langueur des sables
A travers Cayor et Baol[1] de sécheresse[2] où se tordent les bras les baobabs[3] d'angoisse[4]
Tout le long du jour, tout le long de la ligne
Par les petites gares uniformes, jacassantes petites négresses à la sortie de l'Ecole et de la volière
Tout le long du jour, durement secoué sur les bancs du train de ferraille[5] et poussif et poussiéreux[6]
Me voici cherchant l'oubli de l'Europe au cœur pastoral du Sine[7].

---

[1] Région sablonneuse de l'ouest du Sénégal
[2] drought
[3] Arbre des régions tropicales
[4] anguish
[5] iron
[6] dusty
[7] Région natale de L.S. Senghor.

### Une Main de lumière

*Une main de lumière a caressé mes paupières[1] de nuit*
*Et ton sourire s'est levé sur les brouillards qui flottaient monotones sur mon Congo[2].*
*Mon cœur a fait écho au chant virginal des oiseaux d'aurore[3]*
*Tel mon sang[4] qui rythmait jadis le chant blanc de la sève[5] dans les branches de mes bras.*

*Voici la fleur de brousse et l'étoile dans mes cheveux et le bandeau qui ceint le front du pâtre-athlète.*
*J'emprunterai la flûte qui rythme la paix des troupeaux[6]*
*Et tout le jour assis à l'ombre de tes cils[7], près de la Fontaine Fimla[8]*
*Fidèle, je paîtrai les mugissements blonds de tes troupeaux.*
*Car ce matin une main de lumière a caressé mes paupières de nuit*
*Et tout le long du jour, mon cœur a fait écho au chant virginal des oiseaux.*

---

[1] *eyelids*
[2] Fleuve (*river*) africain, qui a une valeur symbolique pour le poète
[3] dawn
[4] blood
[5] sap
[6] flocks
[7] eyelashes
[8] Petit village, où L. S. Senghor a passé une partie de son enfance

## APPENDIX P
## GROUP ACTIVITY – SENEGAL

> Ha ! Le Sénégal...

Mettez-vous en groupe de 2 ou 3.

Maintenant, vous allez imaginer un **voyage** au Sénégal. Voici les photos que vous avez prises avec votre appareil photo digital. Choisissez-en 5 à 7. Et à partir de ces photos, écrivez (en discutant avec votre groupe) une description de 8 phrases minimum de votre voyage. Vous pouvez choisir le présent ou le passé (*passé composé ou imparfait*). Mais attention ! Il est important que vous utilisiez **quatre (4) pronoms relatifs (*lequel, lesquels, laquelle, lesquelles*)** précédés de **prépositions (*pendant, dans, sur, etc*)**, pour lier (*link*) vos phrases.

    Par exemple : L'avion *dans lequel* je voyage est un Boeing 747.

    En résumé :    - décrivez votre voyage au Sénégal en français
                     - à partir de 5 à 7 photos
                     - au présent ou au passé
                     - 8 phrases minimum
                     - utilisez quatre (4) pronoms relatifs (*lequel, lesquels, laquelle, lesquelles*) précédés de prépositions (*pendant, dans, sur, etc.*)

Vous pouvez utiliser les idées suivantes pour vous guider: villes, activités, temps (*weather*), durée (*length of trip*), nourriture, vêtements, votre opinion du voyage, différences avec les Etats-Unis

                                                                                                      Bon voyage !

APPENDIX Q
SPEC - SENEGAL

SPEC # 2 (Senegal)
TITLE: pre-test / post-test I / post-test II for experiments on doctoral research
LEVEL: third-semester French students

**General Description:** The objective of this test is to study the effect of content-enriched instruction through the integration of content and language forms (grammar and vocabulary). Beside learning about the culture(s) of the target language, the learners are exposed to grammar and lexical items that they can practice with the theme of the culture through task-based activities. In this specific testing situation, subjects will show their acquisition of cultural, lexical and grammatical knowledge, presented to them through a cultural lesson on Senegal. The test is valid for checking the cultural, grammatical and lexical knowledge presented in the lesson, as it specifically asks participants to recall items from the lesson.

**Prompt Attribute 1:** Subjects will be asked to answer questions concerning the culture of Senegal. On each of the tests, 7 questions, related to the content of the cultural lesson, will be asked. Subjects will have to answer in English.
The scoring will be done as follow : # 1, 2, 3, 4, 7: 1 pt right answer / ½ pt right answer with spelling errors / 0 pt wrong/no answer. # 5: 3 pts 3 right answers / 2 pt 2 right answers / 1 pt 1 right answer / ½ pt off for each spelling error. # 6: 1 pt right answer / ½ pt right month or day / 0 pt wrong/no answer

**Prompt Attribute 2:** Subjects will be asked to translate into French from English 7 non- or false-cognate words that were presented during the cultural lesson on Senegal. The list of words were chosen, as they did not appear earlier in the curriculum, supporting the need to be new to the participants.
The scoring will be done as follow : # 8-14 : 1 pt right answer / ½ pt right answer with spelling errors or partial answer / 0 pt wrong/no answer

**Prompt Attribute 3 for pre-test:** Subjects will fill in blanks with a relative pronoun, using a preposition given below the blank. The translation in English is provided in order to give the meaning. An example will be presented to them in order to clarify. The reason for this type of activity is to show if the learners are able to produce the targeted grammatical forms. Seven items compose this section.
The scoring will be done as follow : # 15 - 21: 4 pts right answer / 3 pts right order + agreement but wrong form of agreement (1 error) fem. or pl. / 2 pts right order but wrong form of "lequel" pronoun / 2 pts wrong order but right form of "lequel" pronoun / 1 pt right order but wrong pronoun

**Prompt Attribute 3 for post-tests:** Subjects will fill in blanks with a relative pronoun, using a preposition given below the blank. The translation in English is provided in order to give the meaning. An example will be presented to them in order to clarify. The reason for this type of activity is to show if the learners are able to produce the targeted grammatical forms. Ten items compose this section, as distracters are integrated. Distracters are defined as relative pronouns *lequel* and its variations WITHOUT a preceding preposition.

The scoring will be done as follow: Don't count # 16, 18, 21. #15, 17, 19, 20, 22, 23, 24: 4 pts right answer / 2 pt right order but wrong form of "lequel" pronoun / 2 pt wrong order but right form of "lequel" pronoun / 1 pt right order but wrong pronoun / 0 pt all wrong answer/no answer

**Prompt Attribute 4:** Subjects will have to write a paragraph of 7 sentences, using four grammatical structures targeted in the lesson they have learned (relative pronouns). The topics will be related to vacations they spent.

The scoring will be done as follow : 1 pt per correct form of "lequel" (take off ½ for minor errors) / 1 pt for correct preposition (meaning and form) (take off ½ for minor errors) / 1 pt for correct order of preposition + "lequel" / 1 pt for trying

**Sample Item 1:**
Here are 22 questions that are divided in three categories: the first one (7 questions) concerning facts about Senegal, the second one (14 questions) concerning what you know about the French language, and the third one asking you to write a little paragraph. If you don't know the answer, simply leave it blank.

**I. Culture**
**Fill in the blank with a short but clear answer in English:**
1. What is the capital of Senegal? _____

**Sample Item 2:**
**II. Language**
 A. Translate the following words in French:

8. A goat _____

**Sample Item 3 :**
 B. Below are sentences about Senegal. Complete the sentences by filling the blanks using the words, if applicable, and the translations given below, as it is shown in the example. *

Example : Le thé attaya, <u>dans lequel</u> on peut mettre beaucoup de sucre, est un rituel
    populaire.  dans

 (The attaya tea, in which we can put a lot of sugar, is a popular ritual)

15. Le pays du Sénégal, _____ on trouve beaucoup de langues, a une culture très riche.      **dans**
*(The country of Senegal, **in which** one finds many languages, has a very rich culture.)*

208

Sample Item 3 :
> B. Below are sentences about Senegal. Complete the sentences by filling in the blanks with and appropriate French expression. In formulating your answers, use the provided English translations.
>
> *Example :*    **Le thé attaya, *qui* peut être très sucré, est un rituel populaire.**
>
> (The attaya tea, which can be very sweet, is a popular ritual)

15. Le pays du Sénégal, _____ on trouve beaucoup de langues, a une culture très riche.
*(The country of Senegal, **in which** one finds many languages, has a very rich culture.)*

**Sample Item 4:**
**III. Spring break.**

Spring Break was just around the corner. What did you do? In a paragraph of a minimum of seven (7) sentences, describe what you did and where you went. Give detailed descriptions using four (4) relative pronouns (i.e. linking pronouns) "lequel" (and its variations: laquelle, lesquels, lesquelles) with a preceding prepositions such as: avec , pour, sans dans, pendant, etc. (e.g. *dans lequel*). Use the past tense (*passé composé or imparfait*) in your sentences.

APPENDIX R
PRE-TEST – SENEGAL

## Le Sénégal

Here are 22 questions that are divided in three categories: the first one (7 questions) concerning facts about Senegal, the second one (14 questions) concerning the French language, and the third one asking you to write a short paragraph. If you don't know the answer, simply leave it blank.

### I. Culture:
**Fill in the blank with a short but clear answer in English:**
1. What is the capital of Senegal?  _____
2. What is the name of the first president?  _____
3. What is the name of the annual race? _____
4. How many official languages are there in Senegal? _____
5. Name at least three (3) languages spoken in Senegal? _____
6. What is the date of the Senegalese national day? _____
7. What is the name of a famous Senegalese singer? _____

### II. Language
#### A. Translate the following words in French:
8. A field _____
9. Iron _____
10. Bitter _____
11. A truck _____
12. A masterpiece _____
13. The countryside _____
14. A race _____

**B. Below are sentences about Senegal. Complete the sentences by filling the blanks using the words, if applicable, and the translations given below, as it is shown in the example. \***

Example : Le thé attaya, <u>dans lequel</u> on peut mettre beaucoup de sucre, est un rituel populaire.                       **dans**

(The attaya tea, in which we can put a lot of sugar, is a popular ritual)

15. Le pays du Sénégal, _____ on trouve beaucoup de langues, a une culture très riche.        **dans**
(The country of Senegal, **in which** one finds many languages, has a very rich culture.)

16. La Tabaski, _____ on mange beaucoup, est un fête religieuse.
**pendant**
*(The Tabaski, **during which** people eat a lot, is a religious holiday.)*

17. Il y a environ 10 millions d'habitants _____ on trouve une grande diversité ethnique.  **parmi**
*(There are about 10 million inhabitants **among whom** one can find a vast ethnic diversity.)*

18. Les traditions, _____ la culture sénégalaise est basée, sont importantes à toutes les ethnies.  **sur**
*(The traditions, **on which** the Senegalese culture is based, are important for all ethnies.)*

19. Le Sénégal est une république _____ il y a un président démocratiquement élu.  **dans**
*(Senegal is a republic **in which** there is a president democratically elected.)*

20. La musique, _____ on peut s'exprimer est une partie essentielle de la vie sénégalaise.  **avec**
*(Music, with which one can express themselves, is an essential part of Senegalese life.)*

21. Au Sénégal, il y a beaucoup de fêtes, _____ on aime manger beaucoup et render visite à sa famille.  **pendant**
*(In Senegal, there are many holidays, during which people like to eat and visit their families.)*

### III. Summer Break.

Summer Break seems already far away! What did you do? In a paragraph of a minimum of seven (7) sentences, describe what you did and where you went. Give detailed descriptions using four (4) relative pronouns (i.e. linking pronouns) "**lequel**" (and its variations: *laquelle, lesquels, lesquelles*) with a preceding prepositions such as: **avec , pour, sans, dans, pendant,** etc. (e.g. *dans lequel*). Use the past tense (*passé composé* or *imparfait*) in your sentences.[15]

In summary: 7 sentences with 4 composed relative pronouns in the past tense.

_____
_____
_____
_____

---

[15] The scoring for this section went as follow:
4 points total per form present in the writing, divided as:
- 1 pt per correct form of the comparative or superlative
- 1 pt for correct agreement adjective
- 1 pt for correct meaning regarding the preceding preposition
- 1pt for trying

APPENDIX S
POST-TEST I - SENEGAL

**Le Sénégal**

This activity contains 25 questions divided in three categories: the first one (7 questions) concerns facts about Senegal, the second one (17 questions) concerns the French language, while in the third one you are asked to write a short paragraph. If in the first two categories, you do not know an answer, simply leave the answer blank.

**I. Culture:**
**Fill in the blank with a short but clear answer in English:**
1. What is the capital of Senegal? _____
2. What is the name of the Senegal first president? _____
3. What is the name of Senegal's annual race? _____
4. How many official languages are there in Senegal? _____
5. Name at least three (3) languages spoken in Senegal
_____
6. What is the date of the Senegalese national holiday? _____
7. What is the name of a famous Senegalese singer? _____

**II. Language**
    **A. Translate the following words in French:**
8. field _____
9. iron _____
10. bitter _____
11. truck _____
12. masterpiece _____
13. countryside _____
14. (sports) race _____

    **B. Below are sentences about Senegal. Complete the sentences by filling in the blanks with and appropriate French expression. In formulating your answers, use the provided English translations.**

    Example :    *Le thé attaya, **qui** peut être très sucré, est un rituel populaire.*

        (The attaya tea, which can be very sweet, is a popular ritual)

15. Le pays du Sénégal, _____ on trouve beaucoup de langues, a une culture très riche.
*(The country of Senegal, **in which** one finds many languages, has a very rich culture.)*

16. La religion principale, _____ est la religion musulmane, est pratiquée par plus de 90% des Sénégalais.

*(The main religion, **which** is the muslim religion, is practiced by more than 90% of the population.)*

17. La Tabaski, _____ on mange beaucoup, est une fête religieuse.
*(The Tabaski, **during which** people eat a lot, is a religious holiday.)*

18. La population sénégalaise, _____ est d'environ 10 millions, est composée d'une grande diversité ethnique.
*(The Senegalese population, **which** is about 10 million, is composed of a large ethnic diversity)*

19. Les traditions, _____ la culture sénégalaise est basée, sont importantes à toutes les ethnies.
*(Ttraditions, **on which** the Senegalese culture is based, are important for all ethnicities.)*

20. La musique, _____ on peut s'exprimer est une partie essentielle de la vie sénégalaise.
*(Music, **with which** one can express oneself, is an essential part of Senegalese life.)*

21. Le franc CFA, _____ est la monnaie sénégalaise, est aussi la monnaie commune des autres pays africains francophones.
*(The CFA franc, **which** is the senegalese currency, is also the common currency of the Francophone African countries.)*

22. Au Sénégal, il y a beaucoup de fêtes, _____ on aime manger beaucoup et rendre visite à sa famille.
*(In Senegal, there are many holidays, **during which** people like to eat and visit their families.)*

23. Le mouton, _____ on célèbre les grands événements, est une des viandes préférées des Sénégalais.
*(Mutton, **with which** people celebrate big events, is one of the favorite meat dishes of the Senegalese.)*

24. Le Sénégal est une république _____ il y a un président démocratiquement élu.
*(Senegal is a republic **in which** there is a democratically elected president.)*

### III. Summer vacation.

The summer is already far but try to remember it. What did you do? In a paragraph of a minimum of seven (7) sentences, describe what you did and where you went. Give detailed descriptions using **four (4) relative pronouns "lequel"** (and its variations: *laquelle, lesquels,* *lesquelles*) with a preceding preposition such as: **avec , pour, sans, dans, pendant**, etc. (e.g. *dans lequel*). Use the past tense (*passé composé* or *imparfait*) in your sentences.[16]

In summary: write at least 7 sentences with four (4) relative pronouns preceded by a preposition in the past tense.

_____
_____
_____
_____

---

[16] The scoring for this section went as follow:
4 points total per form present in the writing, divided as:
- 1 pt per correct form of the comparative or superlative
- 1 pt for correct agreement adjective
- 1 pt for correct meaning regarding the preceding preposition
- 1pt for trying

APPENDIX T
POST-TEST II - SENEGAL

**Le Sénégal**

This activity contains 25 questions divided in three categories: the first one (7 questions) concerns facts about Senegal, the second one (17 questions) concerns the French language, while in the third one you are asked to write a short paragraph. If in the first two categories, you do not know an answer, simply leave the answer blank.

**I. Culture:**
**Fill in the blank with a short but clear answer in English:**
1. What is the capital of Senegal? _____
2. What is the name of the Senegal first president? _____
3. What is the name of a famous Senegalese singer? _____
4. What is the name of Senegal's annual race? _____
5. What is the date of the Senegalese national holiday? _____
6. How many official languages are there in Senegal? _____
7. Name at least three (3) languages spoken in Senegal
_____

**II. Language**
    **A. Translate the following words in French:**
8.     truck            _____
9.     field             _____
10.   (sports) race    _____
11.   iron              _____
12.   bitter           _____
13.   countryside      _____
14.   masterpiece      _____

    **B. Below are sentences about Senegal. Complete the sentences by filling in the blanks with and appropriate French expression. In formulating your answers, use the provided English translations.**

    Example :     Le thé attaya, **_qui_** peut être très sucré, est un rituel populaire.

                    (The attaya tea, which can be very sweet, is a popular ritual)

15. La religion principale, _____ est la religion musulmane, est pratiquée par plus de 90% des Sénégalais.
(*The main religion, **which** is the muslim religion, is practiced by more than 90% of the population.*)

16. La Tabaski, _____ on mange beaucoup, est une fête religieuse.
*(The Tabaski, **during which** people eat a lot, is a religious holiday.)*

17. La population sénégalaise, _____ est d'environ 10 millions, est composée d'une grande diversité ethnique.
*(The Senegalese population, **which** is about 10 million, is composed of a large ethnic diversity)*

18. Le pays du Sénégal, _____ on trouve beaucoup de langues, a une culture très riche.
*(The country of Senegal, **in which** one finds many languages, has a very rich culture.)*

19. Les traditions, _____ la culture sénégalaise est basée, sont importantes à toutes les ethnies.
*(Ttraditions, **on which** the Senegalese culture is based, are important for all ethnicities.)*

20. Le franc CFA, _____ est la monnaie sénégalaise, est aussi la monnaie commune des autres pays africains francophones.
*(The CFA franc, **which** is the senegalese currency, is also the common currency of the Francophone African countries.)*

21. Au Sénégal, il y a beaucoup de fêtes, _____ on aime manger beaucoup et render visite à sa famille.
*(In Senegal, there are many holidays, **during which** people like to eat and visit their families.)*

22. La musique, _____ on peut s'exprimer est une partie essentielle de la vie sénégalaise.
*(Music, **with which** one can express oneself, is an essential part of Senegalese life.)*

23. Le mouton, _____ on célèbre les grands événements, est une des viandes préférées des Sénégalais.
*(Mutton, **with which** people celebrate big events, is one of the favorite meat dishes of the Senegalese.)*

24. Le Sénégal est une république _____ il y a un président démocratiquement élu.
*(Senegal is a republic **in which** there is a democratically elected president.)*

**III. A past vacation.**

Think of a fun vacation you have had in the past. What did you do? With whom were you? Where was it? What was the weather like? In a paragraph of a minimum of seven (7) sentences, describe your vacation, using **four (4) relative pronouns** "**lequel**" (and its variations: ***laquelle,*** *lesquels, lesquelles*) with a preceding preposition such as: **avec , pour, sans, dans, pendant**, etc. (e.g. ***dans lequel***). Use the past tense (***passé composé*** or ***imparfait***) in your sentences.[17]

In summary: write at least 7 sentences with four (4) relative pronouns preceded by a preposition in the past tense.

_____
_____
_____
_____
_____

---

[17] The scoring for this section went as follow:
4 points total per form present in the writing, divided as:
- 1 pt per correct form of the comparative or superlative
- 1 pt for correct agreement adjective
- 1 pt for correct meaning regarding the preceding preposition
- 1pt for trying

APPENDIX U
QUESTIONNAIRE

I would like to ask for another favor concerning the research project you have conducted for me. After looking at the videos and at the results of the students, I have had a few questions that came up to mind. I was wondering if you could spend a few minutes answering the following questions, in order to help me understand teachers' techniques. Please, be as open as possible! Thank you! ☺ If you could send back, by attachement, this questionnaire by **this coming Sunday**, it would be wonderful! Thank you again and I deeply appreciate all your help!
Frédérique
*Please answer the questions by explaining or by circling.*

**General questions:**
1. For how long have you taught French? _____

2. Have you received formal training in foreign language teaching / pedagogy? Yes   No

3. If yes on 2, what type of training did you receive?
   _____
   _____

4. Last semester, I videotaped the cultural lesson you taught for me. How did you like it? And why?
   _____
   _____

5. Do you think your students liked it?           Yes           No

**Your beliefs:**
6. Do you believe that there are no situations in which the first language (English) should be used in the classroom?           Yes           No

7. Do you believe that the foreign language (French) should only be used to learn about grammar and usage of the foreign language?     Yes           No

8. Do you believe that your students generally feel anxious when you only use the foreign language (French)?           Yes           No

**Your language use:**
9. Usually, do you use occasionally some English when you teach a French class?
                                                  Yes           No

10. What are your reasons?
    _____

11. Do you use English to explain some difficult grammar points?
    no          yes sometimes          yes often          yes always

12. Do you use English to give directions?
    no          yes sometimes          yes often          yes always

13. Do you use English to explain some difficult lexical points (i.e. vocabulary)?
    no          yes sometimes          yes often          yes always

14. Do you use English to explain some cultural facts?
    no          yes sometimes          yes often          yes always

15. Do you use English when you are individually talking to students (when they work in groups or alone)?
    no          yes sometimes          yes often          yes always

16. Do you use English to talk about quizzes, tests, homework, etc.?
    no          yes sometimes          yes often          yes always

17. Do you use English to explain course policies or other administrative information?
    no          yes sometimes          yes often          yes always

18. Do you use English before class starts?
    no          yes sometimes          yes often          yes always

19. Do you use English after class?
    no          yes sometimes          yes often          yes always

20. Do you use English to rely better/to feel closer with your students?
    no          yes sometimes          yes often          yes always

21. If you do not mind, I might contact you for more information. Please, let me know if this is okay:
    Yes     No

**Thank you!**

APPENDIX V
QUESTIONNAIRE (2)

Please, forgive me for all this harassment, but I have a few more questions to ask you about your personal beliefs. I would really appreciate if you could take a few minutes to answer this questionnaire. Thank you! Please send it by this Sunday. Once again, I deeply thank you for your previous help. You are helping me more than what you can imagine. Frédérique

1. Can you rank the following language component in order of importance according to your personal beliefs (feel free to have a same number for 2 or more, if you think they are as important) 1 being the most important - 5 being the least important
   _____ Grammar                    _____ Written comprehension
   _____ Culture                    _____ Vocabulary
   _____ Oral comprehension         _____ Communication
                                              (being able to communicate)

Please circle the best answer:
2. The formal study if grammar is essential to eventual mastery of a foreign language.
Agree strongly     Agree          Undecided          Disagree slightly     Disagree strongly

3. Students generally like the study of grammar
Agree strongly     Agree          Undecided          Disagree slightly     Disagree strongly

4. It is generally more important to practice a foreign language in situations simulating real life (i.e., interview, role plays, etc.) than to analyze and practice grammatical patterns.
Agree strongly     Agree          Undecided          Disagree slightly     Disagree strongly

Please write complete answers:
5. Do you believe grammar is an important part of the language? Why?
_____
_____
_____

6. According to your knowledge of language teaching theories, how do you think <u>grammar</u> should be taught?
_____
_____
_____

7. According to your knowledge of language teaching theories, how do you think <u>vocabulary</u> should be taught?

8. According to your personal experience, how do you think grammar and vocabulary should be taught?

9. What language (French or English) should be used to teach grammar? Explain why.

10. If you encounter a difficult grammar point, how do you usually handle the situation?

11. If you encounter a difficult vocabulary point, how do you usually handle the situation?

12. Do you usually use grammatical jargon (i.e. prépositions, verbes, complément d'objet direct…)? Why? Or why not?

13. Une dernière question: J'ai besoin d'un pseudonyme pour vous mentionner dans mon étude. Quel prénom aimerais-tu que j'utilise quand je parle de ton cours?

MERCI BEAUCOUP!!!
☺

# Wissenschaftlicher Buchverlag
kostenfreie
## Publikation
von
# wissenschaftlichen Arb

Diplomarbeiten, Magisterarbeiten, Master und Bachel
sowie Dissertationen, Habilitationen und wissenschaftliche

verfügen über eine wissenschaftliche Abschlußarbeit zu aktu
Fragestellungen, die hohen inhaltlichen und formalen Anspr
und haben **Interesse an einer honorarvergüteten Pub**

Dann senden Sie bitte erste Informationen über Ihre Arbe
an info@vdm-verlag.de. Unser Außenlektorat meldet sich umg

VDM Verlag Dr. Müller Aktiengesellschaft & Co. K
Dudweiler Landstraße 125a
D - 66123 Saarbrücken

www.vdm-verlag.de

8. According to <u>your personal experience</u>, how do you think grammar and vocabulary should be taught?

9. What language (French or English) should be used to teach grammar? Explain why.

10. If you encounter a difficult grammar point, how do you usually handle the situation?

11. If you encounter a difficult vocabulary point, how do you usually handle the situation?

12. Do you usually use grammatical jargon (i.e. prépositions, verbes, complément d'objet direct…)? Why? Or why not?

13. Une dernière question: J'ai besoin d'un pseudonyme pour vous mentionner dans mon étude. Quel prénom aimerais-tu que j'utilise quand je parle de ton cours?

MERCI BEAUCOUP!!!<br>☺

## Wissenschaftlicher Buchverlag bietet

kostenfreie

## Publikation

von

# wissenschaftlichen Arbeiten

Diplomarbeiten, Magisterarbeiten, Master und Bachelor Theses
sowie Dissertationen, Habilitationen und wissenschaftliche Monographien

Sie verfügen über eine wissenschaftliche Abschlußarbeit zu aktuellen oder zeitlosen Fragestellungen, die hohen inhaltlichen und formalen Ansprüchen genügt, und haben **Interesse an einer honorarvergüteten Publikation**?

Dann senden Sie bitte erste Informationen über Ihre Arbeit per Email an info@vdm-verlag.de. Unser Außenlektorat meldet sich umgehend bei Ihnen.

VDM Verlag Dr. Müller Aktiengesellschaft & Co. KG
Dudweiler Landstraße 125a
D - 66123 Saarbrücken

www.vdm-verlag.de

LaVergne, TN USA
21 March 2010

176615LV00003B/50/P